MW01260103

Cultural Evolution

Cultural Evolution:
How Darwinian Theory Can Explain Human Culture
and Synthesize the Social Sciences

Alex Mesoudi

University of Chicago Press :: Chicago and London

Alex Mesoudi is lecturer in psychology at Queen Mary, University of London. He is the author or coauthor of articles in such leading journals as *Behavioral and Brain Sciences, Evolution*, and *Psychological Review*.

The University of Chicago Press, Chicago 60637
The University of Chicago Press, Ltd., London
© 2011 by The University of Chicago
All rights reserved. Published 2011.
Printed in the United States of America

20 19 18 17 16 15 14 13 12 11   1 2 3 4 5

ISBN-13: 978-0-226-52043-8 (cloth)
ISBN-13: 978-0-226-52044-5 (paper)

ISBN-10: 0-226-52043-9 (cloth)
ISBN-10: 0-226-52044-7 (paper)

Library of Congress Cataloging-in-Publication Data

Mesoudi, Alex.
    Cultural evolution : how Darwinian theory can explain human culture and synthesize the social sciences / Alex Mesoudi.
        p. cm.
    Includes bibliographical references and index.
    ISBN-13: 978-0-226-52043-8 (alk. paper)
    ISBN-10: 0-226-52043-9 (alk. paper)
    ISBN-13: 978-0-226-52044-5 (pbk. : alk. paper)
    ISBN-10: 0-226-52044-7 (pbk. : alk. paper)   1. Social evolution.
2. Culture.   I. Title.
HM626.M486 2011
306.01—dc22

                                              2010054354

⊚ The paper used in this publication meets the minimum requirements of the American National Standard for Information Sciences—Permanence of Paper for Printed Library Materials, ANSI Z39.48-1992.

Contents

Preface

The year 2009 was the 150th anniversary of the publication of Charles Darwin's *The Origin of Species*. As was the case for the 50th and 100th anniversaries in 1909 and 1959, the 150th anniversary was celebrated with lavish events and prestigious meetings at universities and learned societies around the world, as well as TV series and a movie biopic of Darwin. Few other scientists, and even fewer books, warrant such long-term attention. But this is not merely hero worship on the part of scientists. It is the recognition of a major scientific advance. In *The Origin*, somebody had set out for the first time a tenable scientific explanation for two phenomena that had predominantly been, and often still are, attributed to supernatural, mystical, or religious forces. The first phenomenon is the incredible diversity of biological organisms that we see in the natural world. This diversity ranges from beetles to cacti to hummingbirds to algae to gibbons, to name just a few random examples. Prior to Darwin, the accepted explanation for this diversity was simply that God had created these species in their present forms, for whatever reason he saw fit (he works in mysterious ways, after all). The second phenomenon that Darwin explained was the often intricately complex adaptations that these diverse organisms possess, such as eyes, wings, echolocation systems, and brains. As many theologians have noted, such adaptations have multiple, functionally interrelated parts that appear to work perfectly together, seemingly betraying clear evidence of having been designed by an intelligent being.

Darwin's genius—the reason he is still celebrated today—was to provide the first coherent and workable scientific explanation for these phenomena. According to Darwin, the diversity and complexity of the natural world could be explained using a handful of simple principles, all of which could be demonstrated empirically to be operating in nature: first, that variation exists between individuals; second, that a "struggle for existence" occurs due to limited resources, such as food, nesting space, or mates, and ever-increasing population sizes, such that not every individual has an equal chance of surviving and reproducing; and third, that characteristics are inherited from parent to offspring during reproduction. The consequence is what Darwin called "natural selection": those characteristics that increase an individual's chances of surviving and reproducing are more likely to be inherited by the next generation, and such characteristics will increase in frequency within a population. Over time, beneficial characteristics gradually accumulate and combine to generate the eyes, wings, and so on that had previously been attributed to the actions of a creator. Darwin's work has stimulated a century and a half of enormously productive research in evolutionary biology, which has been devoted to working out the details of Darwin's principles, such as the genetic basis of inheritance, of which Darwin was only dimly aware.

In this book I survey a growing body of scientific research that is based on the fundamental premise that cultural change—by which I mean changes in socially transmitted beliefs, knowledge, technology, languages, social institutions, and so on—shares the very same principles that Darwin applied to biological change in *The Origin* a century and a half ago. In other words, *culture evolves*. This is not a new idea by any means. In fact, Darwin himself would later draw parallels between biological evolution and cultural change, specifically language change:

> The formation of different languages and of distinct species, and the proofs that both have been developed through a gradual process, are curiously parallel . . . The survival or preservation of certain favoured words in the struggle for existence is natural selection.[1]

Darwin wasn't just using an analogy here for purposes of exposition. Language change isn't "a bit like" natural selection, or "resembles in some respects" natural selection, it "is" natural selection, plain and simple. And many other illustrious scientists since then have made similar observations, such as William James, one of the founders of psychology:

> A remarkable parallel . . . obtains between the facts of social evolution on the one hand, and of zoölogical evolution as expounded by Mr. Darwin on the other.[2]

Despite these early pronouncements by prominent scholars of a curious and remarkable parallel between biological and cultural change, only now are scholars beginning to properly apply Darwinian methods, tools, theories, and concepts to explain cultural phenomena. This book is an attempt to summarize and synthesize this growing movement.

In many ways, the problem that Darwin set out to solve—the diversity and complexity of biological organisms—is echoed in the problem faced by those studying culture. Human culture, too, shows enormous diversity: there are approximately 10,000 different religions currently practiced in the world, almost 7,000 different languages spoken, each one of which contains around half a million words, and 7.7 million patented items of technology in the United States alone. Human culture also shows often astounding complexity, such as the intricately detailed ecological knowledge of the behavior of other species that is passed from generation to generation in many hunter-gatherer groups, technological artifacts such as computers or space shuttles that are composed of countless functionally interlinked parts, and political and financial institutions that successfully organize (at least to some degree) the lives of millions of people. This body of diverse and complex culturally transmitted knowledge has allowed our species to successfully colonize virtually every terrestrial environment on the planet, from freezing poles to scorching deserts, from tropical rainforests to mountain ranges. Chapter 1 is devoted to more precisely defining this phenomenon that we call "culture," as well as demonstrating empirically that culturally acquired knowledge significantly shapes various aspects of human behavior, from society-wide patterns of aggression and cooperation to fundamental psychological processes such as how we perceive objects and interpret other people's actions.

In chapter 2, I outline the argument that Darwin's explanation for the diversity and complexity of biological life also applies, in a broad sense, to human culture. That is, cultural change—changes in beliefs, knowledge, technology, social institutions, and so on—shares the same principles that Darwin laid out in *The Origin*. First, culturally acquired traits show variation in their form and expression; second, there is some kind of competition between these cultural variants due to finite resources, such as space in memory, so that not every variant is equally likely to survive and spread; and third, cultural variants are passed from person to person due to cultural transmission. Chapter 2 is devoted to expanding this basic proposition and showing that the resulting theory of cultural evolution is empirically well supported—at least as well supported as the equivalent argument that Darwin made for biological species in *The Origin*.

Equally important as the basic similarity between biological and cultural change, however, are the differences. Beyond the theory outlined by Darwin in *The Origin*, many of the details of biological evolution that have been worked out by biologists since then, such as particulate inheritance (the existence of discrete particles of inheritance, genes), blind variation (new genetic variation is not generated to solve a specific adaptive problem), or Weismann's barrier (the separation of genotypes and phenotypes such that changes acquired in an organism's lifetime are not directly transmitted to offspring), may not apply to cultural evolution. But, crucially, this does not invalidate the basic argument of chapter 2 that culture evolves. It just means that the details of cultural evolution may be different from the details of biological evolution, and it is up to social scientists to fill in those details, just as biologists have done over the past 150 years.

With this in mind, chapter 3 outlines the microlevel details of cultural evolution, drawing on groundbreaking mathematical models developed in the 1970s and 1980s by a handful of pioneering researchers based in California. Some of these resemble the underlying processes of biological evolution, such as drift (changes due to chance events in small populations) or vertical cultural transmission (from one's biological parents, just like genes). Others are unique to culture, such as the Lamarckian-like process of guided variation, where people modify what they learn from others before passing it on. Each of these microevolutionary processes has distinct population-level consequences for cultural evolution, consequences that could only have been worked out with formal mathematical models borrowed from population geneticists.

Chapters 4 and 5 examine cultural macroevolution, which describes the large-scale, long-term patterns and trends that are documented by anthropologists, archaeologists, historians, and linguists. Of course, scholars in these fields have long described and explained large-scale patterns of cultural change without any reference to cultural evolution. Yet these explanations are typically based on informal and nonquantitative methods. We will see how cultural evolution researchers are using rigorous, quantitative methods originally designed to detect and explain patterns and trends in biological evolution, such as phylogenetic analyses and neutral drift models, to uncover patterns and trends in cultural macroevolution with greater certainty than is possible with traditional, nonevolutionary methods.

Chapters 6 and 7 concern two specific methods for studying cultural microevolution: lab experiments and ethnographic field studies. Experiments can be used to simulate cultural evolution under controlled conditions in the lab. This brings all kinds of benefits over purely observational or historical methods. With experiments, for example, we can manipulate variables to determine the causes of cultural phenomena, we can "re-run" history several times to see whether trends are meaningful or due to chance, and we can obtain uninterrupted and complete behavioral data—none of which is possible with purely observational or historical studies of actual cultural change. Ethnographic field studies complement experiments by tracking cultural change within small communities of people, addressing such questions as whether people learn primarily from their parents or from their peers, and how such transmission pathways affect within- and between-group cultural variation.

Chapter 8 examines recent efforts to model economic change as an evolutionary process. Traditional economic theory is not very good at explaining change over time, instead focusing on whether an economic system is in an optimal state at any one point in time. This is problematic when economies are constantly changing, for example, in response to rapid technological change (e.g., in telecommunications or computing), and evolutionary economists have begun to construct an evolutionary theory of economic systems in which change rather than stasis is the default. Other researchers have argued that cultural evolutionary processes, specifically the process of cultural group selection, can potentially explain puzzling findings from various economic experiments that suggest that people are typically far more cooperative than they should be if they are just maximizing their own utility in a purely self-interested manner, as assumed by traditional, nonevolutionary economic theory.

Chapter 9 asks whether any species other than humans have culture. To a large extent, this depends on how we define "culture" to start with. It is clear, however, that a surprisingly large number of other species possess at least some of the key elements of human culture, such as the ability to learn from other individuals and to maintain stable between-group differences in behavior that might be described as cultural "traditions." Yet only humans appear to have *cumulative* culture, where modifications are built up over successive generations. Why only humans have cumulative cultural evolution is at present a mystery, but this avenue of study promises to shed light on the origin and basis of human culture.

In the final chapter, I argue that all the research that I have discussed here is indicative of a coming "evolutionary synthesis" for the social sciences. For all the brilliance of *The Origin of Species*, it was not until the so-called "evolutionary synthesis" of the 1930s and 1940s that evolutionary biology really took off as a coherent and successful discipline. Prior to this synthesis, biology was fractionated into several isolated disciplines composed of experimentalists, theoretical modelers, field naturalists, paleontologists, and so on. Each discipline had its own theoretical assumptions that often conflicted with those of other disciplines. During the synthesis, scientists within each discipline came to accept the same basic assumptions, thus synthesizing biology within a single Darwinian theoretical framework. More specifically, it was recognized during this period that broad trends and patterns in biological macroevolution, such as patterns of adaptive radiation in the biogeographical record or periods of change and stasis in the fossil record, could be explained in terms of the small-scale microevolutionary processes studied by experimentalists and model builders, processes such as natural selection, sexual selection, and drift. I argue in chapter 10 that the social sciences are currently in a similarly fractionated state as the biological sciences were prior to the 1930s. However, if culture does indeed evolve in a similar way to species, then a similar "evolutionary synthesis" might be possible for the social sciences. That is, large-scale trends or patterns of cultural macroevolution, as studied by archaeologists, historians, historical linguists, sociologists, and anthropologists, might be explained in terms of small-scale microevolutionary cultural processes, as studied by psychologists and other behavioral scientists. We can see the emergence of a unified science of culture, one that transcends traditional social science disciplinary boundaries.

This view of a single, overarching science of culture, unified around a Darwinian evolutionary framework and incorporating anthropology, archaeology, economics, history, linguistics, psychology, and sociology, may seem naive. Anyone who has studied a social science subject at university level will probably be aware that there is little theoretical common ground, or even communication, between many of the different branches of the social sciences. Yet the current state of the social sciences, composed as they are of theoretically incompatible and mutually incomprehensible disciplines, is hugely problematic. Valuable findings and theories are rarely transferred across disciplinary boundaries to stimulate work in other fields, and scholars waste time reinventing discoveries that have already been made in other disciplines. Consequently, while there are pockets of rigorous and high-quality research being carried out within specific social science disciplines, it is lamentable that so little progress has been made over the past few decades in understanding one of the most intriguing and astounding phenomena known to science—human culture—especially when so much progress has been made in the natural and physical sciences over the same period. My aim in this book is to nudge the social sciences along a little by showing that there is a growing interdisciplinary body of work that is making significant progress in explaining culture scientifically.

Acknowledgments

This book is the cumulative product of the influence of many people over several years. Henry Plotkin, Kevin Laland, Andrew Whiten, and Michael O'Brien have been particularly important in shaping my thinking on many of the issues covered here. I am also grateful to the following people for reading and commenting on one or more chapters, and whose advice has undoubtedly improved it: Robert Aunger, Elodie Briefer, Kevin Laland, Stephen Lycett, Michael O'Brien, Alan McElligott, Richard Nelson, Peter Richerson, Jamie Tehrani, Peter Turchin, and Andrew Whiten. Finally, I thank my editor at University of Chicago Press, David Pervin, who provided unwavering support and a much-needed outsider's perspective.

1   A Cultural Species

Humans are a cultural species. We acquire a multitude of beliefs, attitudes, preferences, knowledge, skills, customs, and norms from other members of our species cultur- ally, through social learning processes such as imitation, teaching, and language. This culturally acquired infor- mation affects our behavior in quite fundamental ways. People who grow up in different societies exhibit mea- surably different ways of thinking and behaving because they acquire different cultural norms and beliefs from other members of their societies. Culturally transmitted technology, from stone tools to automobiles to the inter- net, and culturally transmitted political, economic, and social institutions have drastically changed our environ- ments and our lives in a relatively short period of time. No other species on the planet exhibits such rapid and effective cultural change.

As a result, any explanation of human behavior that ignores culture, or treats it in an unsatisfactory manner, will almost certainly be incomplete. Yet a large number of social and behavioral scientists—many psychologists, economists, and political scientists, for example—either implicitly or explicitly downplay or ignore cultural influ- ences on human behavior, instead focusing on the be- havior and decisions of single individuals with little or no consideration of how that behavior and those decisions are affected by culturally acquired norms and beliefs. Other social scientists—many cultural anthropologists, archaeologists, sociologists, and historians, for example—*do* acknowledge the importance of culture, yet their methods and approaches often lack the scientific rigor and precision needed to satisfactorily explain how and why culture is the way that it is and how it affects behavior in the way that it does. Consequently, while the natural and physical sciences have made huge progress in the last century or so in explaining the hidden mysteries of life, matter, and the universe, the social sciences have failed to provide a unifying and productive theory of cultural change. The different branches of the social sciences remain fractionated, each speaking their own, often mutually unintelligible, languages and holding assumptions and theories that are mutually incompatible. Indeed, a good example of this mutual incompatibility concerns the very definition of "culture" itself, which varies greatly from discipline to discipline. It is necessary, then, to clearly specify the definition of "culture" that will be used in the rest of this book, before going on to demonstrate the extent to which culture shapes our behavior.

What Is Culture?

"Culture" is one of those concepts, like "life" or "energy," that most people use in everyday speech without giving much thought to its precise meaning. In fact, people often use it in several different, but overlapping, senses. For example, it might be used to identify a specific group of people, usually within a single nation, such as "French culture" or "Japanese culture." Or it might be used in the sense of "high culture," such as literature, classical music, and fine art, as is the focus of many "culture" sections of Sunday newspapers. Or it might be used to describe a seemingly shared set of values or practices within a group or organization. For example, during the financial crisis that began in 2007, many commentators lamented the "culture of greed" that seemed to be prevalent within the banking industry, as it emerged that CEOs were still receiving huge bonuses even as their banks were being bailed out using public money.

When scientists use the term "culture," they usually mean something broader, something that encompasses all three of the definitions above. Although literally hundreds of definitions of culture have been proposed across the social sciences over the years, the definition that I will adopt in the rest of this book is that *culture is information that is acquired from other individuals via social transmission mechanisms such as imitation, teaching, or language.*[1] "Information" here is intended as a broad term to refer to what social scientists and lay people might call knowledge, beliefs, attitudes, norms, preferences, and skills, all of which may be acquired from other individuals via social transmission and consequently shared across social groups. Whereas genetic information is stored in sequences of DNA base pairs, culturally transmitted information is stored in the brain as patterns of neural connections (albeit in a way that neuroscientists are only beginning to understand), as well as in extrasomatic codes such as written language, binary computer code, and musical notation. And whereas genetic information is expressed as proteins and ultimately physical structures such as limbs and eyes, culturally acquired information is expressed in the form of behavior, speech, artifacts, and institutions.

This definition of culture encompasses in one way or another all of the colloquial uses of culture noted above. Culture includes the Japanese grammar and vocabulary, Japanese norms, and Japanese customs that a Japanese child acquires that contribute to maintaining the specific "Japanese culture." The skill required to use chopsticks, for example, is stored in the brains of virtually all Japanese people, is acquired from other people via imitation or teaching, and is expressed behaviorally in the form of chopstick use. Cultural groups are not always the same as nation-states, though: there is substantial variation in the customs and values of people living in different regions of Japan, while Japanese customs such as chopstick use have diffused to many other nations. Culture also includes the literature, music, and art that make up "high culture," although it is by no means limited to this. Celebrity gossip about the latest relationship problems of Hollywood movie stars is just as much a part of human culture as are the works of William Shakespeare. And culture includes those norms and practices that may have been transmitted from banker to banker via imitation or direct instruction that create and maintain selfish behavior within an organization.

According to this definition, culture is defined as information rather than behavior (in anthropological jargon, it is an *ideational* definition of culture). Restricting our definition of culture to information does not mean to say that culturally acquired information does not *affect* behavior. Of course it does, otherwise it would be a useless concept for explaining human behavior. However, as anthropologist Lee Cronk makes clear, it is important to distinguish between culture and behavior for two reasons.[2] First, if behavior is the thing we are trying to explain, then including it in the definition of culture makes cultural explanations for behavior circular. A thing cannot explain itself, at least not in any useful sense. And second, there are other causes of behavior besides culture. In fact, this is a useful way of defining culture: by what it is not. First, as noted above, culture can be distinguished from information that we acquire *genetically*, from our biological parents, which is stored as DNA base pair sequences and expressed as proteins and, ultimately, as entire organisms. Second, culture can be distinguished from information that we acquire through *individual learning*, which describes the process of learning on our own with no influence from other individuals. While individually learned information, like culturally acquired information, is stored in the brain, it is not acquired from other individuals via cultural transmission. This distinction between genetically, culturally, and individually acquired information is important, because even if we observe variation between people and groups in some behavioral practice, we cannot automatically assume that the explanation of this behavioral variation is culture. Take variation in alcohol drinking, for example. Some variation in alcohol drinking is most likely cultural in origin, for example, resulting from the culturally transmitted norms prohibiting the drinking of alcohol found in religions such as Islam, or the more informal prodrinking norms found in certain social groups such as university fraternities and sororities. But some variation might be the result of individual learning, where a person independently decides to drink (or not to drink) alcohol because they like (or dislike) its taste or its effects. Other variation in alcohol drinking might be genetic. Indeed, certain genetic alleles have recently been found to increase a person's risk of alcohol dependency such that people with these alleles have higher alcohol intake than people without these alleles. Many East Asians, on the other hand, lack a different genetic allele that would allow them to digest alcohol, potentially decreasing the frequency of alcohol drinking in that group.[3]

How Important Is Culture?

Given these alternative explanations for human behavioral variation, how can we be sure that culture really is important, compared to genes and individual learning? Here are three examples, one from political science, one from economics/cultural anthropology, and one from psychology, that illustrate the importance of culture in shaping our behavior.

Civic Duty: From Europe to America. It is often said that the United States is a nation of immigrants. Leaving aside the issue of the several million Native Americans who already lived on the continent, the early European settlers of North America did indeed come from various countries, including Britain, Germany, Italy, the Netherlands, and Scandinavia. As anyone who has traveled across Europe will be aware, while the inhabitants of each of these countries are broadly similar in their beliefs and attitudes (at least compared to, say, Japan or India), there are also significant differences between European countries. One such difference relates to values and attitudes concerning civic duty. These include various traits that can be considered beneficial to a liberal democratic society, such as the tendencies to donate to charity and conduct voluntary work, to vote in elections, to organize local pressure groups and labor unions, to regularly read newspapers (and thus be able to make informed democratic decisions), and to support social equality and representation for minorities. Some countries, such as Denmark, Norway, and Sweden, are high in average civic duty. Their inhabitants willingly donate to charity, vote, volunteer, and so on. Other countries, such as Italy and Spain, rank somewhat lower in average civic duty. Their inhabitants are less likely to, among other things, donate to charity, vote, and volunteer.

To political scientists Tom Rice and Jan Feldman, this cultural variation in civic duty presented a natural experiment that could test to what extent cultural differences persist over time.[4] Rice and Feldman reasoned that if values related to civic duty are faithfully passed via cultural transmission from parent to child and teacher to pupil, down the generations, then perhaps the civic duty of contemporary Americans could be predicted by the specific European country that their settler ancestors came from. So Rice and Feldman calculated the civic duty for Americans of various European ancestries. They did this using the answers to such questions as "Do you regularly read a newspaper?," "Did you vote in the last presidential election?," and "Generally speaking, would you say that most people can be trusted or that you can't be too careful in dealing with people?," and whether they agreed with such statements as "Most public officials are not really interested in the problems of the average person" and "Women should take care of running their homes and leave running the country up to men."

Rice and Feldman's results were just as they predicted. Americans who claim to be descended from settlers from European countries that have high civic duty, such as Denmark, Norway, and Sweden,

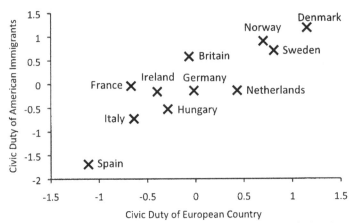

FIGURE 1.1 The correlation between civic duty of European populations and the civic duty of contemporary Americans who claim to be descended from those European populations. Values are composite z-scores from various measures of civic duty. Data from Rice and Feldman 1997.

themselves have relatively high civic duty. Americans who claim to be descended from European countries that have low civic duty, such as Italy and Spain, have relatively low civic duty. This can be seen in figure 1.1. Rice and Feldman's explanation for this match is that values related to civic duty, such as beliefs that voting or donating to charity are important and desirable things to do, have been culturally transmitted by imitation or teaching from parent to child or teacher to pupil over the several successive generations from original European settlers to present-day Americans. This would have occurred despite extensive interaction with other Americans of different descent, despite a declaration of independence and a civil war, and despite differences between Europe and the United States in geography and ecology. And a subsequent study by Tom Rice and Marshall Arnett showed that values related to civic duty can have important consequences.[5] They found that the average civic duty measured in different states at several points during US history significantly predict later socioeconomic development. For example, states that scored highly in civic duty in the 1930s were found to have relatively higher levels of personal income and education in the 1990s than states that scored low in civic duty in the 1930s. The reverse was not true: socioeconomic performance in the 1930s did not predict civic duty in the 1990s. So civic duty seems to be responsible for later socioeconomic development. The way in which it did this is not entirely clear, but we might imagine that states in which the residents more strongly value representative democracy elect more effective and honest public representatives, or perhaps rich residents of such states give more to charity, thus reducing inequality and raising average income. In any case, Rice and colleagues' work illustrates how people's cultural values can persist over several generations and significantly shape people's behavior and the society in which they live.

Is Fairness Universal? Rice and colleagues' studies are intriguing, but limited somewhat because they rely on self-reported measures of civic duty. Someone who says that it is important to vote or donate to charity is not necessarily someone who actually votes or donates to charity. An alternative way of exploring cultural variation is by directly measuring people's behavior in a controlled experimental setup.

One aspect of civic duty is fairness, and its flipside, selfishness. People high in civic duty tend to value fairness in personal interactions (e.g., business dealings), with each party getting a fair deal, while people low in civic duty tend to eschew the ideal of fairness and attempt to selfishly maximize their own personal gain at the expense of the other person. One way that experimental economists have tested people's sense of fairness/selfishness is known as the ultimatum game. The ultimatum game is played by two players, a proposer and a responder. The proposer must divide up a sum of money, say $100, into two portions, one that the proposer can keep and the other that is given to the responder to keep. For example, the proposer might split the $100 equally into two $50 portions (a fair offer), they might offer $20 and keep $80 for themselves (a selfish offer), or they might offer $80 and keep $20 (a generous offer). The responder can then decide whether to accept this offer, in which case they both get the amounts specified by the proposer, or reject the offer, in which case neither the proposer nor the responder get anything. Typically, the game is played just once and both players are anonymous, in order to avoid complications like pacts, promises, and reputation. The amount of money to be divided is also fairly substantial in order to motivate the players to give serious responses.

In a typical sample of US college students, the most common offer made by proposers is 50 percent, a fair and equal split. And responders react in a way that suggests they also have a sense of fairness: any offer less than 20 percent is rejected half the time.[6] It seems that responders have a sense of fairness, rejecting offers that they perceive as being unfair. Proposers, knowing this, make fair offers. So these experimental findings show that US college students are not entirely selfish and, consistent with the existence of civic duty, exhibit some degree of charity to others and a sense of fairness.[7]

Just as civic duty varies across countries and states, so too fairness responses in the ultimatum game vary across different societies. A team of cultural anthropologists led by Joseph Henrich of the University of British Columbia ran ultimatum game experiments in fifteen small-scale societies in twelve countries across the world.[8] These societies had diverse lifestyles, ranging from nomadic herders to hunter-gatherers to small-scale farmers. In each case, two randomly chosen members of the society played the ultimatum game anonymously and for a large potential reward, just as the US college students did. The results showed substantial variation between different societies in their offers. The Lamalera of Indonesia and the Aché of Paraguay, for example, both most commonly offered 50 percent of the sum to responders, just like US students. The Machiguenga of Peru and the Hadza of Tanzania, in contrast, most commonly offered just 20–25 percent. The acceptance thresholds also varied: the Quichua of Ecuador never rejected any offers, even those well below 50 percent, while the Au of Papua New Guinea rejected more than a quarter of all offers made, even those above 50 percent.

How can this variation between societies in fairness be explained? Individual-level variables, such as sex, age, wealth, and education, failed to predict behavior in the ultimatum game, both across societies and within each society. Instead, what predicted behavior best were the characteristics of the players' societies, primarily the degree to which economic life in that society depends on cooperation with people outside of one's family. Societies in which ultimatum game offers were lowest, such as the Machiguenga, had few economic dealings in their everyday life with people outside the family. Societies in which higher offers were made were much more integrated within market economies, frequently trading and cooperating with other people in their daily lives. The 50/50-splitting Lamalera, for example, hunt whales off the coast of Indonesia. Whale hunting is no easy task, and large crews of Lamalera in several boats are needed to stand a chance of making a successful kill. Because success depends on the cooperation of several people, the whale meat is divided into equal parts and shared among each crew member. In other words, the need for cooperation has resulted in the emergence of relatively strong fairness norms, which, Henrich et al. argue, are invoked in the ultimatum game and result in fair offers. So the bottom line: people in different societies exhibit different degrees of fairness because they have acquired different fairness norms from other members of their society, which in turn have emerged because of different requirements of life in those societies.

Eastern versus Western Thinking. One of the lessons of Henrich et al.'s study is that American college students are not necessarily representative of our species as a whole, a message that is slowly permeating the discipline of economics. Another discipline that is slowly beginning to recognize this is psychology. For much of its hundred-or-so-year history, experimental research in psychology has been carried out predominantly by Western (i.e., Western European and North American) psychologists on Western participants, who are typically well-educated, middle-class, financially well-off college students. Despite this patently narrow sample, major discoveries made by Western psychologists have often been heralded as major discoveries about universal, specieswide human psychological processes. In recent years, however, a growing number of cultural psychologists have begun to actually test this claim and have repeatedly found significant differences between the psychological processes of people from different societies.[9]

A good example relates to what Western psychologists have called the fundamental attribution error. This is the tendency, found in Western participants, to explain other people's actions in terms of stable, underlying dispositions. For example, if asked to explain why a student failed an exam, a Westerner might respond that the student was lazy and had not revised well enough, or that they were simply not smart enough. Westerners are much less likely to consider situational factors that are beyond the control of the student, such as that the student was badly taught, they were feeling unwell, or their questions didn't come up. This tendency is called an "error" because it persists even when it is obviously incorrect. The classic experimental demonstration of this in the 1960s had American participants read student essays that were either for or against Fidel Castro's communist regime in Cuba.[10] Half the students were told that the essay writers had been given a free choice as to whether to argue for or against the regime; the other half were told that the essay writers had been assigned the position at random. They were then asked to judge the extent to which the essay writers themselves supported Fidel Castro. As expected, the participants who were told that the essay writers had had a free choice said that those who chose to write a supportive essay really did support Castro more than those who wrote critical essays. Surprisingly, however, so did the participants who were told that the essay writers had had no choice: they also rated writers of supportive essays as having more positive attitudes toward Castro than writers of critical essays. In other words, the participants ignored the situational context—the fact that the essay writers were assigned to a position at random—and erroneously attributed the essay content to the writer's attitudes.

Until the mid-1990s it was generally believed that the fundamental attribution error was a universal characteristic of human psychology (it was, after all, called "fundamental"). When cultural psychologists started to test non-Western participants using tasks similar to the Castro study, however, they found that the fundamental attribution error was much smaller, if not absent altogether. Michael Morris and Kaiping Peng, for example, asked American and Chinese participants to read a newspaper report of a real-life murder case in which a Chinese physics student named Gang Lu shot his PhD advisor, several bystanders, and then himself after he lost an award competition and failed to get an academic job.[11] American participants, more than Chinese participants, attributed the behavior of Lu to internal dispositions, agreeing more with statements such as "Lu had chronic personality problems," "Lu drove himself crazy by putting too much pressure on himself," and "If Lu couldn't win, he didn't care about anything else." Chinese participants were more likely to appeal to situational explanations, agreeing more with statements such as "The recession has hurt the job market, which places stress on people seeking a new job," "The advisor failed in his duties to help Gang Lu and respond to his increasing frustration," and "American movies and television glorify violent revenge tactics."

Similar cross-cultural studies comparing North American and East Asian participants have revealed many other differences in thinking styles. Numerous psychological phenomena once thought to be human universals have been found to be weaker or absent in non-Western, typically East Asian, populations, such as cognitive dissonance (the anxiety brought about by simultaneously holding contradictory beliefs). Other studies have revealed differences in basic processes of attention, memory, and perception. For example, East Asian participants show better memory for the position of an object relative to other objects, while Western participants show better memory for the features of single objects. Psychologist Richard Nisbett and colleagues have argued that these East-West differences can be described along a single dimension, with an East Asian thinking style characterized as "holistic," and a Western thinking style characterized as "analytic."[12] Eastern holistic thinking focuses on the relations between objects and people (recognizing, for example, the role of situational factors in the murder case), whereas Western analytic thinking focuses on the characteristics and dispositions of individual objects and people. In short, the consensus from recent research in cultural psychology is that our thinking and behavior is deeply influenced by culture.

Culture, Environment, or Genes?

The examples given above all suggest that there are nontrivial differences between the members of different societies or different groups in various aspects of behavior and thinking. Can we be sure, however, that these differences really are cultural? Remember that there are two other ways in which people can acquire information: genetically and via individual learning. Perhaps the civic duty values that appear to have persisted over several generations have been inherited not culturally but genetically: perhaps Scandinavians are genetically predisposed to be more civic-minded than Italians, and this genetic variation has persisted in the modern-day United States. Or perhaps the variation in fairness revealed by the ultimatum game is the result of individual learning: each member of a relatively "fair" society lives in a (nonsocial) environment that has led them each to independently develop strong fairness norms, whereas members of less fair societies have each independently developed less fair norms.

These explanations need to be seriously considered, as many influential traditions within several social and behavioral science disciplines would favor genetic or individual learning explanations for human behavioral variation. The two dominant schools of thought of twentieth-century psychology, associative learning theory and cognitive psychology, both focus on individual learning while largely ignoring social learning and culture. Learning theorists such as J. B. Watson and B. F. Skinner sought to explain human behavior in terms of simple individual learning processes such as classical conditioning, where people learn associations between different stimuli in their environments (the original example of this being Pavlov's dogs learning to associate the sound of a bell with the appearance of food). Cognitive psychologists delve deeper into the underlying knowledge structures that shape people's behavior, such as the abstract categories that we use to classify objects (e.g., "furniture" or "animal") and use to infer the characteristics of novel objects without having to undergo trial-and-error associative learning. But like learning theorists before them, cognitive psychologists typically do not treat learning from the nonsocial environment and learning from other people any differently, if indeed they consider the latter at all. Similarly, economists of the "rational choice theory" school typically assume that people individually calculate costs and benefits of different behaviors, with little cultural influence. And an approach known as "cultural ecology" or "cultural materialism" within cultural anthropology, often associated with anthropologists Julian Steward and Marvin Harris, assumes that behavioral practices and technology can be seen as adaptations to local conditions rather than as culturally acquired.[13]

Other disciplines stress the role of genes. Evolutionary psychologists, for example, typically explain human behavior in terms of genetically evolved adaptations and downplay or ignore the role of culture. While admitting in theory a role for "transmitted culture," that is, the definition of culture given earlier in the chapter, evolutionary psychologists such as John Tooby and Leda Cosmides typically focus instead on what they call "evoked culture."[14] According to the evoked culture argument, much behavioral variation between groups of people can be explained as different genetically encoded responses triggered by different ecological conditions, a sort of mix of genes and individual learning. Tooby and Cosmides use a jukebox analogy to explain this. Imagine two jukeboxes with an identical set of songs programmed into each. Despite being identical, one jukebox might be playing a Beatles song and another jukebox playing a Bob Dylan song in response to the selections of different people. In the same way, two people living in two different societies might exhibit different behaviors because different (nonsocial) environmental cues trigger those behaviors from the identical underlying behavioral repertoire. This is very different to the "social transmission" definition of culture given earlier. If evolutionary psychologists are correct, then transmitted culture plays little or no role in shaping human behavioral variation, and a theory of cultural evolution would be unnecessary. So it is important to demonstrate that individual learning and genes cannot fully explain human behavioral variation and that culture plays an important role.

Individual Learning Alone Cannot Explain Human Behavioral Variation. If individual learning were responsible for variation in human behavior, then we would expect to see a close match between a person's behavior and the nonsocial ecological conditions in which that person lives, such as climate, terrain, or local animal and plant species. Different ecological conditions would cause people to independently invent similar solutions to the problems posed by those ecological conditions.

Numerous examples collected by cultural anthropologists and sociologists show this not to be the case. Indeed, there seems to be a "double dissociation'" between behavior and ecology. Two societies living in the same environment can have entirely different behavioral practices. For example, the Amish Mennonite religious groups live in the same ecological conditions in Pennsylvania as non-Amish Pennsylvanians, yet they retain quite distinct customs and practices, such as the use of horse and buggy rather than motor vehicles. Conversely, two societies with very similar behavioral practices can live in entirely different environments. For example, Britain and Australia have extremely different ecologies, yet British immigrants to Australia have maintained many British customs, laws, practices, and of course, the English language (albeit with many peculiar changes to proper English).

These anecdotal observations are confirmed by more systematic, statistical analyses. Anthropologist Barry Hewlett, along with biologists Annalisa De Silvestri and Rosalba Guglielmino, compared 109 different customs found in thirty-six ethnic groups across Africa.[15] Examples of the customs that they examined included type of marriage system (e.g., monogamous vs. polygamous), the presence or absence of intensive agriculture, and beliefs in interventionist versus noninterventionist gods. Just four of these 109 customs reliably varied according to ecological conditions (classified as desert, savannah, or forest), suggesting that local adaptation to ecological conditions through individual learning had little influence. The others correlated best either with family lineages, suggesting cultural transmission within families, or with geographical closeness, suggesting cultural transmission between neighboring groups.

Genes Alone Cannot Explain Human Behavioral Variation. The implication of Rice and Feldman's study is that values related to civic duty have been culturally transmitted down the generations. An alternative explanation, however, is genes. Perhaps the variation in civic duty in both European countries and their US descendents is genetic, rather than cultural. This is also a potential explanation for the findings of Hewlett, De Silvestri, and Guglielmino from Africa, which found that many practices correlate with family lineages. Such a pattern could also be explained by genetic inheritance, given that genes flow along family lineages as well as cultural information.

It is important first to be clear about exactly what genes are supposed to explain. There is no doubt that the psychological mechanisms that allow us to do things like imitate other people or learn languages are the product of genetic evolution. Such complex capacities did not spring from nowhere, unless one wishes to invoke creationism. However, we are not interested here in these underlying *capacities*, so much as the *contents* of culture: the specific beliefs, attitudes, skills and values that are transmitted using these genetically evolved capacities. And in particular, whether variation in these beliefs, attitudes, skills, and values both within and between groups can be explained primarily in terms of genetic variation or cultural variation.

The vast majority of between-group behavioral variation in humans simply cannot be explained by genetic differences. Behavioral geneticists, by comparing identical twins (who are genetically identical) and fraternal twins or siblings (who share on average half their unique genetic variation), estimate that most behavioral and cognitive traits, such as IQ, personality, and psychopathology, have a heritability of around 40–50 percent. That is, around half the variation in behavior between people living in the same society can be attributed to genes.[16] That leaves around 50–60 percent for culture. But the crucial point is that these differences are *within* societies, not *between* societies: for the kind of between-society differences discussed above, genetic influence will be substantially lower. Recent worldwide analyses estimate that the vast majority of human genetic variation (93–95 percent) is found within populations and just a tiny proportion (5–7 percent) between populations, and that this between-population genetic variation is far too small to explain documented behavioral variation in customs, practices, and languages.[17]

Immigration also counts against purely genetic explanations of human behavioral variation. Recall the aforementioned differences between the holistic thinking style of East Asians and the analytic thinking style of Westerners. What happens when people who grew up in East Asia emigrate to North America, or vice versa? Do the immigrants' children inherit the psychological characteristics of their parents, suggesting a genetic basis for these differences? Or do the immigrants' children adopt the psychological characteristics of the local society, suggesting a cultural basis? The evidence clearly favors the latter cultural explanation. When East Asians migrate to North America, this first generation tends to retain the psychological traits of their society of origin. However, their children, who grew up in the United States or Canada, show psychological characteristics that are much closer to their local Western society than to those of their parents. By the third generation, the psychological traits of people of East Asian descent are indistinguishable from their peers of European descent.[18] Substantial genetic change does not occur in just two generations: it must be the result of acculturation to local norms.

Other aspects of human behavior can change even more rapidly and offer further evidence against purely genetic explanations. Technology, for example, has changed incredibly quickly over the last few hundred years[19]: a gap of just sixty-six years separated the first powered flight by the Wright brothers and Neil Armstrong stepping foot on the moon. Social customs show similarly monumental change in relatively short periods of time: just forty-five years separate the Civil Rights Act of 1964, which ended racial segregation in the United States, with the election of Barack Obama in 2008 as the first African American president. These time periods are roughly equivalent to one or, at most, two biological generations. Given that genetic evolution operates gradually over many generations, genes simply cannot account for change this rapid. And these are just the big changes: think of the even more rapidly changing fashions and fads in clothing and popular music that change on the order of weeks and months.[20]

More Evidence for Culture: Children Are Cultural Sponges. These examples suggest that much behavioral variation between societies can be explained in terms of cultural transmission: people acquire knowledge, customs, attitudes, values, and so on from other members of their society. More proximate research on the learning habits of children supports this conclusion. Children seem to be predisposed to rapidly and automatically acquire huge amounts of information from other people. They are, in a sense, "cultural sponges," soaking up knowledge from those around them. A well-studied example is language. By the time they reach adulthood, children have a vocabulary of 60,000 words. This means that they must be learning, on average, 8–10 words every day.[21] As anyone who has tried to learn a second language as an adult can attest, this is no mean feat. Yet young children do this with little direct instruction. This general finding extends beyond words to all kinds of actions and beliefs. In one recent study conducted by developmental psychologists Derek Lyons, Andrew Young, and Frank Keil, for example, three- to five-year-old children were shown by an adult how to open an unusual box to retrieve a toy inside.[22] Some of the actions performed by the adult were functional, such as unscrewing a lid, while others were nonfunctional, such as tapping the side of the box with a feather. Yet despite their obvious irrelevance, the latter nonfunctional actions were faithfully copied by the children. This was found even when the nonfunctional actions were identified by the adult as being "silly and unnecessary," when the children were alone and unobserved, and when the children were rewarded for opening the box as quickly as possible. In sum, children can't help copying.

Evolutionary anthropologist Michael Tomasello has argued that it is our capacity to rapidly and accurately acquire huge amounts of information culturally that sets humans apart from other species. One study conducted by Esther Herrmann, Tomasello, and others illustrates this.[23] Herrmann et al. gave a battery of intelligence tests to two-year-old human children, adult chimpanzees, and adult orangutans. Some of these tests tapped physical intelligence, such as the ability to keep track of the number of objects in a display or the ability to use a tool to retrieve some food. Other tests tapped what Herrmann et al. called cultural intelligence, such as imitating the solution to a problem, communicating with the experimenter to retrieve a reward, or following the experimenter's gaze. There were no significant differences between the children, chimps, and orangutans on any of the tests of physical intelligence. On the tests of cultural intelligence, however, the children greatly outperformed both other species. Even at this early age, the minds of human children seem to be designed to acquire knowledge from other individuals, a finding that has been found in study after study.[24]

Culture Is Genetically Adaptive. A more theoretical line of support for the claim that humans are a cultural species comes from a set of theoretical models that show that it is often genetically adaptive for individuals to acquire information culturally.[25] In other words, it often in our genes' interests (metaphorically speaking) to forego direct control over behavior and let culture take over. While this might seem counterintuitive, the theoretical models show exactly why, in evolutionary terms, culture is adaptive. These models typically specify a population of hypothetical individuals tasked with discovering the correct "behavior" to carry out in their particular environment, such as what kind of food to eat or what stimuli in their environments constitute threats to be avoided. Each individual is assumed to possess one of three genotypes, each of which specifies a different way of discovering the best behavior to carry out: an "innate" genotype that directly specifies its bearers' behavior genetically, with that behavior fixed at birth and unable to be changed via learning; an "individual learning" genotype that causes its bearers to randomly try out different behaviors and stick with the one that gives the highest payoff; and a "cultural" genotype that causes its bearers to copy the behavior of another individual in the population. The modeler then allows the different types of individuals to compete with one another over several generations to see which genotype does best.

According to these models, learning, either individual or cultural, is favored over innateness when environments change relatively rapidly, because genes cannot respond to rapid change that occurs within a single biological generation. Once we receive our genes from our parents we are stuck with them, and novel changes in the world that occur within one's lifetime cannot be anticipated directly by those genes. Individual learning is a way for genes to indirectly respond to rapid, within-generational change: if a new potential food item or predator suddenly appears in the environment, then individual learners can discover whether the item is edible or whether the potential predator really is dangerous. However, individual learning is also often costly: trying out various novel food items one finds in one's environment is a risky way of identifying what is edible and what is poisonous. Culture allows individuals to forego these costs: eating whatever other individuals are eating is a much safer way of identifying edible food items, given that you can observe whether the other individuals are getting sick or not.[26] Culture also allows us to acquire and use things like cars and computers that could never have been invented by a single individual in their lifetime from scratch purely via individual learning. These theoretical findings that culture can be genetically adaptive fit well with the evidence reviewed so far that much of human behavior is shaped by culture rather than directly by genes or via individual learning.

Problems with How Culture Is Studied

Culture is thus clearly important in shaping various aspects of human behavior. So why are so many social and behavioral scientists reluctant to acknowledge this? To some extent it is quite understandable. For many economists, cognitive psychologists, and evolutionary psychologists, explanations of human behavior in terms of "culture" are simply meaningless. As economists Luigi Guiso, Paola Sapienza, and Luigi Zingales write:

> Until recently, economists have been reluctant to rely on culture as a possible determinant of economic phenomena. Much of this reluctance stems from the very notion of culture: it is so broad and the channels through which it can enter economic discourse so ubiquitous (and vague) that it is difficult to design testable, refutable hypotheses.[27]

The evolutionary psychologists John Tooby and Leda Cosmides are similarly disparaging about typical cultural explanations of human behavior in the social sciences. They describe the "Standard Social Science Model," in which every aspect of human behavior is explained in terms of some mysterious force called "culture," and mock its use in the social sciences during the mid- to late twentieth century to simultaneously explain everything and nothing:

> The invocation of culture became the universal glue and explanatory variable that held social science explanations together: Why do parents take care of their children? It is part of the social role their culture assigns to them. Why are Syrian husbands jealous? Their culture tied their status to their wife's honor. Why are people sometimes aggressive? They learn to be because their culture socializes them to be violent. Why are there more murders in America than in Switzerland? Americans have a more individualistic culture. Why do women want to look younger? Youthful appearance is valued in our culture. And so on.[28]

These complaints are somewhat justified. Historically, social scientists studying cultural phenomena have been reluctant, and even unable, to specify in precise terms exactly how culture operates beyond some vague and informal notion of "socialization" or "social influence." As Guiso, Sapienza, and Zingales note, when a concept is imprecise, then one cannot generate specific predictions, often via formal models, which can then be tested quantitatively through systematic experimentation or real-world measurement. This gives noncultural disciplines that *do* employ formal models and quantitative methods, such as evolutionary psychology or economics, an intrinsic advantage in explaining human behavior. In the chapters that follow I will argue that the theory of cultural evolution offers a fully scientific, quantitative, and rigorous way of understanding and explaining cultural change. But first, it is useful to examine in more detail the problems with how culture is typically studied in the social sciences.

The Perils of Hermeneutics, Reflexivity, and Social Constructionism. In the past few decades cultural anthropology has undergone something of a crisis. The principle methodology of cultural anthropology is ethnography, in which an anthropologist lives in a particular society for an extended period of time and observes and interviews the members of that society. The ethnographer's aim is to describe the studied people's lives, typically through the production of written descriptions. In the early years of cultural anthropology, attempts were then made to quantify the information contained in these ethnographies and to assemble these data into large cross-cultural databases. This allowed systematic cross-cultural comparisons to be made and gave early anthropologists a way to test hypotheses concerning how and why different cultural practices spread from society to society.[29]

In the latter part of the twentieth century, however, the ethnographic method, and the systematic cross-cultural comparisons that resulted from it, came under attack from various directions. Scholars working within what is called the "hermeneutic" or "textualist" school of thought, such as Clifford Geertz and James Clifford, attacked the validity of the ethnographic method. They argued that any example of written text, including an ethnography, will necessarily reflect the many implicit and subjective assumptions of its writer, assumptions that the writer acquires from members of his or her own society. Because ethnographers' assumptions will be different to those of the people being studied, who acquired different assumptions from their own society, these critics argue that an ethnographer can never accurately capture the true experiences of those people. A similar criticism arose in the guise of "reflexivity," the idea that the very act of observing another person's actions changes those actions, making observational methods intrinsically flawed. And another line of attack came from social constructionists, led by sociologists such as Bruno Latour, who conducted ethnographic studies of practicing scientists. Having observed numerous examples of how social factors—the ideological beliefs of scientists, for example—can shape scientific findings, Latour concluded that science is largely a social construction rather than an objective means of acquiring accurate knowledge.[30]

As a result of these challenges to the validity of ethnographic fieldwork and to the objectivity of the scientific method in general, most contemporary cultural anthropologists have largely abandoned any attempt to quantify the behavior of people living in different societies and to scientifically test hypotheses concerning behavioral variation. Seemingly accepting the criticisms fully, many ethnographers do not now claim to be conducting scientific research and make no claims of even trying to achieve objective findings, instead producing subjective and qualitative descriptions ("thick descriptions") of people's lives in particular social contexts.

The social constructionists and others have valid points: of course the assumptions of the ethnographer will affect their conclusions, the act of observing may well affect those being observed, and nobody who has had firsthand experience of working in a university science department will deny that social factors play some role in the scientific process. But this does not mean that ethnography cannot ever be scientifically useful, that insights cannot be gained from quantitative studies of human behavior, that cross-cultural comparisons are meaningless, and that science is entirely subjective. There are many ways of reducing the likelihood of subjectivity and bias in observational studies. Field biologists, for example, who have produced thoroughly scientific observational field studies of nonhuman animal behavior, get around the problem of observer bias by using multiple observers, some of whom are blind to the hypothesis under study, then quantifying the interobserver reliability (the extent to which different observers' observations agree). And if observer bias *is* detected, then statistical techniques can be used to correct that bias.[31] Regarding the social constructionists' criticism that social factors influence the scientific process, while this may be the case, ultimately the objective tools of the scientific method—hypothesis testing, falsification, replication, quantitative statistical analyses, and so on—result in a much more accurate understanding of the world than the nonscientific alternative of compiling subjective and superficial descriptions of people's lives.

Culture Is Not Static. Other branches of the social sciences that are fully scientific and methodologically rigorous, including economics, social/cultural psychology, and much of sociology, suffer from a different problem. These disciplines often treat culture as a static background variable that influences certain aspects of human behavior, rather than as something that itself changes and is itself a product of human behavior. Take cultural psychology, for example. As noted above, much recent research has demonstrated that what were once thought to be psychological universals are actually characteristics that are specific to Western countries. Many of these differences relate to quite fundamental psychological processes, such as the way that people view objects and attribute causes to behavior. Whereas Westerners tend to focus on individual objects in a scene and explain behavior in terms of stable dispositions, people who grew up in East Asian countries pay more attention to the relations between objects and explain behavior more in terms of social relationships. As argued above, patterns of immigration show that such differences cannot be attributed to genes or individual learning: they are cultural differences. Yet this still leaves much to explain: how exactly does "culture" give rise to these differences?

Many explanations of cultural variation given by cultural psychologists tend toward the descriptive. For example, the thinking of Westerners is labeled as "analytic," while that of East Asians as "holistic." Western selves are described as "independent" while East Asian selves are described as "interdependent."[32] While these labels are useful for connecting related findings under umbrella categories, they do not really explain the origin of these differences. Occasionally, historical scenarios are proposed as explanations of current cross-cultural variation. It has been argued, for example, that Eastern thinking is holistic because East Asian societies are more collectivist, which in turn is because the ancient Chinese agricultural system of rice farming necessitated the cooperation of large numbers of people. The analytic thinking that developed in the West can be attributed to a more individualistic Western European society, which originated in the ancient Greek farming methods of herding and fishing, which were more solitary activities.[33] However, these historical scenarios are still quite descriptive and speculative, and they fail to specify exactly how agricultural practices translate into psychological traits, or the transmission mechanisms by which these traits have persisted over successive generations.

Economists Richard Nelson and Sidney Winter have long made a parallel argument concerning economics.[34] Mainstream economics, they argue, is unrealistically focused on static equilibria. A typical economic model specifies a set of decisions that a firm can carry out in response to a set of external conditions, such as supply and demand in the market, and internal conditions, such as stock levels, assuming that firms are attempting to maximize profits. Rigorous mathematical modeling techniques can be used to determine the static equilibrium, or stable state, of the economic system at which all economic forces balance out, such as when supply matches demand. While such equilibria describe real economic conditions reasonably well at a single point in time, Nelson and Winter argue they are not so good at explaining changes in economic systems over time. Economic growth that is driven by technological change is particularly poorly described by static equilibria, given that technology such as telecommunications and computing exhibit continual growth and change. The inability of economists to foresee the 2007 global recession is a forceful reminder of this limitation. Again, a way is needed of combining the rigor of economic models with a proper treatment of change over time.

Disciplinary Fragmentation. An adequate understanding of culture is also hindered by the fragmentary structure of the social sciences. There is little exchange of theories and findings between economists, sociolo-

gists, linguists, historians, psychologists, anthropologists, and archaeologists. In many cases these disciplines hold mutually incompatible
assumptions. In other cases, different disciplines end up reinventing
concepts from scratch that other disciplines have known about for
years, because of the lack of communication. This should not be the
case, if every social science discipline is supposed to be studying the
same phenomenon—culture—and it is certainly not conducive to scientific understanding.

Compare this situation to that of the biological sciences, which for
decades have been unified under a single theoretical framework: Darwinian evolutionary theory. Each branch of biology, from field studies
to laboratory experiments to mathematical models to the study of the
fossil record, is united by a unifying theory with a shared set of common assumptions. As a result, there is frequently the mutually productive exchange of ideas, theories, and methods across these branches:
an experimentalist might, for example, try to recreate in the lab the
pattern of "punctuated equilibria" observed in the fossil record (i.e.,
long periods of stasis interspersed by brief periods of rapid biological
change) in order to better understand the underlying processes that
drive it. A field biologist might measure the strength of natural selection in a wild population in order to check the validity of mathematical
models of selection, after which the modelers revise and improve their
models.[35] This back and forth both within and across subdisciplines
has resulted in huge progress in biologists' understanding of biological change and diversity, which would not have been possible in the
absence of a common, unifying theoretical framework.

Conclusion: Culture Is important, But Inadequately Studied

So despite the importance of culture in shaping various aspects of
human behavior, there are several problems with the way in which
culture is studied and conceptualized across the social sciences, such
as the lack of quantitative, formal methods and scientific hypothesis
testing, the treatment of culture as static rather than dynamic, and a
general lack of communication of findings and methods across different branches of the social sciences. In the chapters that follow, I argue
that the theory of cultural evolution, based on the premise that culture evolves according to similar Darwinian principles as do biological species, provides solutions to all of the problems just outlined: it
fully recognizes the role of culture in explanations of human behavior;
it provides formal, quantitative methods that can be used to explain

cultural phenomena in a way that explicitly incorporates change over time; and it provides a common theoretical framework around which the different branches of the social sciences can be synthesized. The next chapter introduces the basic theory of cultural evolution and the evidence supporting this theory.

2 Cultural Evolution

The concept of cultural evolution—the idea that culture evolves and that useful parallels can be drawn between biological and cultural change—has had a long and often controversial history in the social sciences. Ever since the publication of *The Origin of Species* in 1859, scholars have attempted to use ideas from biology to understand cultural change. Evolutionary approaches to culture have, at different times over the past century and a half, been both the dominant paradigm for understanding cultural change and also deeply unpopular and virtually taboo. There have also been several different theories of "cultural evolution," from nineteenth-century progressive theories of cultural evolution to more recent fads such as memetics. Not all of these bear much resemblance to evolution as either Darwin, or modern biologists, would recognize it. So it is crucial to specify exactly what is meant by a theory of cultural evolution and also to show that this theory is empirically supported.

While biology has undoubtedly changed in the 150 years since its publication, *The Origin* remains one of the most compelling descriptions of biological evolution ever written, and the basics of Darwin's argument have not considerably changed.[1] A clearer picture of a theory of cultural evolution can, I think, be achieved by going back to this original source.[2] Darwin famously described

The Origin as "one long argument." This argument can be seen as comprising three elements, or preconditions: variation, competition, and inheritance.[3] First, individuals within a species *vary* in their characteristics. For example, finches might vary in the size of their beaks, with some finches having larger beaks than other finches. Second, there is *competition* between individuals. This competition may be over food, nesting space, mates, or any other limited resource. As a result, not all individuals will have an equal chance of surviving and reproducing. Moreover, an individual's characteristics affect its success in this competition to survive and reproduce. For example, finches with larger-than-average beaks might be able to open a wider range of seeds than finches with smaller-than-average beaks. These large-beaked finches will get more food, thus increasing their chances of survival to reproductive age and of successfully raising offspring compared to small-beaked finches. We can say here that larger-beaked finches have higher fitness than smaller-beaked finches, where fitness refers to the success of an entity in reproducing. Finally, offspring *inherit* characteristics from their parents. For example, large-beaked finches will, on average, give birth to similarly large-beaked offspring. Over time, this variation-competition-inheritance cycle results in evolutionary change, defined as a change in the frequency of a trait in a population over time. Finches with larger beaks obtain more food and so have more offspring on average than finches with small beaks. Because those offspring inherit large beaks from their parents, the next generation will, on average, have slightly larger beaks than the parental generation. The same happens in the subsequent generation: larger-beaked finches will have more offspring than smaller-beaked finches, and the third generation will have slightly larger beaks again. Over successive generations, beak size gradually increases. Indeed, this very process of finch beak evolution was observed in the 1970s on the Galápagos Islands, when a drought drastically reduced the number of seeds in the environment. Large-beaked finches were able to open a wider range of seeds than small-beaked finches, were more likely to survive and reproduce, and so average beak size in the population increased.[4]

So this was Darwin's basic idea—that all biological change can be described in terms of just three basic preconditions: variation, competition, and inheritance. If any of these cannot be demonstrated, then evolution simply does not happen (indeed, this is an important and often underappreciated point: that the theory of evolution is falsifiable). Since *The Origin*, biologists have established without a shadow of a doubt that Darwin's theory is correct as applied to biological change.

Does Cultural Change Exhibit Darwin's Three Preconditions?

But what about cultural change? Can we also show that culture exhibits these three key preconditions specified by Darwin? If so, then this would provide justification for describing cultural change as a Darwinian evolutionary process. Let's take each in turn.

Precondition One: Variation. Darwin documented, in often excruciating detail, the variation between individuals of several species, especially pigeons:

> The proportional width of the gape of mouth, the proportional length of the eyelids, of the orifice of the nostrils, of the tongue (not always in strict correlation with the length of beak), the size of the crop and of the upper part of the oesophagus; the development and abortion of the oil-gland; the number of the primary wing and caudal feathers; the relative length of wing and tail to each other and to the body; the relative length of leg and of the feet; the number of scutellae on the toes, the development of skin between the toes, are all points of structure which are variable.[5]

And this goes on for several pages. But Darwin had good reason to go into such painstaking detail. If every individual were identical, then there would be nothing for natural selection to select, and no meaningful change could take place. As Darwin noted, "These individual differences are highly important for us, as they afford materials for natural selection to accumulate."[6]

Since *The Origin*, biologists have confirmed and quantified the extent to which biological organisms vary. There are, for example, an estimated 1.8 million extant biological species, while in terms of within-species variation, humans and mice have around 20,000–25,000 protein-coding genes, *Drosophila* have 13,000, and rice has 46,000.[7] Biologists have also determined exactly how variation is generated, in the form of genetic mutation and recombination, and established that novel variation is blind with respect to fitness (i.e., beneficial mutations are no more likely to arise when they are needed than when they are not needed). The equivalent processes that are responsible for variation in cultural evolution and the issue of blind variation will be discussed later in this chapter. For now, let us stick with the direct comparison with *The Origin* and, like Darwin, simply try to demonstrate that cul-

ture varies and remain temporarily ignorant of the causes of this variation. Indeed, this echoes the position of Darwin, who admitted that
"our ignorance of the laws of variation is profound."[8]

That culture also varies is patently obvious. People vary in their
religious beliefs, in their political views, in their scientific knowledge,
in their skills, and so on. The manifestation or expression of these
mental aspects of culture also, as a result, varies, such as variation in
buildings and tools. But following Darwin's lead, can we go beyond
informal observation and give documented examples of this variation?
And furthermore, can we in any way quantify this variation? Technology provides a good source of data regarding cultural variation. Historian Henry Petroski documents the variation found in forks of the late
1800s, each designed for a slightly different function, listing "oyster
fork-spoon, oyster forks (four styles), berry forks (four styles), terrapin,
lettuce and ramekin fork . . . large salad, small salad, child's, lobster,
oyster, oyster-cocktail, fruit, terrapin, lobster, fish, and oyster-cocktail
fork . . . mango, berry, ice-cream, terrapin, lobster, oyster, pastry,
salad, fish, pie, dessert, and dinner fork."[9] These vary in the number of
tines, the dimensions (length, width, thickness), the shape of the tines,
the shape of the handle, the material used, and so on, reminiscent of
the minute variation documented by Darwin for pigeons.

The patent record provides a good way of measuring technological
variation on a grosser scale. A staggering 7.7 million patents were is-
sued in the United States alone between 1790 and 2006.[10] Because a
successfully patented invention must, by law, be demonstrably different to all existing patents, each of these 7.7 million patents describes
unique variation. Other databases do the same for other aspects of culture. Take religious beliefs: the World Christian Encyclopedia estimates
that there are over 10,000 distinct religions worldwide.[11] Within each
of these 10,000 religions there is further variation: Christianity can be
divided into 33,830 denominations, for example. Languages also vary:
there are an estimated 6,800 languages currently spoken worldwide.[12]
Again, within each language there is further variation: the Oxford
English Dictionary contains over 615,000 different words, with the
average person using 16,000 words every day.[13] And just as dictionar-
ies contain a record of linguistic variation, encyclopedias contain a
record of general knowledge. In August 2009, the English-language
Wikipedia added its three-millionth page (it was about Beate Eriksen,
a Norwegian soap opera actor). The combined number of Wikipedia
entries across all languages is, at the time of writing, 9.25 million,

while even this is just a fraction of the more than 25 billion website pages on the internet.[14]

There are, of course, caveats to these figures. Some might quibble with the methods of data collection, or how the different units (words, religions, technologies, web pages) are defined. It also presupposes that this variation is discrete and can be counted, rather than being continuous, in which case there would be no discrete units (e.g., words, patents) to count. Another important issue is the distinction between variation of the same type of cultural trait (e.g., different types of fork), analogous to within-species variation, versus variation between different types of cultural trait (e.g., forks and tractors), analogous to between-species variation. This is important because competition will be most extreme in the former case, between similar traits that serve the same purpose and so are competing for the same cultural "niche." These are all important issues, and no doubt methods for quantification can be improved. But it is reasonable to conclude that there is huge variation in human culture, on the order of millions to billions of variants, and that this variation can be documented and quantified. We can therefore state with some certainty that the first of Darwin's preconditions—variation—is present in culture.[15]

Precondition Two: Competition. Darwin talked about competition in terms of a "struggle for existence," asking rhetorically, "can we doubt (remembering that many more individuals are born than can possibly survive) that individuals having any advantage, however slight, over others, would have the best chance of surviving and of procreating their kind?"[16]

Inspired by the ideas of the economist and demographer Thomas Malthus, Darwin argued that this struggle for existence results from the fact that populations tend to increase in size exponentially, generating inevitable shortages of finite resources such as food, living space, and mates. There will therefore be competition for these limited resources, with only a subset of the population likely to survive and reproduce. This competition between individuals might be direct and physical, such as when jackals fight over a fresh carcass or when stags lock antlers in order to impress onlooking females. However, Darwin also stressed that competition need not be literal or direct. A single individual can also be said to struggle for existence in the face of the physical environment, such as when "a plant at the edge of a desert is said to struggle for life against the drought."[17] Here, competition between different plants is indirect, with the plants best able to deal with dry conditions more likely to survive and reproduce than less able plants. This indirect competition is not what most people think of as "competition," and to avoid this confusion modern biologists tend to use the phrase "differential fitness" instead of "competition."[18] I will continue to use the word "competition" because it is less cumbersome and maintains the link with Darwin's terminology in *The Origin*. But really "competition" is shorthand for "differential fitness," which simply says that some individuals are more likely to survive and reproduce than other individuals, and these differences in survival and reproduction are linked in some way to their characteristics.

Intuitively, there must be some form of competition in culture given the extent of the variation observed even in such things as forks, let alone religions and languages. It is surely impossible for any single person to possess the knowledge and skills to manufacture 7.7 million distinct inventions, or to learn every one of the 6,800 languages in existence. And even if some linguistic genius *could* learn 6,800 languages, they could only ever speak one language at any one time. This highlights the finite resources that are acting upon culturally acquired information: there are limitations on memory capacity and on the time it takes to learn and express knowledge.

Evidence supports this intuitive reasoning. That technology and language are subject to competition due to finite resources is highlighted by the phenomenon of extinction, just as extinction of species is the product of biological competition. The extinction of various forms of technology has been documented by historians and anthropologists, such as the loss of various technologies and practices from the islands of Oceania (e.g., the canoe, pottery, the bow and arrow, and circumcision) and the loss of artifacts such as bone tools and skills such as fishing in prehistoric Tasmania following isolation from mainland Australia.[19] There is also an extremely high extinction rate of languages at present, much higher than the extinction rate of any biological species.[20] And within languages, it has been shown that numerous irregular verbs have, throughout history, gradually been whittled down to just a handful, based on how often those verbs are used.[21] Irregular verbs that are used often, such as "to go" with its irregular past tense of "went," are easier to remember, less likely to be regularized, and so more likely to survive in the vocabulary. Indeed, this process in which easily remembered words are more likely to survive was presaged by Darwin himself:

> A struggle for life is constantly going on amongst the words and grammatical forms in each language. The better, the shorter, the easier forms are constantly gaining the upper hand.[22]

Archaeologists, too, have documented many examples in which one type of artifact or technology has increased in frequency over a specific time period, while a different type of artifact or technology shows a corresponding decrease over the same time period. This is consistent with the former replacing the latter as a result of competition between the types. Examples include painted pottery replacing corrugated pottery in New Mexico or the replacement of spear-throwing technology with bow-and-arrow technology in North America.[23]

At a more proximate level, evidence from experimental psychology provides details of how different ideas compete for memory space. Classic experiments have demonstrated the existence of "interference effects" in memory.[24] In these experiments, subjects are asked to read and recall lists of words. Subjects show significantly worse recall of the words when they have to read another list of words while they are trying to remember the first list. This suggests that the second list is interfering with recall of the first. And if one cannot recall a word, one cannot pass it on to another person, and the word declines in frequency in the population as a whole. Interestingly, this interference is greater when the distractor words are similar in meaning to the target words, suggesting that, as Darwin noted, competition is greatest between similar kinds, because they are competing for the same cultural niche:

> [I]t is the most closely allied forms—varieties of the same species and species of the same genus or of related genera—which, from having nearly the same structure, constitution, and habits, generally come into the severest competition with each other.[25]

We therefore see competition in culture both at the psychological level, in the form of competition for space in memory, and also the effects of that competition, in the form of the extinction of various cultural practices and forms. Cultural traits, like biological organisms, take part in an endless struggle for existence.

Precondition Three: Inheritance. The third of Darwin's preconditions for evolution was inheritance, and he was direct about its importance:

"Any variation which is not inherited is unimportant for us."[26] Darwin noted that individuals that are more likely to survive and reproduce during the struggle for existence will often pass on their traits or characteristics to their offspring. If those characteristics were at least partially responsible for the parents' increased chances of survival and reproduction, then there will be a gradual increase in fitness and adaptation to the local environment. Inheritance therefore allows beneficial traits to be preserved in successive generations. Without inheritance, beneficial traits are not preserved, and evolution cannot occur.

Although inheritance was necessary for Darwin's argument, for him "the laws governing inheritance are quite unknown"[27] beyond the basic observation that offspring resemble parents more than a randomly chosen member of the species. It was not until the rediscovery of Gregor Mendel's pea-plant experiments, and further experiments in the early twentieth century, that the details of genetic inheritance were worked out. So for the moment let's ignore the details of cultural inheritance and simply ask whether cultural information can be successfully reproduced, or transmitted, from one person to another.

As discussed in chapter 1, there is voluminous evidence from cross-cultural comparisons that people acquire beliefs, attitudes, skills, and knowledge from other people via cultural transmission. Early immigrants to the United States have passed values related to civic duty down successive generations via cultural transmission, people in small-scale societies transmit norms relating to fairness as evidenced by cultural variation in the ultimatum game, and holistic and analytic thinking styles have been transmitted from generation to generation in East Asia and the West, respectively. Evidence from studies of contemporary immigrants confirms that this inheritance is cultural rather than genetic, given that in only one or two generations the children of immigrants are indistinguishable from long-term residents, rather than their more immediate genetic ancestors.

Such cross-cultural studies are complemented by more direct experimental studies that demonstrate person-to-person cultural transmission of behavior, attitudes, and opinions. Classic experiments conducted by social psychologist Albert Bandura in the 1960s showed that children will readily imitate the behavior of adult demonstrators.[28] Children who saw an adult acting aggressively toward a large inflatable "Bobo" doll themselves later showed more aggressive actions toward the doll than children who did not see any aggressive actions, or who saw an adult behaving nonaggressively. Other classic experiments conducted by social psychologist Solomon Asch show how adults readily adopt the opinion of others in simple tasks, such as matching a line to one of a set of other lines of varying length, even when the other people's answers (actually stooges of the experimenter) are patently false.[29] These experimental studies are complemented by questionnaire studies showing strong parent-offspring correlations in traits that are unlikely to be entirely genetic, such as religious beliefs and hobbies, as well as similarly high correlations between unrelated peers in such traits, which cannot be genetic.[30]

In a sense, however, mere person-to-person transmission of information is not enough for a fully Darwinian cultural evolution. Darwin famously described biological evolution as "descent with modification." By this he meant that for biological evolution to work, minor modifications must not merely be inherited from parent to offspring in a one-to-one fashion, inheritance must be faithful enough such that the modifications are preserved over several successive generations and potentially combined with other beneficial traits. Only then can we explain the complex adaptations involving several functionally interrelated parts, such as eyes or wings, that are the result of the accumulation of numerous separate modifications over countless generations.

We can similarly demonstrate the gradual accumulation of modifications in culture. Historians have repeatedly shown how technological artifacts rarely, if ever, spring from nothing. Instead, successful innovations are always slight modifications of what went before, or the combination of previously separate innovations. Historian George Basalla gives the example of the steam engine.[31] Rather than suddenly emerging fully formed from James Watt's inventive mind, as suggested by some popular accounts, Watt's steam engine was actually a modified version of the preexisting Newcomen steam engine, with which Watt had had extensive experience, and which in turn was a modification of a previous model, and so on back through history. Bodies of knowledge also accumulate gradually in the same way that technological artifacts do. Mathematics, for example, has evolved through the accumulation of successive innovations by different individuals in different societies over vast periods of time, with each new innovation paving the way for the next. Even the basic base-10 decimal system took over 4,000 years to emerge. Only after the Sumerians began to use written symbols to represent numbers in around 2400 BC could the Babylonians invent the place value system, in which the position of a digit with respect to the decimal place determines its value. This then allowed the Hindus and Mayans to invent a written symbol for zero, which in turn made calculations easier. This accumulation of directly related successive inventions proceeded for centuries, with major additions from the Greeks (e.g., geometry), Arabs (e.g., algebra), and Europeans (e.g., calculus), through to present-day mathematics.[32]

Human culture therefore also exhibits the last of Darwin's three preconditions for evolution, inheritance. Cultural variants can be passed faithfully from one individual to another, just as genes are passed from parent to offspring in biological evolution. Moreover, this cultural inheritance is of sufficiently high fidelity that it can successfully support the gradual accumulation of modifications, just as Darwin observed for lineages of biological organisms.

Further Parallels

As well as demonstrating the existence of these three key characteristics of Darwinian evolution—variation, competition, and inheritance—Darwin also showed that these characteristics can explain the hitherto mysterious biological phenomena that had puzzled naturalists for centuries. Three such phenomena are adaptation, maladaptation, and convergence. So if culture is Darwinian, then we should expect to see these emergent phenomena in culture also.

Adaptation. One of Darwin's greatest achievements was to provide a scientific explanation for the often striking fit between organisms and their environments, in the form of adaptations:

> We see these beautiful co-adaptations . . . in the structure of the beetle which dives through the water; in the plumed seed which is wafted by the gentlest breeze; in short, we see beautiful adaptations everywhere and in every part of the organic world.[33]

Natural selection provides a scientific explanation for this organism-environment fit. Over successive generations, individuals that are better at interacting with and gaining resources from their environments—individuals that are faster or more efficient at swimming through water, for example—are more likely to survive and reproduce than less effective individuals. We see the outcome of this gradual selection process in the form of, for example, streamlined body shapes that make swimming faster and more efficient. More complex adaptations, such as the eye, may have multiple working parts all interacting with one another in a precise manner. These can equally be shown to be the product of gradual natural selection through the accumulation of successive beneficial modifications, from concave pits of photosensitive cells to adjustable lenses, each of which improved an organism's ability to sense light and movement in their environments.

We can also observe cultural adaptations that are exquisitely designed for a particular purpose or for use in a particular environment but that are the result of cultural rather than biological evolution. An example might be the bow and arrow, which features multiple working parts all interacting with one another in a precise manner. For example, the San people of Botswana have 1-meter-long bows with strings made of animal tendons, arrow shafts made of reeds, arrowheads of ostrich bone (or more recently, barbed wire) that are poisoned using beetle larva, and quivers made of tree roots.[34] These components together form a "beautiful co-adaptation" that is highly suited to its function and features many functionally interrelated parts. The examples of cumulative cultural evolution given above, such as modern mathematics or the steam engine, also constitute cultural adaptations. Indeed, these examples highlight the power of cultural processes in generating adaptations that single individuals could never have come up with on their own.

Maladaptation. While it was important for Darwin to demonstrate that his theory could explain adaptations, it was equally important to demonstrate that species are not perfectly adapted to their environments. Perfect adaptation would, after all, be consistent with the action of an omniscient creator designing every species to a perfect standard. To counter this view, Darwin gave examples of maladaptation, where a species is ill fitted to its environment. This might occur when the environment in which a species lives changes in some way, or when a species moves into a new environment. Although drastic mismatches between the species and the new environment are likely to lead to extinction, when the mismatch is not so drastic then minor remnants of adaptations to the previous environment may often persist despite no longer serving any purpose. Examples include the small and functionless skeletal hind limbs of whales and snakes that have been preserved from their quadrupedal ancestors but which no longer serve any function. Vestigial organs such as these provide evidence for descent, and therefore for Darwinian evolution.

Aspects of culture can also be described as vestigial, where once-adaptive cultural adaptations become maladaptive when environments change. A familiar example is the QWERTY keyboard, which comprises a configuration of keys designed to make typing as slow and awkward as possible. In the context in which it emerged, the QWERTY keyboard was highly functional because fast typing caused early typewriter keyboards to jam. Modern keyboards no longer have this limitation, yet the suboptimal QWERTY keyboard configuration remains.[35] Vestigial features are also common in technological artifacts, especially when new raw materials become available. Indeed, George Basalla notes that such cases are common enough to merit their own label, namely, a "skeuomorph," which is defined as an "element of design or structure that serves little or no purpose in the artifact fashioned from the new material but [which] was essential to the object made from the original material."[36] Stone columns, for example, often retain the masonry joints of their wooden precursors, despite no longer serving a function.

Convergence. Finally, Darwin observed that isolated species could evolve similar traits due to convergent evolution to similar environments. He himself drew a cultural analogy here:

> [I]n nearly the same way as two men have sometimes independently hit on the very same invention, so natural selection . . . has sometimes modified in very nearly the same manner two parts in two organic beings, which owe but little of their structure in common to inheritance from the same ancestor.[37]

Familiar examples of convergence in biological evolution include the independent evolution of wings in bats, birds, and insects, or streamlined body forms in fish and cetaceans. Indeed, convergence is now considered to be one of the strongest forms of evidence for natural selection, given the unlikelihood that similar forms would evolve independently in unrelated lineages unless they are adaptations to similar environments.

In culture, Darwin famously confirmed the first part of his observation above when both he and Alfred Russel Wallace came up with the theory of natural selection at the same time. Other examples of parallel inventions or discoveries in culture include writing, which was invented independently by the Sumerians around 3000 BC, the Chinese around 1300 BC, and the Mexican Indians around 600 BC.[38] Convergent cultural evolution may also produce artifacts that perform the same function but do so in different ways, such as knives and forks in Europe and chopsticks in China, both used to handle hot food.[39]

Darwinian versus Spencerian Theories of Cultural Evolution

Given the many parallels outlined above between biological and cultural change, including several parallels pointed out by Darwin himself, it is not surprising that theories of cultural evolution began to appear not long after the publication of *The Origin of Species*. Many of these were proposed by influential early anthropologists such as Edward Burnett Tylor in Britain and Lewis Henry Morgan in the United States.[40] Unfortunately, the evolutionary theory that they applied to culture bore little resemblance to Darwin's theory and more closely resembled the rather un-Darwinian "progressive" evolutionary ideas of Darwin's contemporary, Herbert Spencer.[41] Spencer saw evolution as embodying a process of inevitable progress along a ladder of increasing complexity, from simple microorganisms, to more complex plants and animals, and ultimately to humans. Following Spencer, Tylor and Morgan saw cultural evolution as also embodying some form of inevitable progress. For them, cultural change could be described as the movement of societies along fixed stages of ever-increasing complexity. For example, Morgan presented seven stages through which every human society supposedly has passed or will pass in the future: lower, middle, and upper savagery, then lower, middle, and upper barbarism, and finally civilization. According to Morgan, each of these periods "has a distinct culture and exhibits a mode of life more or less special and peculiar to itself."[42] For example, "lower barbarism" begins with the appearance of speech and ends with the invention of fire, while "middle barbarism" begins with the domestication of animals and ends with the appearance of iron smelting. (For computer game enthusiasts, it's a lot like the fixed stages of technological advancement seen in Sid Meier's Civilization games.) Morgan then goes on to classify contemporary societies as each having advanced to one of these levels. Australian aborigines, for example, he classified as having achieved "middle savagery," while Central American "Village Indians" were placed at "middle barbarism." European societies, and their recent colonial off-shoots such as the United States, were placed at the top of this cultural ladder, and non-European societies were explicitly compared with ancestral stages of European societies. For example, contemporary (to Morgan) Central American "Village Indians" had reached the same stage as ancient Britons, and had not yet achieved the stage attained by "Italian tribes shortly before the founding of Rome."[43]

There are many problems with these early "progress" theories of cultural evolution. First, they are rather tainted by the racist and colonialist social views of the Victorian societies in which they emerged. The idea that non-Western societies were "less evolved" than contemporary Britain or America provided an attractive "scientific" justification for what today are considered to be rather distasteful social and political attitudes. Beyond their political implications, however, it is crucial to recognize that these progress theories bear little resemblance to the evolutionary theory that Darwin proposed in *The Origin*, nor to what modern-day biologists understand by evolution, and nor, indeed, to the theory of cultural evolution presented in this book. As the biologist Stephen Jay Gould has repeatedly argued, biological evolution is explicitly nonprogressive.[44] Species do not progress along fixed stages from simple microorganisms to more complex plants and animals. Humans are not at the top of the evolutionary ladder, because there is no ladder of which to be at the top. There is only local adaptation to local environments, which does not necessarily translate into global increases in fitness, and does not result in inevitable and entirely predictable evolutionary change along a prespecified course.

Similarly, as argued in the 1920s by anthropologists such as Franz Boas and his followers, there is little historical or ethnographic evidence that different societies pass through exactly the same stages in the same order, and contemporary non-Western societies cannot be meaningfully equated with ancient European societies.[45] More fundamentally, societies do not constitute self-contained wholes in the form of distinct stages. Ideas, technologies, and people can move from one society to another, such that different societies may share some aspects of culture and differ in others. Finally, progressive theories are inadequate because they do not specify the processes that are responsible for this supposed cultural progression. It seems that societies somehow magically jump from one stage to the next once they have accumulated the necessary inventions (e.g., the use of fire or pottery).[46]

Unfortunately, while progress theories of biological evolution were quickly purged from biology, progress theories of cultural evolution persisted well into the twentieth century.[47] To this day, many anthropologists and sociologists are wary of modern theories of cultural evolution because of their (unfounded) association with politically motivated and scientifically dubious nineteenth-century progress theories of cultural evolution. It is crucial to recognize, therefore, that

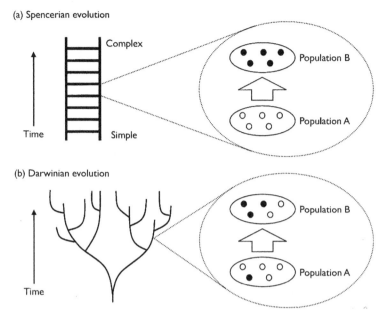

(a) Spencerian evolution

Complex

Population B

Population A

Time   Simple

(b) Darwinian evolution

Population B

Population A

Time

FIGURE 2.1 The conceptual differences between Spencerian and Darwinian evolution. (a) Spence-rian evolution involves movement up a ladder of increasing complexity, from simple to more complex stages. The inset shows how populations (e.g., species or societies) are considered to be homoge-nous types. (b) Darwinian evolution is treelike rather than ladderlike. There is no inevitable increase in complexity, and many branches go extinct. The inset shows how variation within populations (e.g., species or societies) gradually changes over time.

the progressive Spencerian theory of evolution is fundamentally differ-ent to Darwin's population-based theory of evolution. This difference is illustrated in figure 2.1. Spencer's theory views species as a group of homogenous individuals that all share the same essential qualities. Evolutionary change occurs when one species abruptly steps up to the next rung of the evolutionary ladder to become a new, more "com-plex" species. The same was true of Spencerian theories of cultural evolution, except instead of species there are societies that move up a stagelike ladder. Darwin's theory, on the other hand, focuses instead on the variation *within* populations (e.g., in beak size) and how this variation gradually changes over time. Given enough time, a popula-tion might change enough to warrant being called a new species, but this change is internally driven by selection and other processes act-ing on the individuals within the population, rather than propelled by an externally triggered shift. This change in thinking, from essential-ist, ladderlike thinking to variation-focused, Darwinian "population" thinking, has been described as one of Darwin's major contributions to science.[48] Furthermore, Darwinian evolution does not require that species increase in complexity over time. Traits may be lost, and species frequently go extinct (the dead-end branches in figure 2.1b). This makes Darwinian evolution more treelike than ladderlike, as lineages branch off from one another in a haphazard, nonlinear manner. The theory of cultural evolution discussed in this book is Darwinian, not Spencerian.

Darwinian versus Neo-Darwinian Theories of Cultural Evolution

Another important distinction to make is between Darwinian theories of cultural evolution and *neo-Darwinian* theories of cultural evolution. The evidence reviewed above demonstrates that cultural change is Darwinian in that it exhibits those properties of variation, competition, and inheritance that Darwin outlined in *The Origin*. Yet Darwin often had little idea—and in some cases was dead wrong—about exactly how these processes worked at a microlevel: where new variation comes from and how it is generated, the precise forms of competition that act to sort different variants, and the mechanisms by which traits are inherited from parent to offspring. In the decades following publication of *The Origin*, a group of biologists known as experimental geneticists conducted a series of ingenious breeding experiments in order to work out these "microevolutionary" details. *Microevolution* describes those small-scale, individual-level processes that act to change trait frequencies within a single population, and can be contrasted with *macroevolution*, which describes large-scale patterns and trends above the species level, such as the emergence and diversification of new species due to adaptation.

The microevolutionary details worked out by experimental geneticists include the findings that genetic inheritance is *particulate* (it involves the transmission of discrete units of information in an all-or-nothing manner) and *non-Lamarckian* (changes to an organism during its lifetime, such as the loss of a limb or the overuse of a muscle, are not directly transmitted to offspring), and that genetic mutation is blind with respect to selection (genetic mutations are no more likely to arise when they are needed than when they are not needed). Adding these microevolutionary details to the basic theory of Darwinian evolution gave rise to what became known as the neo-Darwinian theory of evolution.

Several researchers have subsequently argued that these neo-Darwinian details also apply to cultural evolution: that cultural transmission is particulate, cultural evolution is strictly non-Lamarckian, and cultural mutation is blind with respect to selection. However, many social scientists have argued that these neo-Darwinian details do not apply to cultural change. In many cases these criticisms appear to be valid, or at least potentially valid. The following sections examine in more detail these three neo-Darwinian principles first as applied to biological evolution and then whether they also apply to cultural evolution.

Is Cultural Transmission Particulate? A common observation by animal and plant breeders of Darwin's day was that traits appear to blend when they are inherited: a large pigeon and a small pigeon would have intermediately sized offspring, for example. This suggested to many early biologists, Darwin included, that biological inheritance is a process of blending, where offspring take an intermediate form between their two parents. However, Austrian monk Gregor Mendel showed through breeding experiments with pea plants that this blending is just superficial, and at a microlevel biological inheritance is in fact particulate not blending. In other words, biological inheritance involves the transmission of discrete units of inheritance (called genes) that are transmitted in an all-or-nothing fashion. We either inherit one version (or allele) of a gene or another version, and these discrete units do not blend together to produce an intermediate allele halfway between our two parents' alleles. Eye color is the classic example, where the child of a brown-eyed parent and a blue-eyed parent will have either brown or blue eyes, not a mixture of brown and blue. While other traits such as height or skin color do appear to blend and take on any value on a continuum, such cases are now known to be caused by lots of discrete underlying alleles jointly determining such characters. For example, in 2009 a team of researchers showed that the striking variation in the coats of different dog breeds, from shaggy-coated bearded collies to smooth-coated Chihuahuas, is controlled by just three discrete genes.[49]

Does cultural inheritance similarly involve the particulate, all-or-nothing transmission of discrete units of cultural information? This is a central assumption of the neo-Darwinian theory of cultural evolution called *memetics*. Memetics originated in the final chapter of Richard Dawkins's hugely influential book *The Selfish Gene*, where he coined the term "meme" to describe a discrete unit of cultural inheritance, or cultural replicator, that operates within human culture.[50] He described this as the cultural equivalent of the biological replicator, the gene, such that the differential selection and transmission of these memes would make cultural change an evolutionary process. Although Dawkins primarily intended the meme concept to be a way of highlighting how his replicator-centered theory of evolution was not limited to just genes, others such as philosopher Dan Dennett and psychologist Susan Blackmore have developed the meme concept into a full theory of memetics.[51] Memetics makes the neo-Darwinian assumption that culture can be divided into discrete units that are inherited in a particulate fashion, like genes. It also assumes that memes are transmitted with high fidelity, this being one of the defining characteristics of a replicator according to Dawkins.

However, whereas genetic inheritance is particulate, cultural inheritance in many cases appears to be nonparticulate. As anthropologist Maurice Bloch puts it, "culture simply does not normally divide up into naturally discernable bits."[52] Think of political beliefs, which vary on a continuum from extreme left-wing to extreme right-wing, or archaeological artifacts such as arrowheads, which vary continuously in their length and width. There is also evidence that cultural traits blend when transmitted. During language acquisition, children appear to blend the speech sounds of their parents and their peers, resulting in a shift toward the average pronunciation of several people.[53] Social psychologists have similarly found that people adopt the blended average of other people's judgments of ambiguous stimuli, such as the extent to which a small point of light appears to be moving in a pitch-black room.[54]

Now, a limitation of such studies is that they might be at entirely the wrong level of analysis: artifacts, speech sounds, and stated beliefs are the outward behavioral expressions of information stored in the brain and as such are the cultural equivalents of phenotypic traits such as height or skin color. As we saw for the biological case, even though phenotypic traits such as height may vary continuously and appear to blend in offspring, they are nevertheless determined by discrete underlying units of inheritance (genes). In the same way, it may be that continuous, blending cultural traits such as speech sounds and expressed political values are determined at the neural level by discrete cultural units of transmission. This is ultimately an issue for neuroscientists studying how information is represented in the brain and how it is transmitted from one brain to another. Given our current lack of understanding of such issues, it is impossible to say with certainty whether cultural transmission, at the neural level, is particulate or nonparticulate. Without this evidence, a cautious working assumption should be that cultural variation may, in some cases, be continuous, and that cultural transmission may, in some cases, be blending.[55]

Is Cultural Evolution Lamarckian? Another common belief of early biologists, including Darwin, was that changes that occurred to an organism in its lifetime were directly (i.e., genetically) transmitted to its offspring. This inheritance of acquired characteristics is often called "Lamarckian" after the eighteenth-century French biologist Jean-Baptiste Lamarck.[56] The textbook example of Lamarckian inheritance involves giraffes: a Lamarckian explanation of long giraffe necks is that giraffes in one generation stretch to get leaves on high tree branches; their neck muscles stretch and lengthen slightly as a result of this stretching, and their offspring directly inherit these elongated neck muscles. Successive generations of stretching resulted in the long necks we see today. The alternative to this Lamarckian explanation instead invokes selection: some giraffes happen to have been born with long necks, some with short necks; those with longer necks can reach higher branches, get more food, and have more offspring; those offspring inherit the long necks of their parents, and so long-neck genes gradually spread in the population.

Careful experiments conducted by geneticists such as August Weismann in the 1890s showed that the former Lamarckian mechanism does not operate in biological evolution. Weismann and others showed, for example, that rats who had their tails cut off gave birth to offspring with fully intact tails, indicating that acquired changes are not transmitted genetically. This led to a distinction between the *genotype*, the genetic information inherited by offspring, and the *phenotype*, the expression of the genotype in the form of anatomical and physiological structures. Changes to the phenotype are not directly transmitted to the genotype; they cannot pass what became known as "Weismann's barrier." In neo-Darwinian evolutionary theory, therefore, selection is the main process that causes biological change, and Lamarckian inheritance is strictly absent.[57]

Is cultural evolution Lamarckian? Obviously it is not literally Lamarckian in the sense that the knowledge and skills we learn during our lifetimes, such as how to play the violin or do differential calculus, are not transmitted genetically to our offspring. But several researchers have argued that cultural evolution is Lamarckian in the sense that the knowledge and skills that we learn can be directly transmitted to others culturally, rather than genetically. As Stephen Jay Gould put it, "cultural evolution is direct and Lamarckian in form: The achievements of one generation are passed by education and publication directly to descendants."[58] Others, such as economists Geoffrey Hodgson and Thorbjørn Knudsen, maintain that cultural evolution, like biological evolution, is strictly non-Lamarckian even in this sense. Still others, such as philosopher David Hull, have argued that the term "Larmarckian" cannot be meaningfully applied to cultural evolution.[59] Clearly much disagreement exists over this issue.

Whether cultural evolution can properly be described as Lamarckian depends on how one defines the equivalent of the genotype-phenotype distinction in culture. The ideational definition of culture given in chapter 1 implies that the cultural equivalent of the genotype is the information stored in people's brains that represents their beliefs, attitudes, values, skills, knowledge, and so on. The cultural equivalent of the phenotype is the expression of that information in the form of behavior, speech, and artifacts. It is the latter—the phenotype equivalent—that is copied during cultural transmission: we do not directly acquire neural patterns of activation in people's brains; we copy people's behavior, we listen to what they say, and we read what they write. If we then modify the acquired beliefs, knowledge, and skills in some way before transmitting them to someone else, we can be said to be engaging in Lamarckian cultural inheritance.

The history books are full of apparent examples of the inheritance of acquired cultural change, where single inventors have individually modified an existing technology that has then spread to other members of society. For example, in the 1760s James Watt dismantled and tinkered with the workings of the preexisting Newcomen steam engine.[60] The Newcomen engine uses the condensation of steam to create a vacuum underneath a piston. The greater pressure acting from above then forces the piston down. Over the next two decades Watt made several modifications to this preexisting design, such as having a separate compartment for condensing the steam, which allowed the piston chamber to remain hot continuously. Watt's improved steam engine, which first appeared in 1784, diffused across the world and dominated engine design for the next fifty years. So here we have one individual (Watt) acquiring information from another (Newcomen, via his engine), modifying it in some way, and transmitting the modified information to others, in a manner that can be described as Lamarckian. So given the assumptions made earlier, we can say that cultural evolution can be described as Lamarckian, and the neo-Darwinian requirement that inheritance is strictly non-Lamarckian does not apply to cultural evolution.

Is Cultural Evolution Blind? A third neo-Darwinian assumption is that mutation is blind or undirected, such that novel genetic mutations are no more likely to arise when they are needed (i.e., when they will confer a fitness benefit on their bearer) than when they are not needed. This was demonstrated definitively in the 1940s in experiments conducted by Salvador Luria and Max Delbrück.[61] In these experiments, different colonies of initially genetically identical bacteria were exposed to a virus. Luria and Delbrück reasoned that if mutations that conferred resistance to the virus occurred randomly, then different colonies would vary in their level of resistance, as only some colonies would happen to have these beneficial mutations. If, on the other hand, mutations conferring resistance appeared nonrandomly and were triggered by the presence of the virus, then all colonies should have the same level of resistance. The former was found, indicating that beneficial mutations occur randomly and not in response to a particular adaptive problem. This finding that genetic mutation is blind with respect to fitness reinforces the notion that biological evolution is undirected or unguided by any kind of foresight.

A neo-Darwinian theory of cultural evolution that incorporates the principle of blind variation is psychologist Donald T. Campbell's "blind-variation-and-selective-retention" (BVSR) theory.[62] Campbell argued that blindly generated cultural variants are subject to consistent selection criteria, and the positively selected variants are preserved. One of the key assumptions of BVSR theory, as its name suggests, is that new cultural variation arises blindly, with no foresight directing the course of cultural evolution. This resembles the neo-Darwinian assumption of blind, or nonadaptive, mutation as established by Luria and Delbrück for genetic variation. Consequently, BVSR theorists such as psychologist Dean Keith Simonton have conducted extensive historical studies of creativity and discovery in order to test this blind variation hypothesis.[63]

Is cultural evolution blind? On the face of it, no: cultural evolution appears to be guided by the intentional actions of people who possess at least some degree of foresight, potentially increasing the likelihood of adaptive cultural mutations. Inventors and scientists strive to solve a particular problem, military commanders plot the course of a coming engagement, and advertisers plan marketing campaigns, for example. This is a point frequently made by social scientists. Sociologist Ted Benton remarks that "Darwin's mechanism of natural selection assumes that mutations are random with respect to the selective pressures which affect their chances of replication. In the case of the activities which lead to social change . . . human agents act intentionally to produce anticipated outcomes: they are not 'blind watchmakers.'"[64] On the other hand, historical analyses of scientific and technological change suggest that cultural change is not quite so directed, and foresight not quite as accurate, as commonly assumed.[65] Historical figures often claim retrospectively to have guided cultural change in particular directions, yet such claims may have the benefit of hindsight and be self-servingly exaggerated.[66] However, there is a general lack of systematic evidence regarding this issue, at least compared to the careful experiments conducted by Luria and Delbrück in biology. We should therefore be prepared to accept that cultural evolution may, at least in some instances, be directed rather than blind and that there is a valid difference here between cultural and biological evolution.

Cultural Evolution Is Darwinian, But Not Neo-Darwinian. This lack of correspondence between neo-Darwinian evolutionary theory and cultural change has often led to the wholesale rejection of any kind of evolutionary theory of culture. Stephen Jay Gould, for example, argued on the basis of the aforementioned differences that "biological evolution is a bad analogue for cultural change,"[67] while John Maynard Smith, one of the most highly regarded biologists of the twentieth century, argued that the

> explanatory power of evolutionary theory rests largely on three
> assumptions: that mutation is nonadaptive, that acquired char-
> acters are not inherited, and that inheritance is Mendelian—
> that is, it is atomic, and we inherit atoms, or genes, equally
> from our two parents, and from no one else. In the cultural
> analogy, none of these things is true. This must severely limit
> the ability of a theory of cultural inheritance to say what can
> happen and, most importantly, what cannot happen.[68]

This wholesale rejection of the application of evolutionary theory to culture is unfounded once we make a distinction between Darwinian and neo-Darwinian evolution. Whereas cultural evolution does not appear to resemble neo-Darwinian evolution, with its strict assumptions of blind mutation and particulate, non-Lamarckian inheritance, cultural evolution can still be described as Darwinian, given the evidence reviewed above that it exhibits the basic Darwinian properties of variation, competition, and inheritance.[69] Variation that is nonrandom is still variation, and inheritance that is Lamarckian and nonparticulate is still inheritance. Indeed, it is an interesting historical point that Darwin himself held distinctly non-neo-Darwinian beliefs concerning biological evolution, such as in blending and Lamarckian inheritance.

What is needed is a theory of Darwinian cultural evolution that explicitly incorporates non-neo-Darwinian microevolutionary processes such as blending inheritance, Lamarckian inheritance of acquired characteristics, and nonrandom variation, as well as other processes that may have no parallel whatsoever in biological microevolution. Such a theory is presented in chapter 3. However, further examination of the history of biology suggests that simply having the correct microevolutionary processes in place was not enough to make every biologist agree on a single, unifying theoretical framework. It is instructive for the social sciences to examine why not.

Bridging the Micro-Macro Divide

The Micro-Macro Problem in Early Biology. Even after experimental geneticists such as Mendel and Weismann had established the neo-Darwinian microevolutionary principles of particulate, non-Lamarckian inheritance and random variation, these microevolutionary principles were not readily accepted by other biologists studying macroevolution, such as naturalists documenting spatial macroevolutionary patterns by comparing the species found in different regions and paleontologists documenting temporal macroevolutionary trends in the fossil record. As biologist Ernst Mayr notes:

> Through the first third of the twentieth century the gap between the experimental geneticists and the naturalists seemed so deep and wide that it looked as if nothing would be able to bridge it . . . The members of the two camps continued to talk different languages, to ask different questions, to adhere to different conceptions.[70]

One particularly fierce argument raged over Lamarckian inheritance and the strength of selection.[71] Naturalists had by this time documented immense diversity in living species as a result of expeditions such as Darwin's own voyage on the *Beagle*, as well as equally diverse forms found in the fossil record, such as the many dinosaur species uncovered in the late nineteenth century. The only process that is strong enough to generate such diversity, the naturalists reasoned, was Lamarckian inheritance. After all, if an organism could directly transmit beneficial changes to its offspring, then meaningful change could occur in just a single generation and myriad diverse forms could rapidly emerge. The non-Lamarckian alternative, natural selection, seemed to the naturalists to be far too weak to generate the diversity that they had documented. Selection, they thought, was severely limited because it relied on the chance occurrence of beneficial mutations. And even when a beneficial mutation did happen to arise, it must spread gradually over the course of several generations as those individuals that possessed the beneficial mutation had more offspring than those that didn't possess the beneficial trait. This advocacy of Lamarckian inheritance over selection put the naturalists in direct conflict with experimental geneticists such as Weismann who, as we saw above, had shown experimentally that inheritance is strictly non-Lamarckian.

A second division between the experimental geneticists and the naturalists concerned particulate inheritance and gradualism.[72] Experimental geneticists such as Mendel had shown that biological inheritance involves the all-or-nothing transmission of discrete units (genes), with evolutionary change occurring when one of these discrete units mutates into a different version. Several experimental geneticists, most notably Richard Goldschmidt, saw this as inconsistent with Darwin's assertion in *The Origin* that biological change is gradual. Goldschmidt and others instead advanced a saltationist theory of evolution, in which major evolutionary change, such as the appearance of new species, occurs in a sudden, single-generation leap, equivalent to a massive mutation. While most of these mutants will be maladaptive, or nonviable, a rare mutant (a "hopeful monster" as Goldschmidt put it) might happen to be adaptive, and thus an entirely new species is born. Naturalists and paleontologists, on the other hand, saw saltationist theories of evolution as entirely inconsistent with their observations of macroevolution. The fossil record, rather than showing sudden jumps, generally records gradual change in species over time. Rather than birds evolving from dinosaurs in a single dramatic mutation, paleontologists were finding transitionary forms such as *Archaeopteryx* that indicated gradual, incremental evolutionary change. The same applied to geographical variation in species, which tended to be gradual rather than abrupt. The finch species found by Darwin on the Galápagos, for example, while being measurably different in beak size and shape, were nevertheless all minor variations on the same design (i.e., the common ancestor).

The Evolutionary Synthesis in Biology: The Benefits of Formal Models. These disagreements between the experimentalists and the naturalists were caused largely by flawed, informal reasoning on both sides regarding the relationship between micro- and macroevolution: the naturalists' informal intuition that selection (a microevolutionary process) is too weak to generate the rich species diversity they had observed (a macroevolutionary pattern), and the experimentalists' intuition that particulate inheritance (a microevolutionary process) was incompatible with gradual change (a macroevolutionary trend). What was needed was a way to more precisely test these intuitions regarding the macroevolutionary consequences of different microevolutionary processes. In the 1920s and 1930s a group of mathematically inclined biologists, primarily R. A. Fisher and J. B. S. Haldane in the United Kingdom and Sewell Wright in the United States, developed a set of mathematical tools, known as population genetic models, that allowed these informal intuitions to be tested far more precisely than is possible with informal, verbal arguments and thought experiments.[73] These population genetic models can be seen as methods of evolutionary "bookkeeping." Just as a bookkeeper compiles a record of all of the financial transactions that act to change a company's stock levels or profit margin, so a population geneticist compiles a record of all of the natural processes that act to change gene frequencies in a population over time. The modeler specifies a set of alternative genes (or alternative versions of a gene, known as alleles) in a population. Then they specify a set of processes (e.g., mutation or different kinds of selection) that change the variation in genes in the population in a single generation. Mathematical modeling techniques are then used to predict the long-term changes in genetic variation over time, identifying, for example, whether one allele will entirely replace another allele, or whether the two alleles will coexist at some stable equilibrium.[74]

In the 1920s and 1930s, Fisher, Haldane, Wright, and others used population genetic models to resolve the disagreements that separated the naturalists and experimentalists. They showed mathematically that selection, far from being the weak, insignificant force assumed by the naturalists, was in fact an extremely potent force.[75] Their models showed, for example, that a gene that conferred an advantage of just 1 percent (i.e., its bearers were 1 percent more likely to reproduce than individuals without the gene) could spread to half of a population in just 100 generations. Although quite long in terms of human generations, for most species 100 generations is quite short. And compared to the complete history of life on earth, it is but the blink of an eye. Fisher and Haldane therefore showed that the naturalists' assumption that selection was too weak to effect meaningful biological change

was incorrect and that recourse to Lamarckian inheritance was unnecessary. Once the naturalists accepted this, reconciliation with the
anti-Lamarckian experimentalists soon followed. Fisher also showed
mathematically that continuous phenotypic variation, like that seen
in height or skin color, could arise from the combined action of multiple discrete genetic characters, each of which has a small individual
effect. This reinforced Mendel's experimental demonstration that biological inheritance is particulate. He then showed that gradual phenotypic change could occur as mutations appear in just a subset of the
underlying discrete characters. Because each discrete character has a
small individual effect, this does not result in the massive phenotypic
mutations envisioned by the experimental geneticists who advocated
saltationism. Thus the experimental geneticists' informal intuition
that particulate inheritance inevitably leads to abrupt, discontinuous
change became untenable; they abandoned saltationism and accepted
the gradualism of the naturalists.

Once the population geneticists had used formal models to resolve
these disagreements, the two previously separate camps—experimental
geneticists studying microevolution and naturalists studying macroevolution—came together during a short ten-year period from 1937
to 1947 in what is known as the evolutionary (or modern) synthesis to
form what we now recognize as evolutionary biology.[76] Essentially this
synthesis represented a bridging of the micro-macro divide: macroevolutionary patterns documented by naturalists, such as gradual change
and species diversity, were shown to be consistent with the microevolutionary processes that had been demonstrated experimentally by the
geneticists, such as particulate and non-Lamarckian inheritance. As
Mayr put it:

> The proponents of the synthetic theory maintain that all evo-
> lution is due to the accumulation of small genetic changes,
> guided by natural selection, and that transspecific evolution is
> nothing but an extrapolation and magnification of the events
> that take place within populations and species . . . it is mislead-
> ing to make a distinction between the causes of micro- and
> macroevolution.[77]

Although this synthesis was by no means comprehensive and complete
(a major omission, for example, was development), the bridging of
the micro-macro divide within a common neo-Darwinian theoretical

framework set the stage for huge advances in the study of biological evolution.

The Micro-Macro Divide in the Social Sciences. The micro-macro divide that afflicted the biological sciences in the early twentieth century has a striking parallel in the social sciences today. The divide in the social sciences is between the microlevel, that is, those small-scale, individual-level processes that act to change the frequency of culturally transmitted traits within a single population, and the macrolevel, that is, large-scale patterns and trends at or above the level of entire societies, such as cross-cultural differences in civic duty or cognition, or long-term historical trends such as the rise and fall of the Roman empire or the diversification of Indo-European languages. Just like the geneticist-naturalist divide in presynthetic biology, these two levels are often studied entirely separately, by different scholars in different disciplines, and with little attempt to ensure that the findings at one level are consistent with the other, or to use the findings of one to explain observations at the other. Psychologists, for example, study the behavior of single individuals (as in cognitive psychology), or at most the behavior of individuals interacting within small groups (as in social psychology), under controlled conditions in the laboratory. Cultural anthropologists, meanwhile, often focus on macrolevel, societywide cultural variation in customs and practices, and archaeologists deal with macrolevel cultural change over time, such as the spread of a particular arrowhead design over several centuries. Other disciplines exhibit an internal micro-macro split. Economics is partitioned into microeconomics, the study of individual-level processes such as how the decisions of individual buyers and sellers affect supply and demand for goods, and macroeconomics, the study of population-level variables such as GDP and unemployment rates. Similarly, microsociology is concerned with the analysis of individual behavior (or "agency"), while macrosociology deals with population-level phenomena such as social structure. Linguistics has microlevel branches such as psycholinguistics, concerned with how individuals acquire and use language, and macrolevel branches such as historical linguistics, concerned with how entire languages change over hundreds or thousands of years.

This micro-macro divide is problematic for two reasons. First, macrolevel researchers are often unwilling to explain macrolevel patterns and trends that they document in terms of underlying individual-level processes. This reluctance has its origin in the ideas of many influential early social scientists. For example, cultural anthropologist Alfred Kroeber saw culture as a "superorganic" phenomenon that cannot be reduced to individual-level psychological ("mental") processes:

> Mental activity . . . proves nothing whatever as to social events. Mentality relates to the individual. The social or cultural, on the other hand, is in its very essence non-individual. Civilization, as such, begins only where the individual ends.[78]

Similarly, one of the founders of sociology, Emile Durkheim, argued that:

> In no case can sociology simply borrow from psychology any one of its principles in order to apply it, as such, to social facts. Collective thought, in its form as in its matter, must be studied in its entirety, in and for itself, with an understanding of its peculiar nature.[79]

This unwillingness to reduce cultural phenomena down to individual behavior persists to this day. While macrolevel disciplines such as cultural anthropology, historical linguistics, history, and macrosociology have documented patterns of cultural change, such as the rise and fall of the Roman empire or the diversification of Indo-European languages, and patterns of cross-cultural variation in, for example, supernatural and religious beliefs, marriage systems, or agricultural methods, they have generally failed to explain these patterns of change and variation in terms of the behavior and psychological processes of the people who are responsible for those patterns. This reluctance to reduce cultural phenomena to individual psychological processes may have its roots in the mind-body dualism inherent in many of the nonscientific approaches to culture such as social constructionism that were discussed in chapter 1.[80] Yet reductionism is a key tool of the scientific method and is responsible for huge advances in the physical and natural sciences, whether it is the reduction of matter to atoms and subatomic particles in physics or, as we have seen in biology, the reduction of macroevolutionary patterns such as adaptation and speciation to microevolutionary processes such as natural selection and particulate inheritance.

The second problem is the opposite of the first: micro-level disciplines such as psychology have failed to acknowledge the extent to which macrolevel cultural processes shape individual behavior.[81] Psychologists, for example, tend to focus on single individuals and their behavior in nonsocial experimental situations in the lab, or at most interactions within small groups. Similarly, economists typically assume that people make economic decisions in isolation from other people by rationally assessing the costs and benefits of different options. Yet as reviewed in chapter 1, recent findings from cultural psychology have demonstrated that culture shapes numerous aspects of human behavior to a degree not hitherto suspected, from cooperative tendencies to basic processes of attention and perception. Although these are significant findings, they are rather recent and have yet to permeate most of psychology. A similar situation pertains to economics, in which the lack of consideration of cultural processes such as conformity (sometimes called "herd behavior") has limited economists' understanding of macroevolutionary phenomena such as market bubbles and crashes.[82] As economist Herbert Gintis notes:

> Sociology and anthropology recognize the importance of conformist transmission but the notion is virtually absent from economic theory. For instance, in economic theory consumers maximize utility and firms maximize profits by considering only market prices and their own preference and production functions. In fact, in the face of incomplete information and the high cost of information-gathering, both consumers and firms in the first instance may simply imitate what appear to be the successful practices of others.[83]

Microlevel disciplines such as psychology and microeconomics remain largely divorced from the real-world patterns of cultural change and variation documented by macrolevel disciplines such as cultural anthropology, and archaeology. Without such links, the validity of microlevel experiments and theories concerning human behavior remain in doubt.

Conclusion: A Darwinian Theory of Culture Can Synthesize the Social Sciences

Given that cultural change, like biological change, is Darwinian, perhaps a similar evolutionary synthesis to that which occurred in the biological sciences in the 1940s might be possible for the social sciences. Just as the evolutionary synthesis in biology solved the micro-macro problem by showing, through the use of formal, quantitative models, how microevolutionary processes are consistent with, and indeed explain, macroevolutionary patterns, an equivalent evolutionary synthesis in the social sciences would use similar models to show how cultural macroevolution, as studied by macroeconomists, macrosociologists, historical linguists, historians, cultural anthropologists and archaeologists, is consistent with, and indeed explicable from, microevolutionary processes studied by microeconomists, microsociologists, psycholinguists, neuroscientists, and psychologists. Yet it is crucial that the differences between biological and cultural evolution are incorporated into these models, given that cultural evolution does not exhibit the same neo-Darwinian microevolutionary processes as does biological evolution. The following chapter outlines the pioneering work of a handful of scholars who in the 1970s and 1980s attempted to construct a formal theory of Darwinian cultural evolution taking these differences into account.

3

Cultural Microevolution

The first attempts to construct formal models of cultural evolution along the lines of those models that stimulated the evolutionary synthesis in biology appeared in the 1970s and 1980s with the groundbreaking work of two pairs of researchers working in California: Luigi Luca Cavalli-Sforza and Marc Feldman of Stanford University, and Robert Boyd and Peter Richerson of the University of California (UCLA and UC Davis). Their work is primarily encapsulated in two books: Cavalli-Sforza and Feldman's 1981 book *Cultural Transmission and Evolution: A Quantitative Approach*, and Boyd and Richerson's 1985 book *Culture and the Evolutionary Process*.[1] Cavalli-Sforza, Feldman, Boyd, and Richerson simply applied the same mathematical "bookkeeping" methods developed by Fisher, Haldane, Wright, and others to culture, on the assumption that biological and cultural change are at heart both Darwinian systems. In a typical cultural evolution model, a population is assumed to be composed of a set of individuals, each of whom possesses a particular set of cultural traits. A set of microevolutionary processes is specified that changes the variation in those traits over time. The variation is then transmitted to the next generation, simulating the process of cultural transmission from individual to individual.[2] Mathematical techniques or computer simulations are used to explore the long-term changes in cultural variation over time (e.g., whether one cultural trait drives another to extinction, or whether two or more traits coexist in stable equilibrium), and possibly also the spatial distribution of cultural variation (e.g., whether different semi-isolated groups come to have the same or different cultural traits), that result from different microevolutionary processes. These microevolutionary processes concern the sources of cultural variation, the forms of cultural selection (i.e., the reasons why some traits are more likely than others to be acquired and transmitted), and the details of the cultural transmission processes that are responsible for passing traits to the next generation.

Table 3.1 lists some of the microevolutionary processes that were modeled by Cavalli-Sforza, Feldman, Boyd, and Richerson.[3] These processes include pathways and modes of cultural transmission, including vertical (from one or both parents), oblique (from unrelated elders), and horizontal (within generations); one-to-one and one-to-many transmission; and the particulate versus blending distinction. Variation may be created in an entirely random fashion, akin to genetic mutation, or it might be introduced in a directed, Lamarckian manner (known as "guided variation"). Cultural selection occurs when one cultural trait is more likely to be acquired than an alternative trait. This may occur for various reasons, and considered below are three kinds of cultural selection: content biases, frequency-dependent biases, and model-based biases. Cultural drift occurs when cultural variation changes because of random processes, such as the chance loss of rare traits in small populations. Two final processes are natural selection, where cultural traits increase or decrease in frequency because of their effect on an individual's survival and biological reproduction, and migration, where traits diffuse from group to group. Each of these processes has different macroevolutionary consequences for how culture as a whole changes over time or becomes patterned in space. The rest of this chapter discusses these processes and their consequences in more detail.

Quantitative models such as those built by Cavalli-Sforza, Feldman, Boyd, and Richerson have several advantages over the informal verbal arguments and thought experiments often employed in the social sciences.[4] Rather than appealing to some vague process of "socialization" or "social influence" to explain how cultural traits persist over time, the modeler is forced to precisely define different microevolutionary processes and their consequences. Models let the researcher keep track of several simultaneously acting (and interacting) processes that are

Table 3.1 Processes that cause changes in cultural variation over time

Process	Description
TRANSMISSION:	
Pathway	
Vertical	Transmission from biological parents (either uniparental or biparental)
Oblique	Transmission from unrelated members of the parental generation
Horizontal	Transmission from unrelated members of the same generation
Scope	
One-to-one	Face to face learning from one individual to another
One-to-many	One individual influencing many others via mass education or mass media
Mechanism	
Blending	Adopting the average value of a continuous trait from more than one model
Particulate	All-or-nothing transmission of discrete cultural traits
VARIATION:	
Cultural mutation	Generating innovations entirely at random
Guided variation	Individuals modify acquired information according to individual cognitive biases
CULTURAL SELECTION:	
Content biases	Preferentially adopting traits based on their intrinsic attractiveness
Model-based biases	Preferentially adopting traits based on characteristics of the model, e.g. their prestige, age, or similarity
Frequency-dependent biases	Preferentially adopting traits based on their frequency, e.g. conformity (copying the most popular trait)
CULTURAL DRIFT	Random changes in cultural trait frequencies due to cultural mutation, random copying and sampling error
NATURAL SELECTION	Cultural traits spread due to their effect on biological survival and reproduction
MIGRATION:	
Demic diffusion	Cultural traits spread as their bearers move between groups
Cultural diffusion	Cultural traits spread across group boundaries due to cultural transmission

Note: see text for details.

virtually impossible to keep track of without mathematical tools. Variables, such as the strength of a particular cultural selection bias or probability of learning from one's parents versus one's peers, can be systematically manipulated one at a time in order to understand their consequences for long-term cultural change and variation. And finally, quantitative models generate clear predictions that can be tested in the lab or in the real world.

Cavalli-Sforza, Feldman, Boyd, and Richerson showed that it is possible to build a useful theory of cultural evolution that is fully Darwinian, yet differs in many of its underlying microevolutionary assumptions from biological evolution. Just like Fisher, Haldane, and Wright did in the 1920s, they laid the groundwork for a synthetic theory of cultural evolution. However, the rather complicated mathematics contained in Cavalli-Sforza and Feldman's 1981 book and Boyd and Richerson's 1985 book has largely prevented their insights from receiving the recognition that they deserve in the social sciences. So the following sections review these models in an accessible, nonmathematical manner, as well as cite empirical research that supports the models' assumptions and predictions.

Cultural Transmission

Pathways and Scope. One of the more obvious apparent differences between biological and cultural evolution involves the potential transmission pathways that each involves. Genetic inheritance is often thought of as exclusively vertical and biparental, with genetic information transmitted in equal amounts from two parents to a single offspring. In culture, on the other hand, one can learn beliefs, ideas, skills, and so forth, not just from one's biological parents (termed "vertical cultural transmission") but also from other members of the parental generation ("oblique cultural transmission") and from members of one's own generation ("horizontal cultural transmission"). One can even learn from members of later generations, such as when parents copy their children's clothing styles (much to the annoyance of their children). Within each of these there are further distinctions that one could draw. Vertical cultural transmission might be mother-biased or father-biased, for example. Oblique or horizontal cultural transmission could occur on a one-to-one basis, as is common in small-scale hunter-gatherer societies in which learning is face-to-face, or it may be one-to-many, as is permitted by the mass media and mass education in postindustrial societies.

In fact, many of these pathways of cultural transmission have parallels in biological evolution. Bacteria and plants often transmit genetic material horizontally between unrelated organisms, while even in diploid species such as humans there are phenomena such as sex-linked genes and genomic imprinting, where genes from one parent are more likely to be inherited or expressed than genes from the other.[5] Nevertheless, most quantitative models of genetic inheritance are indeed based on the assumption of vertical inheritance, making it necessary to construct models tailored specifically to the cultural case. So in the 1970s and 1980s Cavalli-Sforza and Feldman constructed models of different cultural transmission pathways and explored the consequences of each pathway on the speed of cultural evolution (e.g., the rate at which a novel, advantageous trait spreads through the population) and the consequences of each pathway for between- and within-group cultural variation. In very general terms, Cavalli-Sforza and Feldman's models showed that when cultural transmission is one-to-one or one-to-few, as exemplified by vertical cultural transmission or face-to-face learning in a small hunter-gatherer community, then rates of cultural change are relatively slow. Cultural evolution gets faster as transmission becomes one-to-many, as exemplified by oblique or horizontal transmission via the mass media or mass education. This is because a single leader or teacher can rapidly spread a novel idea or practice to a large number of people in a much shorter time (days, weeks, or months) compared to one-to-one transmission, particularly vertical transmission, which is limited by biological generation spans of several decades. This can be seen formally in figure 3.1a, which shows how the same initially

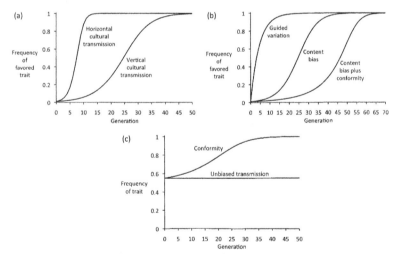

FIGURE 3.1 Long-term, population-level consequences of different cultural evolutionary processes. (a) Horizontal cultural transmission spreads an initially rare yet beneficial cultural trait faster than does vertical cultural transmission. (b) Different processes generate differently shaped curves describing the diffusion of an initially rare yet beneficial cultural trait: guided variation generates r-shaped curves, content bias generates S-shaped curves, while content bias plus conformity generates S-shaped curves with an initial long tail. (c) Conformity drives whichever trait is initially most common to 100 percent, whereas non-conformist, unbiased transmission does not change trait frequencies, assuming no intrinsic advantage to either trait.

rare but beneficial cultural trait spreads through a population faster via horizontal transmission than vertical transmission, all else being equal.[6] As well as the speed of cultural evolution, transmission pathways also affect spatial patterns of cultural variation. One-to-many horizontal transmission has the potential to rapidly spread a cultural trait across an entire group, thus creating within-group homogeneity. If different leaders/teachers spread different traits in different groups, then different groups will be characterized by different traits, thus generating cross-cultural variation. Purely vertical transmission, on the other hand, would take much longer to homogenize groups in this way as it only transmits traits within single families. Vertical transmission is therefore more likely to maintain variation within groups.

Having constructed these mathematical models of cultural transmission pathways and generated predictions regarding their expected spatial and temporal consequences, Cavalli-Sforza and Feldman then collected empirical data to test those predictions in the real world.[7] In the early 1980s they gave Stanford University students surveys asking them about their religious and political beliefs, their sports and entertainment preferences, and their daily habits. They also gave the same survey to the students' parents and friends, allowing the researchers to infer potential transmission pathways. If a student was similar to their parents in a particular cultural trait, then we can infer that this trait is subject to vertical transmission, whereas greater similarity to their friends would indicate an influence of horizontal transmission. Of course, these are big inferences. Similarity between parents and offspring could be caused by genetic inheritance rather than cultural inheritance, while friends could be similar not because of any direct transmission but rather because similar people tend to associate with one another. Nevertheless, the findings of the Stanford survey seemed to fit with model predictions about rates of change. Religious traits were the most influenced by vertical transmission, in particular by mothers. Indeed, whether a student identified themselves as Roman Catholic, Protestant, or Jewish was strongly predicted by their mother's religious affiliation (interestingly, fathers' religious affiliation had no influence at all). This might explain why religious beliefs appear to change little over hundreds or thousands of years, and why identifiable religions such as Christianity, Judaism, and Islam have survived for so long. Other traits, on the other hand, showed no significant parental influence and a much greater influence of friends. These were primarily related to entertainment and popular culture, such as film preferences, belief in UFOs, or a tendency to jog. Again, such traits historically seem to change much more rapidly than, say, religious beliefs. Movie tastes seem to change by the decade, with Westerns in the 1950s replaced in popularity with sci-fi films such as *Star Wars* in the late 1970s. Think also of the jogging epidemic that swept the United States in the 1970s, a horizontally transmitted trait that was probably captured in the Stanford survey. Today, mass media such as cable television and the internet have greatly facilitated the scope of one-to-many transmission to an unprecedented extent. Fashions and fads can spread across the world in a matter of days. This is in striking contrast to the small-scale hunter-gatherer communities in which humans have lived for most of their evolutionary history in which transmission was face-to-face, and consequently much slower.

Particulate versus Blending Cultural Transmission. As discussed in chapter 2, while genetic inheritance is known to be particulate, cultural transmission may well operate via the blending of continuous, nondiscrete cultural variation. While this has been used by some to dismiss cultural evolution as invalid, this dismissal is based on informal reasoning. A better approach is to build formal quantitative models that incorporate blending inheritance and continuous variation to see whether such microevolutionary principles really are inconsistent with macroevolutionary cultural patterns, just as Fisher and Haldane did for biological evolution. In the 1980s Cavalli-Sforza, Feldman, Boyd, and Richerson modeled both the inheritance of continuous cultural traits that could take any value within a specific range, and blending inheritance, where individuals who are exposed to the cultural traits of more than one person adopt the average of all of those traits.[8] These models showed that blending inheritance results in the reduction of cultural variation in the population. Indeed, if blending inheritance is the only process acting on cultural variation in the population, then it eliminates that variation completely. Imagine a population of individuals that varies in a continuously measured trait, say political attitude ranging from extreme left to extreme right and any value in between. In each new generation (which might be biological generations, but could equally be much shorter, such as election cycles), every member of the population chooses two other members of population at random and adopts the blended average of each of their attitudes. Sometimes two extreme left-wing (or two extreme right-wing) attitudes will blend together, which will result in no change. But occasionally, extreme left-wing attitudes will blend with extreme right-wing attitudes, resulting in intermediate attitudes. Over time this will happen to all extreme attitudes, leaving only intermediate attitudes. Because the average of two intermediate attitudes is an intermediate attitude, the population becomes entirely intermediate.[9]

Obviously, in the real world blending inheritance cannot be the only process operating on cultural evolution, otherwise we would not see the enormous cultural variation documented in the previous chapter: 7.7 million patents, 10,000 religions, 6,800 languages, and so on. There must, then, be other processes at work. The mathematical models constructed by Cavalli-Sforza, Feldman, Boyd, and Richerson point to two such cases in which the homogenizing effect of blending inheritance is counteracted by other cultural processes.[10] The first is when the cultural mutation rate is high, for example, when there are a lot of errors in cultural transmission, such that new variation is introduced into the population at an equal or faster rate as blending inheritance removes it. While this is not the case in biological evolution—genetic mutation rates are far too low to replenish genetic variation—cultural transmission appears to exhibit far more copying error. People tend to copy ideas, beliefs, skills, and knowledge from other people in a rough-and-ready way, often grasping the gist of an idea but filling in the details themselves in ways that change the information, akin to mutation.[11] The second case is where people preferentially learn from other people who are similar to them in their cultural traits (the cultural equivalent of what biologists call "assortative mating"). This creates subgroups within the population that are homogenous in their cultural traits. Looking across the entire population, however, there may be substantial variation between these different subgroups. For example, if Republicans only ever copy ideas and beliefs from other Republicans, and Democrats only ever copy other Democrats, then blending inheritance will make people within these two groups homogenous in their beliefs. Yet across the country, big differences of opinion on various issues (healthcare, taxation, gun control, etc.) will be maintained between Republicans and Democrats. Indeed, recent social network analyses of the internet blogosphere seem to empirically confirm this Democrat-Republican separation, with left-wing bloggers seldom linking to right-wing bloggers and vice versa.[12] These cultural evolutionary analyses therefore show that interesting and realistic patterns of cultural evolution can emerge despite (or even because of) the presence of blending cultural inheritance, because high mutation rates or assortative cultural transmission can counteract its homogenizing effect.

Guided Variation (or Lamarckian Inheritance)

Like blending inheritance, the observation that cultural change appears to be Lamarckian is also often used to reject the theory of cultural evolution. Yet this criticism is similarly based on informal intuition rather than formal analysis. Earlier we saw how population geneticists such as Fisher and Haldane showed mathematically that Lamarckian inheritance is not needed to explain the diversity and complexity that is observed in the natural world. But this doesn't mean that Lamarckian inheritance is incompatible with Darwinian evolution, only that it is unnecessary. Using models similar to those of population geneticists, cultural evolution modelers have shown that potentially realistic cultural evolutionary dynamics can emerge even if one assumes that cultural inheritance is Lamarckian. Boyd and Richerson have modeled the Lamarckian inheritance of cultural information, calling it "guided variation." In their model of guided variation, one individual acquires information from a second individual, and then modifies that information according to their own individual learning processes. This modified information is then transmitted to other individuals in the population.

Boyd and Richerson's model of guided variation shows that this Lamarckian inheritance of acquired characteristics causes the population to move toward, and eventually converge upon, whatever behavior is generally favored by individual learning.[13] This occurs even when the individually favored behavior is initially entirely absent from the population. This model of guided variation also addresses the issue of blind versus directed mutation encountered in chapter 2, where the neo-Darwinian assumption that mutation must be random with respect to fitness does not appear to apply to cultural change that is directed by inventors or scientists in a nonrandom fashion. The process of guided variation embodies this nonrandom introduction of new variation. If it is assumed that this new variation is adaptive, then cultural evolution can be said to be directed, not blind.

On the face of it, Lamarckian-like guided variation doesn't seem very Darwinian. Indeed, guided variation seems more akin to the Spencerian notion of evolution described in chapter 2 and depicted in figure 2.1a, where an entire population shifts in a prespecified direction (albeit without the fixed stages or racist connotations of Spencerian evolution). Contrast this with selection, depicted in figure 2.1b, where certain variants are more likely than other variants to be preserved. Cultural selection is discussed in detail in the next section. However, it is important here to note that the two processes are not incompatible. It is true that if Lamarckian-like guided variation were the only process acting in culture, and if everyone had the same individual cognitive biases that favored the same cultural traits, then Darwinian models wouldn't be much use. All that would be needed to explain cultural change is knowledge of a single individual's preexisting cognitive biases. However, neither of these assumptions is likely to be true. People do not have identical cognitive processes: different people come up with different solutions to problems and modify culturally acquired information in different ways. Cultural selection can then act on these different traits. For example, returning to the example of James Watt's modification of the Newcomen steam engine mentioned in the previous chapter, although Watt's steam engine became the industry standard, other inventors modified the basic Newcomen engine in different ways. The Russian inventor Ivan Polzunov came up with a two-cylinder steam engine in 1763, while John Smeaton had earlier improved the dimensions of the Newcomen engine to maximize the steam pressure on the piston. Yet none of these modifications were as successful as Watt's engine, which we might assume was the result of cultural selection favoring Watt's engine in the marketplace.

Another important point is that guided variation is itself the product of selection. The cognitive processes that each individual uses to modify culturally acquired knowledge are themselves the product of selection, either natural selection (i.e., biological evolution) or previous cultural selection, a point originally made by Donald Campbell.[14] Exactly how this may have occurred in specific cases, for example, in the case of Watt's steam engine, remains to be determined. We might even imagine a selection process operating within Watt's mind as he tried out different components and combinations of actions. The key point is that a valid and useful Darwinian theory of cultural evolution can be constructed that has Lamarckian-like guided variation as one of several microevolutionary processes, and this should be distinguished from the entirely Lamarckian (and invalid) Spencerian notion of cultural evolution discussed in chapter 2.

Cultural Selection

Content Biases. "Cultural selection" is defined as any condition where one cultural trait is more likely to be acquired and passed on than an alternative cultural trait (or no trait at all). Unlike guided variation, cultural selection does not involve any modification of the trait itself, only changes in the frequency of that trait. The most obvious form of cultural selection involves what Richerson and Boyd have called content biases, in which the intrinsic attractiveness of an idea, belief, practice etc. affects its probability of being acquired.[15] Of course, this merely begs the question: what makes a trait "attractive"? There are several different answers to this, representing different cultural selection pressures and explained in terms of individuals' psychological processes. These psychological processes, in turn, have been shaped by prior biological or cultural evolution.

As an example, consider why certain rumors seem to spread so well, such as the following: "An old lady was eating fried chicken at a popular fast food restaurant when she noticed teeth in her chicken. When she looked closer she saw that she was eating a deep-fried rat." Or this one: "A woman who had ordered a mayonnaise-free burger noticed a white liquid oozing out of her sandwich. When she complained it turned out that the white liquid was in fact pus from a cyst that had burst as she bit into the meat." According to Stanford behavioral scientist Chip Heath, the reason why such rumors spread so well is because they elicit strong emotional reactions of disgust, and disgusting stories are particularly well remembered and transmitted. In cultural evolutionary terms, we might describe this as a disgust-based content bias that acts to increase the frequency of more-disgusting stories and rumors. Heath and his colleagues tested this idea by collecting as many urban legends from the internet as they could find.[16] Consistent with the disgust bias hypothesis, participants rated those urban legends that were most common on the internet as more disgusting, and reported that they would be more likely to repeat them to someone else. And when Heath et al. manipulated the "disgustingness" of a selection of urban legends, participants were more likely to say that they would tell the more disgusting versions to their friends than the less disgusting versions. Although this study was limited in that it only asked participants whether they would pass on the different stories rather than actually transmitting them along chains of participants or tracking their transmission in the real world, Heath et al.'s results at least suggest that a disgust bias operates in cultural evolution. This particular content bias is likely to have a biological evolutionary origin, in that things that we find disgusting, such as rotten or infected food, are likely to be harmful in some way, such as by harboring diseases and parasites, and avoiding such harmful things would have increased our ancestors' chances of survival.

A second potential content bias concerns supernatural beliefs. In virtually every society ever studied by anthropologists, people have been found to hold supernatural beliefs that violate at least some laws of physics or biology: ghosts or spirits that can walk through solid walls, deities that can be everywhere at once, people who can transform into bats, wolves, or other animals, and corpses that come alive. Several cognitive anthropologists, including Pascal Boyer and Scott Atran, have suggested that such beliefs are so prevalent because they are "minimally counterintuitive."[17] This means that they violate some of our intuitive folk beliefs, but are consistent with others. For example, ghosts violate certain intuitive rules of folk physics (e.g., they can pass through walls and other solid objects) but they behave in ways consistent with our intuitive rules of folk psychology (e.g., they seek revenge). The violations of our intuition make such concepts salient and thus more memorable than entirely ordinary, intuitive concepts, such as a person who cannot walk through walls and dies of old age. Yet they are not so bizarre and counterintuitive that they are too difficult to remember, such as a jealous Frisbee that turns into a caterpillar every other Thursday.

To test the hypothesis that minimally counterintuitive ideas are selected in cultural evolution, cultural psychologist Ara Norenzayan and colleagues analyzed the Brothers Grimm collection of two hundred folktales.[18] While some of these folktales have spread widely since 1857 when the Brothers Grimm collection first appeared, such as "Rapunzel," "Hansel and Gretel" and "Cinderella," others have fallen into obscurity, such as "Brother Scamp," "The Donkey Lettuce," and "Hans My Hedgehog." Norenzayan et al. first counted the number of reproductions of each story on the internet, giving a rough measure of its current popularity, or "cultural fitness." They then compared the number of counterintuitive elements present in successful stories (which were found on average on 8,404 web pages each) and unsuccessful stories (found on average on 148 web pages each). As predicted, successful folktales had around 2–3 counterintuitive elements while unsuccessful stories had either no counterintuitive elements or several (5–6) counterintuitive elements. In the story of Cinderella, for example, there are just a handful of counterintuitive elements (e.g., the fairy godmother turning pumpkin into coach, mice into horses, and rats into coachmen) among many other intuitive elements (e.g., Cinderella's unhappiness at her stepsisters' harsh treatment, the Prince's desire to find Cinderella, and so on). "The Donkey Lettuce," on the other hand, is full of bizarre events, including birds fighting over a magic cloak, people escaping from murderous giants by riding on clouds, and cabbages that turn people into donkeys (hence the title). It appears, then, that minimally counterintuitive stories have a selective advantage in cultural evolution and represent a second content bias. However, whereas the disgust bias seems to be biologically adaptive, the minimally counterintuitive content bias appears to be a possibly maladaptive by-product of a cognition that strives for accuracy yet also favors unusualness.

As well as purely informational content biases that affect the spread of stories, rumors, and beliefs, sociologists have conducted extensive studies on how behavioral practices and technological innovations spread through societies. This "diffusion of innovations" literature has been summarized by sociologist Everett Rogers, who identified several characteristics of successful innovations.[19] In order to successfully spread, novel innovations must (1) have some relative *advantage* over existing practices or technologies, (2) be sufficiently *compatible* with existing practices or technologies, (3) be *simple* enough to use such that a potential adopter can quickly and easily understand or operate them, (4) be easily *testable* by adopters such that their relative advantage can be discerned, and (5) be *observable* to others, thus facilitating their spread. Each of these represents a broad class of content bias that will cause some traits (e.g., advantageous, compatible, understandable, testable and/or observable traits) to spread at the expense of other traits (e.g., disadvantageous, incompatible, complex, untestable and/or unobservable traits). A good example of an innovation that ticks all of these content bias boxes is the mobile phone. Since first appearing in the early 1980s, the mobile phone has diffused across the world at a phenomenal rate. In December 2008 there were an estimated 4.1 billion mobile phones in use in the world. Assuming each of these is used by a single person, then over 60 percent of the population of the world uses a mobile phone. Indeed, an entire generation is now growing up whose only telephone they ever use is a mobile phone. How did this happen? Mobile phones have the obvious *advantage* over landline phones of being portable, allowing people to communicate with others when they are not at home or in the office. They are *compatible* with existing telephone networks, allowing people with mobile phones to call people with regular phones and vice versa. They are *simple* to use, at least with respect to the basic function of making a call, which requires roughly the same knowledge as making a call on a regular telephone. They are *testable*: a friend's mobile phone is easily borrowed in order to try it out. And their portable nature makes them highly *observable* to others, as mobile phone users are seen in the street, in restaurants, and in other public places.[20]

These content biases can also explain the *lack* of spread of innovations, even where those innovations are advantageous. A case study reported by Rogers tells of a health worker's attempts to get the housewives of a Peruvian village to boil their water before drinking it in order to reduce the spread of waterborne diseases.[21] These attempts were an unqualified failure: during an intensive two-year health education campaign, just 11 of 200 families were persuaded to boil their water. Why did the campaign fail? Most importantly, it was *incompatible* with the villagers' existing folk beliefs concerning food and illness. The health workers tried to explain to the villagers that tiny, invisible pathogens caused illness and that boiling water killed the pathogens. The villagers, on the other hand, believed that all food and drink had intrinsic temperatures unrelated to the actual temperature of the food. According to this belief system, when someone gets ill they should avoid very "cold" food, such as pork, or very "hot" food, such as brandy. Water is seen as very cold, and so only people who were already sick heated their water before drinking it. Heating water before one got sick, as the health workers were suggesting, therefore made no sense to the villagers. Boiling water also suffered from a lack of *testability*: there is no clear, unambiguous link between boiling water and lack of illness. Bacteria cannot be seen, so one cannot see the direct effects of boiling water. And people get sick from sources other than water, such as via airborne particles or insect bites, so even someone who religiously boiled their water would still sometimes get sick.

What are the long-term consequences of cultural selection via content biases? Simple cultural evolution models constructed by Boyd and Richerson show that, rather intuitively, when a content bias acts to favor the acquisition of one trait over another, and this content bias is the only process acting, then the favored trait increases in frequency over time until everyone in the population holds that trait. This general model might be applied to any of the traits that we considered above: a disgusting urban legend versus an emotionally neutral urban legend, a mobile phone versus a landline phone, or not boiling water versus boiling water.

On the face of it, content biases seem very similar to guided variation. Both result from psychological processes, and both result in the spread of traits that are favored by those psychological processes. However, Boyd and Richerson's models show that the two processes have quite different consequences. Guided variation is where people individually modify acquired cultural traits according to their own individual learning biases. Content biases, like other forms of cultural selection, occur when people preferentially choose among existing traits found in the population without changing those traits. Guided variation is an individual process, content bias is a population process. As such, content biases depend on variation in the population to work: if everyone has the same cultural trait, then there is nothing for content biases to select, and so content biases will be impotent. Moreover, the more variation there is in the population, the stronger the content bias will be. If there is lots of cultural variation in the population, then the chances of encountering someone with a different cultural trait is high.[22] Guided variation, on the other hand, is unaffected by cultural variation in the population because it is a purely individual process, and other people's cultural traits are irrelevant.

Anthropologist Joseph Henrich took advantage of this difference to test whether novel innovations spread via content bias or guided variation. Hundreds of studies conducted by sociologists (and reviewed by Rogers) have repeatedly found that the spread of new technologies, practices, and beliefs follows an S-shaped cumulative distribution curve. This means that, if one plots the proportion of the population who has adopted a particular innovation over time, it forms an S-shape, with a slow initial uptake, followed by a rapid increase, and then a final slowdown. The classic demonstration of this S-shaped pattern was Bryce Ryan and Neal Gross's 1943 study of the spread of hybrid seed corn among Iowa farmers. Hybrid seed corn was developed by agricultural scientists in the 1920s and had a yield that was 20 percent higher than that of naturally pollinated seed corn (thus ticking the *advantage* requirement, as well as *compatibility* with existing farming methods). By interviewing every farmer in two small Iowan communities, Ryan and Gross were able to track the adoption of hybrid seed corn over time. They found a slow initial uptake: after five years only 10 percent of farmers had adopted the new seed. In the next three years there was a rapid increase, rising to 40 percent. Over the following years the rate of adoption slowed as fewer farmers were left to potentially convert to the new seed. This slow-rapid-slow S-shaped diffusion curve has been since found to describe the spread of techniques for teaching math among schools, bottle feeding in developing nations, the use of new antibiotics by doctors, and the spread of various commercial products such as televisions, dishwashers, refrigerators, and iPods.[23]

Henrich has argued that these S-shaped diffusion curves are most likely to be the result of content-biased cultural selection as opposed to guided variation.[24] Building on Boyd and Richerson's original work, Henrich modeled the diffusion of a novel and beneficial innovation (e.g., a new hybrid type of seed) in a population of individuals (e.g., farmers) who already possessed an alternative trait (e.g., nonhybrid seed). First Henrich modeled guided variation. Here, change in seed type is generated by the individual modification part of guided variation, given that transmission is unbiased. So during each time period, which could be days, weeks, or months depending on the innovation, each individual engages in their own private, trial-and-error learning. For a farmer, this might be a trial of a new type of seed in a small plot of land (which, incidentally, was actually done by some of the Iowan farmers interviewed by Ryan and Gross). When the new trait gives a higher payoff on average than the existing trait (given a certain degree of random error in the learning process), then the farmer switches to the new trait. From this model, Henrich showed that guided variation did not generate S-shaped curves. Guided variation instead generated r-shaped curves, which show a rapid and steady initial uptake followed by a final slowdown. This can be seen in figure 3.1b above.[25] The reason guided variation generates r-shaped curves is, as noted above, because guided variation is an individual-level process: it does not depend on the variation in the trait in the rest of the population. So the uptake is initially rapid and steady because it does not matter that the trait is initially rare. The subsequent slowdown occurs because the proportion of farmers who still have the original trait gets smaller and smaller toward the end, so there are fewer farmers left to independently discover the superior trait.

Content bias, on the other hand, did generate S-shaped curves, as shown in figure 3.1b.[26] With content bias, there is no individual trial-and-error learning. Individuals are assumed to periodically sample the behavior of another randomly chosen member of the population, and if that person's behavior is intrinsically more attractive than their existing behavior, then they copy it. Again, the reason that an alternative trait might be considered more attractive could be any of those listed above: it elicits emotional reactions, it is cheaper, or whatever. For content-bias-generated S-shaped curves, the slow initial uptake occurs because there is little variation in the population and few opportunities for people to encounter the favored trait. The accelerating increase that follows occurs because more and more models are available to learn from. The final slowdown occurs because of a lack of variation again, this time because everyone already has the favored trait. Henrich's study is a good example of how simple models generate simple predictions (r-shaped vs. S-shaped diffusion curves) that can be tested with actual cultural data sets, in this case reaching the conclusion that the diffusion of most innovations is driven by content-biased cultural selection rather than guided variation.

Frequency-Dependent Bias. Cultural traits do not always spread because of their intrinsic advantages and disadvantages or an inherent psychological attraction. Often it is difficult to figure out what the consequences of different practices are. Imagine you are in a restaurant in a foreign country and you want to order something to eat. The menu is in a language you don't understand, and the waiter does not speak your language. In the absence of any direct knowledge of how each item on the menu tastes, you look around to see what the other customers are eating. The majority of them seem to be eating some kind of chicken-based dish, so you indicate to the waiter that you want that too.

In the scenario above you engaged in frequency-dependent bias: you used the frequency of a trait in the population as a guide as to whether to adopt it, irrespective of its intrinsic characteristics. Specifically, you engaged in positive frequency-dependent bias, or *conformity*, where you chose the most popular trait in the population. The opposite is negative frequency-dependent bias, or *anticonformity*, where the least popular trait is chosen, although I will focus here on conformity. In the absence of any clear differences in the costs and benefits of different choices, or where it is costly or dangerous to calculate such costs and benefits, then frequency-dependent bias offers a cheap shortcut to individual trial-and-error learning.

Social psychologists have long studied conformity in the lab.[27] Classic experiments from the 1950s by Solomon Asch placed a naïve participant in a room with what they thought were other participants, but who were actually confederates of the experimenter. Each "participant" was then asked to select, out loud to the rest of the group, which of three lines matched a target line in length. This task was stunningly easy, and when tested alone virtually every participant got it correct 100 percent of the time. The confederates, however, were instructed to give the wrong answer. When it came to the real participant to answer, who always answered after the confederates, a substantial proportion of them went with the obviously incorrect response given by the confederates. In other words, the pressure to conform to the majority view outweighed individual judgment.

In social psychology experiments such as this, conformity is simply defined as the tendency to copy the most common trait in the group. Cultural evolution modelers have defined conformity in a more precise way than this, however (this is one of the advantages of models: they force one to precisely define one's terms). Conformity, as defined by Boyd and Richerson, is not simply choosing the most common trait in the population. Conformity is where a learner is *disproportionately more likely* to adopt the most common trait in the population, relative to simply copying at random. For example, if you looked around the foreign restaurant and saw ten patrons, seven of whom were eating chicken and three who were eating fish, then if you copied their choice entirely at random, with no conformity, then you would have a 70 percent chance of choosing chicken and a 30 percent chance of choosing fish. So the most popular choice is more likely to be copied, but this is simply because it is more likely to be observed; it has nothing to do with conformity. If you were *conforming*, then you would have a *greater than* 70 percent chance of choosing the chicken, and a *less than* 30 percent chance of choosing the fish. The amount by which the 70 percent is increased (and the 30 percent decreased) is a quantitative measure of the strength of conformity.

This subtle distinction is more important than it initially appears, because models show that the two processes—copying at random and conformity—have very different long-term consequences. Random, unbiased copying does not change the frequency of traits over successive generations. Conformity, on the other hand, causes whichever trait was initially most popular to drive all other traits to extinction. These different long-term consequences are shown in figure 3.1c above,[28] where conformity causes a trait that is initially held by the majority (55 percent) of the population to spread to the entire population. Nonconformist, unbiased transmission, on the other hand, does not change anything, keeping the frequency of the trait at 55 percent.

Is there any evidence that people conform in this way, and that actual cultural traits spread via conformity? Unfortunately, the kind of experiments conducted by social psychologists that are commonly cited as evidence for conformity are rarely suitable for detecting conformity as defined above. Usually every other group member gives the same response, such as all choosing the same incorrect line in Asch's study. This means that random copying would lead the real participant to select the incorrect line, and there is no way to distinguish this from conformity. Recent experiments have attempted to correct this by varying the frequency of the trait in the group, but with only ambiguous evidence for actual conformity.[29]

Better evidence for conformity comes again from Joseph Henrich's analysis of S-shaped diffusion-of-innovation curves. Henrich noted that many diffusion curves have "long tails" at the start, that is, unusually long initial periods during which the frequency of the innovation is very low, before the rapid takeoff. Henrich attributed these long tails to conformity, which would prevent the novel trait from spreading when it is initially very rare. For example, even though farmers' content biases might be favoring the new high-yield hybrid seed corn, their conformist bias would be favoring the most-common existing nonhybrid seed corn (at least until hybrid seed corn becomes more popular). This conformity-generated "long tail" effect is illustrated in figure 3.1b.[30]

This "stickiness" of conformity highlights another of its macroevolutionary consequences. Boyd and Richerson showed that conformity is especially good at generating internally homogenous groups. Any individual who deviates from a group norm would quickly be brought back into line by conformity because deviance is, by definition, rare, and so selected against. Similarly, conformity would cause immigrants moving into a group to quickly adopt the common norms of their new group rather than persist with alternative behaviors practiced in their society of origin. And if different groups converge on different norms, then there will be large differences between groups. Conformity is therefore a potential explanation for the often robust cultural traditions that have been observed by ethnographers over the years, where different societies have maintained their own unique customs and practices even in the face of frequent migration.[31]

Model-Based Biases. A third broad class of cultural selection biases concerns the identity of the person from whom cultural traits are acquired. This person is called a model (not to be confused with a mathematical model). Model-based biases occur when people preferentially adopt certain cultural traits not on the basis of their intrinsic qualities but on the characteristics of the model exhibiting them. For example, people might preferentially copy very prestigious models who have high social status or excel in a particular skill (*prestige bias*). Alternatively, they might preferentially copy models who are similar to them in dress, dialect, or appearance (*similarity bias*), or preferentially copy older models (*age bias*).

Why use characteristics of the model as a guide as to whether to copy them? The general answer to this question is the same as for frequency-dependent biases: because it is a cheaper and easier way of acquiring advantageous cultural traits than via content bias, guided variation, or individual learning, all of which may require some kind of evaluation of the traits' intrinsic characteristics. Simply copying whatever prestigious (or similar, or old) members of society are doing is rather simple to do. The specific answer depends on the particular model-based bias we are talking about. Concerning prestige bias, if you copy the behavior of prestigious people then you stand a chance of becoming prestigious yourself. For example, if you want to become a good golfer, then copying Tiger Woods's swing is probably a good learning strategy to follow. At least it is probably quicker and easier than figuring out on your own, through painstaking trial-and-error individual learning, what a good golf swing is.

Boyd and Richerson constructed models to explore this intuition more formally.[32] They confirmed that a general prestige bias is indeed a good way of acquiring adaptive behavior compared to individual learning and unbiased transmission (random copying). However, this depends on the extent to which indicators of success (e.g., number of golf tournaments won) correlate with the traits that are copied. For some traits this correlation is likely to be high, such as swing technique. For others, however, it is likely to be low. Tiger Woods's choice of cap, for example, probably has little to do with his success at golf. Yet Boyd and Richerson's models suggest that prestige bias can be quite broad and still be effective. Just as it is difficult to determine through individual learning or content biases what the best behavior is in a particular situation, it is also going to be difficult to figure out exactly what it is about Tiger Woods that makes him successful. So it is likely that some traits that have little to do with success get copied as well. Indeed, this is what companies such as Nike are banking on when they pay sportspeople large sums of money to wear their clothing: people following a general "copy-whatever-Tiger-Woods-does" prestige bias will copy, that is, purchase, his choice of Nike caps.

Evidence that people actually use prestige bias comes from a number of sources. Social psychology experiments show that people preferentially copy the choices, attitudes, and behavior of prestigious or successful individuals. For example, participants in experiments have been found to shift their art preferences toward those of another participant introduced as the art director of an advertising firm, but not when the participant is introduced as another student. Other experiments support Boyd and Richerson's specific prediction that prestige bias is broad and not necessarily always adaptive. For example, in another study participants shifted their opinions about student activism toward the opinions of an expert professor, even when the professor's expertise (in Chinese history) was unrelated to the topic. Other studies had participants bet on simulated horse races, finding that participants copied the betting choices of other participants who had been successful previously, even when told that each participant was betting on a different race.[33]

Outside the lab, people in the real world also appear to exhibit prestige bias. The diffusion of innovations literature shows that new products or behaviors often spread because they are exhibited by prestigious or successful individuals, or what are known as "opinion leaders." One study reported by Everett Rogers describes how a new method of teaching math only took off in a particular school district in the 1960s when it was adopted by three particularly influential school superintendents.[34] Similar effects are observed by sociolinguists, where dialect changes are driven by prestigious, high-status speakers in a community. This was demonstrated in a classic sociolinguistic study conducted by William Labov on the New England island of Martha's Vineyard.[35] Labov observed that residents who valued life on the island considered fishermen to have high social status because they represented traditional values of the island. Consequently, these residents could be seen adopting the distinctive dialect of the fishermen. Residents who did not identify with other islanders and wanted to leave, on the other hand, did not copy the fishermen's dialect, because they had a different notion of prestige.

Prestige bias can also lead to a runaway "arms race" between the markers of prestige and the copied traits. To illustrate this, Boyd and Richerson drew an analogy with sexual selection in biological evolution. The population geneticist R. A. Fisher proposed that exaggerated traits such as peacocks' tails are the result of runaway sexual selection. Female peahens choose males on the basis of their tail length: the bigger the better. The reason for this preference is not important, simply that it exists. This is sexual selection. Natural selection also acts, but in the opposite direction: it favors small tails that make males less likely to be seen by, and less likely to be caught by, predators. If sexual selection is stronger than natural selection, then male tail length will increase as males with longer tails will be more likely to mate and reproduce, giving rise to more long-tailed sons in the next generation. Fisher's insight was that female peahens' preference for long tails is also inherited, but by daughters. So the next generation will have not only longer-tailed males (on average) but also females with stronger preferences for long tails (on average). This coevolutionary arms race between preference and trait eventually leads to the elaborate, exaggerated peacock's tail.

Boyd and Richerson argued that a similar process of runaway selection can act on prestige markers and prestige-biased traits.[36] They assumed that, like female peahens' preferences for long tails, indicators of prestige are also inherited along with the prestige-biased trait itself. If prestige bias is stronger than more "rational" biases such as content-biased cultural selection (equivalent to natural selection), then preferences and traits can coevolve in a spiraling arms race to exaggerated values. Take house size as an example. It is not unreasonable to assume that "house size" might well be a marker of prestige, with large houses indicating high prestige. Other, more rational biases, such as content bias, might favor smaller houses that are cheaper to buy, easier to heat, less likely to be burgled, etc. When prestige bias is stronger than content bias, then house size will increase as people copy the "large house" trait of prestigious models. Crucially, these people will also copy the "large houses are good" preference. So large houses and preferences for large houses will be copied together, just like large peacock tails and preferences for large peacock tails. The resulting runaway selection can lead to exaggerated traits, such as the enormous mansions of celebrities and sportspeople (Tiger Woods, for example, lives in a $54 million, 9,000-square-foot mansion in Florida). Boyd and Richerson note other possible examples of this kind of runaway selection, including enormous, 9-by-3-foot yams that are brought to celebratory feasts on the Micronesian island of Ponapae, and extensive whole-body tattoos that until recently were favored by Polynesians.

Cultural Drift

Both guided variation and the various forms of cultural selection act to shift the frequency of cultural traits in a population in a specific, non-random direction, whether it is guided variation shifting traits toward a particular form, content biases favoring certain traits (e.g., disgusting rumors) over others, or conformity favoring the most popular trait. While these directional processes are what people usually think of by the term "evolution," biologists also find it useful to consider the case when no such directional processes are involved. In biology, this kind of evolutionary change is called genetic (or neutral) drift. Such change is, by definition, random: all alleles are intrinsically equally likely to get passed on to the next generation. In small populations, however, accidents of history can lead to big differences in the frequencies of different alleles purely as an artifact of sampling error. The same kind of sampling error can be seen in lotteries, which provides a useful analogy for understanding drift. In the pan-European Euromillions lottery, for example, five numbers are selected at random from a range of one to fifty. We can think of this as a bit like a big "genetic drift" simulator. Imagine that each ball in the lottery represents a different allele in a population. Under the assumption of drift, each allele (ball) is equally likely to get transmitted to the next generation (be drawn). Also assume that there is a small population size such that only a few alleles (balls) will get passed on (get randomly drawn) every generation (draw). So what happens to allele frequencies in our big genetic drift simulator? During the one-year period from September 2008 to September 2009, the most commonly drawn numbers were 4 and 14, each appearing 19 percent of the time. The least commonly drawn numbers were 43, drawn just once, and 27, which was never drawn.[37] If these were alleles, 27 would be extinct and 4 and 14 would be doing great. So quite striking differences in allele frequencies can arise purely from random sampling. Sewall Wright was the first population geneticist to formalize the process of genetic drift, and through his work and the work of later population geneticists such as Motoo Kimura in the mid-twentieth century, drift is now recognized as an important evolutionary process.[38] In fact, drift is now considered by biologists to be the default, null hypothesis in explanations of biological evolution, with natural selection only invoked when it can be demonstrated that observed patterns of change deviate significantly from that expected by chance (i.e., drift).

Cultural drift is the analogous process in cultural evolution and occurs when people copy cultural traits entirely at random in the absence of any of the directional processes considered above. How important is drift in cultural evolution? Surely cultural evolution is far more directed and guided, as we saw with guided variation and content biases, to be subject to random sampling errors? Recent research by Alex Bentley, Matthew Hahn, and Stephen Shennan suggests that drift plays a more important role than one might imagine.[39] Bentley and colleagues adapted mathematical models of genetic drift to fit the cultural case. In one model, they assumed a relatively small population of 250 individuals, each of whom initially possesses a single cultural trait. Every generation, the entire population is replaced with a new set of 250 individuals. Each individual of this generation copies the trait of one of the previous generation entirely at random. There is also a small probability of cultural mutation, where an individual invents a new trait at random. Note how random everything is: models are chosen entirely at random, cultural mutation is entirely random, and each trait is identical in its intrinsic fitness.

The result of this cultural drift model over several generations is what is called a "power-law distribution" of trait frequencies, as shown in figure 3.2.[40] This plots the number of copies of a particular trait on the horizontal axis, against the proportion of all traits that have that number on the vertical axis. Cultural drift generates the negatively sloped straight line shown in figure 3.2. This line tells us that there are a very large number of very rare traits (the left-hand part of the straight line) and a very small number of very popular traits (the right-hand part of the straight line). Other nondrift cultural processes, on the other hand, do not result in straight line power-law distributions.[41] Conformity, for example, generates the dashed line shown in figure 3.2.

Bentley et al. then looked to see whether they could find any cultural data sets that fit this power-law distribution and thus might be subject to cultural drift. In fact, they found several. One of these was the distribution of baby names. We might imagine that parents of newborn babies spend months deliberating over the relative worth of different names, consulting one of the many guides and websites available to help decide on a name that will set their offspring in good stead for the rest of its life. In fact, Bentley et al. found that parents' choices of names for their babies, according to applications for new Social Security cards, showed an excellent fit to a power-law distribution. A very

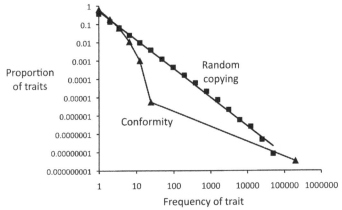

FIGURE 3.2 Cultural trait distributions generated by random copying and conformity. Random copying generates a straight line "power law" distribution, whereas conformity does not. Adapted from Mesoudi and Lycett 2009.

small number of names were very popular. For example, from 2000 to 2008, around 3.6 percent of all newborn boys were called either Jacob, Michael, or Joshua, while 3 percent of girls were called Emily, Madison, or Emma.[42] Conversely, a very large number of names were very rare. During the same period, Zayne, Krish, Stephon, Heriberto, and Jax each made up 0.005 percent of newborn boys' names, while Jaslene, Zara, Dasia, and Finley each accounted for just 0.0075 percent of girls' names. So despite our intuitions, first names appear to evolve as if they were selectively neutral, with no intrinsic fitness differences between different names.

Bentley and colleagues have shown similar power-law distributions for several other data sets, including the frequency with which different technological patents are cited, the frequency of different pottery motifs on seven-thousand-year-old pottery from Western Europe, the frequency of academic jargon words used in the social sciences (e.g., "agency" or "structuration"), the popularity of different songs in the pop music charts, and the popularity of different dog breeds. This last example, regarding dog breeds, illustrates one of the most important uses of the cultural drift model. Because the drift model, by definition, does not incorporate any kind of selection, it constitutes a null hypothesis. Thus, deviation from the drift model indicates cases where selection *is* acting. While the overall changes in dog breed popularity between 1946 and 2001 were found to obey a power-law distribution, thus indicating cultural drift, an interesting deviation occurred. Following the release in 1985 of the Disney film *101 Dalmatians*, new registrations of Dalmatians shot up sixfold, before returning to pre-1985 levels six years later. This was a clear case of Disney-driven cultural selection.

Natural Selection

A distinction can be made between natural and cultural selection. Natural selection involves the differential replication of different genes. Cultural selection involves the differential adoption and transmission of cultural traits. We saw above how cultural selection can change the frequency of cultural traits over time. Bearing the distinction between cultural and natural selection in mind, it is possible to imagine that natural selection can do this, too. Imagine that a particular culturally transmitted trait significantly harms its bearers' chances of surviving. As these bearers die at a faster rate than people without this trait, there will be relatively fewer models available from whom to learn it, and over time its frequency will drop. Examples of survival-reducing cultural traits might be smoking, extreme sports such as skydiving and bungee jumping, or cannibalism. A famous case of the latter occurred among the Fore people of Papua New Guinea in the mid-twentieth century, when the cultural practice of widows eating their dead husbands' brains resulted in the spread of the lethal degenerative neurological disease kuru.[43] In each of these cases, however, natural selection does not appear to be acting very strongly, at least compared to cultural evolutionary processes. Kuru, for example, was stopped not because of its negative effects on survival but because the Australian government prohibited the cultural practice of brain eating. The fact that the Fore did not make the link between the practice of brain eating and kuru was probably because of kuru's lengthy fourteen-year incubation period. Other survival-reducing traits, such as extreme sports, may be counteracted by their benefits, such as a desire for thrill seeking and the increased attractiveness of perceived risk takers. So although survival-related natural selection of cultural traits is possible, it is likely that cultural evolution operates too rapidly for it to be a potent force compared to cultural selection, guided variation, and other cultural processes.

Cultural traits may also affect an individual's fertility. Many culturally transmitted religious beliefs, such as the prohibitions on birth control and abortion found in Catholicism, may increase the fertility of their bearers compared to people of other faiths that do not prohibit birth control and abortion, such as Protestantism or Judaism, or people of no faith at all. If these religious beliefs are transmitted vertically, from parent to child, then the frequency of anti–birth control and anti-abortion beliefs will spread faster than the alternative beliefs. In a previous section we saw that religious beliefs are indeed often strongly vertically transmitted.

However, when cultural transmission is not restricted to the vertical pathway, then biologically maladaptive traits may spread. Models constructed by Cavalli-Sforza, Feldman, Boyd, and Richerson suggest that biologically maladaptive traits can spread if transmission is nonparental and when those traits make their bearers more likely to be copied.[44] An example might be celibacy, as practiced by priests of many religious faiths. Although celibacy reduces one's genetic fitness to zero, the role of priest entails high social status. People engaging in prestige bias might be expected to copy traits associated with priests, one of which is celibacy. Thus, celibacy spreads in the population. Cavalli-Sforza, Feldman, Boyd, and Richerson have suggested that a less extreme version of this process may be responsible for the dramatic reduction in family sizes in postindustrial countries over the last century, known as the "demographic transition." Whereas natural selection favors large family sizes (or as large as resources can support), prestige-biased cultural selection may favor small families because people with small families have more time to devote to attaining social status. Time spent raising children is time that could be spent on things like making sales, campaigning for public office, or publishing academic papers. Other people are more likely to copy the traits exhibited by these high-status individuals, one of which may be the "having a small family" norm. Thus the "having a small family" norm spreads in the population, resulting in smaller family sizes.

So while natural selection may act to change the frequency of cultural traits in the population, in practice it is unlikely to be a strong force compared to other processes such as cultural selection and guided variation. This is because the latter processes can act much faster than natural selection, via nonvertical cultural transmission pathways. This does not mean that natural selection is irrelevant in explaining cultural evolution. Natural selection has undoubtedly shaped the cognitive apparatus through which cultural selection and guided variation act, as we saw in the case of the disgust content bias. This indirect influence is likely to be much more important than any direct effect of natural selection on the frequency of different cultural traits in the population.

Cultural Migration

Cultural migration refers to the movement of cultural traits from one group to another. This has a parallel in migration (or "gene flow") in biological evolution, where genes move from one population to another. Cultural migration can take one of two forms. The first, called *demic diffusion* by Cavalli-Sforza and Feldman, is where people physically move from one population to another and take their cultural traits with them. The other, called *cultural diffusion*, is where cultural traits are transmitted from one population to another without the movement of people, via one of the transmission pathways discussed previously.

Which kind of migration is more important? In prehistoric times, demic diffusion appears to have been the primary means of cultural migration. For example, some 11,000 years ago, farming—the domestication of animals and plants—was invented in the Middle East. About 3,500 years later it had reached Europe. Did it spread via demic diffusion, with farming populations moving into Europe bringing their agriculture with them, or via cultural diffusion, with farming methods transmitted from the original farmers to the preexisting inhabitants of Europe? Recent analyses of mitochondrial DNA extracted from the skeletons of prehistoric Europeans have shown that the DNA of hunter-gatherers and farmers from this time is significantly different, suggesting that the farmers migrated into Europe and replaced the hunter-gatherers, indicative of demic diffusion.[45]

With the advent of mass communication technology such as telephones, television, and the internet, cultural migration has probably increasingly become dominated by cultural diffusion, taking the form of the one-to-many transmission pathway discussed earlier. The spread of hybrid seed corn among Iowan farmers discussed earlier is a case in point and provides a nice link to the prehistoric spread of farming: unlike prehistoric farming methods, hybrid seed corn did not spread because new farmers moved into Iowa with their new seeds and replaced existing farmers with nonhybrid seeds. Rather, the hybrid seed corn diffused culturally among the existing farmers.

Cavalli-Sforza and Feldman modeled migration to explore its macroevolutionary consequences. From the perspective of a single group, cultural migration can be seen as equivalent to cultural mutation in that it introduces new variation into the population. Rather than this new variation being invented by an existing individual, it is brought into the population by an immigrant, or copied from someone outside the group. Across groups, however, migration has the effect of reducing the differences between groups. This makes sense: as traits move randomly from group to group (assuming no other processes are acting), then they will eventually be distributed evenly, just like two liquids or gases diffusing across a permeable membrane. Some other process is needed to maintain between-group differences. Earlier, we saw how conformity is one such process. We might imagine migration and conformity acting against each other to generate the patterns of within- and between-group variation observed in the world and throughout history.

Conclusion: A Quantitative Theory of Darwinian Cultural Evolution

The cultural evolution models constructed by Cavalli-Sforza, Feldman, Boyd, and Richerson in the 1970s and 1980s represent a significant advance over the informal and often empirically unsupported theories presented by advocates of both progressive, Spencerian cultural evolution and neo-Darwinian theories of cultural evolution such as memetics. For the first time, a set of empirically supported microevolutionary principles had been laid out, and their macroevolutionary consequences explored using rigorous mathematical modeling techniques borrowed from biology. Yet Cavalli-Sforza, Feldman, Boyd, and Richerson did not blindly import assumptions from biology. Instead, they modeled cultural microevolutionary processes that were often explicitly different to the biological case, such as blending inheritance and Lamarckian-like guided variation. Having established these microevolutionary processes, the next two chapters turn to cultural macroevolution and ask whether macroevolutionary processes can be similarly quantified using formal evolutionary methods borrowed from biology.

4

Cultural Macroevolution I: Archaeology and Anthropology

The previous chapter focused on the small-scale, micro-evolutionary details of cultural evolution. These details concern the interactions between individuals within a single population over a short period of time, such as who people learn from (e.g., prestigious individuals, or the majority behavior of the entire group), what kinds of information they are most likely to remember and pass on (e.g., disgusting rumors), the pathways of cultural transmission (e.g., vertical or horizontal), the form that that transmission takes (e.g., particulate or blending), and so on. In many cases, connections were drawn between these microevolutionary processes and larger-scale, longer-term macroevolutionary patterns and trends. For example, conformity is predicted to generate stable between-group differences in cultural customs, values, and practices, as members of different groups adopt local norms of behavior. This spatial pattern—large between-group differences and small within-group differences—appears to resemble the distinct ethnic groups observed by ethnographers. Other patterns are temporal, involving the rate of cultural evolution. Most religious beliefs do not change as rapidly as, say, pop music preferences, because the former are transmitted primarily vertically, while the latter are transmitted horizontally and are subject to the random process of cultural drift. Migration, either via demic diffusion (the movement of people) or cultural diffusion (the transmission of information without the movement of people) can result in sweeping large-scale historical changes, such as the spread of agriculture into prehistoric Europe.

However, many of the examples given in the previous chapter of macroevolutionary patterns and trends were still rather informal. If our ultimate goal is to explain macroevolutionary patterns in terms of specific underlying microevolutionary processes and thus bridge the micro-macro divide in the social sciences, then not only must we generate quantitative predictions concerning the macroevolutionary consequences of different microevolutionary processes as outlined in the previous chapter, but we also need some way of rigorously identifying and measuring those macroevolutionary patterns and trends in order to be able to test those predictions. This chapter and the next examine how a group of archaeologists, anthropologists, linguists, and historians have taken evolutionary methods developed by biologists to study biological macroevolution and used them to identify and measure patterns and trends in cultural macroevolution.

Phylogenetics: Reconstructing the Tree of Life (and Culture)

The only diagram to appear in *The Origin of Species*, that of a branching tree, was intended by Darwin to represent the way in which all species are related by descent. To this day, biologists use trees to represent the evolutionary history of groups of species. These trees are now known as phylogenies, and the construction of phylogenies is known as phylogenetics.[1] The construction of phylogenetic trees has become one of the most important tools for explaining patterns and trends in biological macroevolution.

For example, figure 4.1 shows the currently accepted phylogeny of Old World primate species.[2] Species placed closer together on the tree are more closely related. That is, they more recently shared a common ancestor than two species that are further apart on the tree. So the phylogeny in figure 4.1 shows that humans are more closely related to chimpanzees than they are to gorillas, because while humans and chimpanzees share a last common ancestor about six million years ago, the last common ancestor of humans and gorillas (and chimpanzees) lived further back, some seven to eight million years ago. Biological phylogenies can be thought of as just like the human family trees constructed by genealogists, except on a much larger scale. On a family tree, for example, two siblings will be placed closer together than two

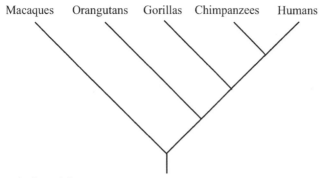

Macaques   Orangutans   Gorillas   Chimpanzees   Humans

FIGURE 4.1 A primate phylogeny.

cousins. This is because the siblings share a more recent "common ancestor," that is, their parents, who are just one generation back. Two cousins, on the other hand, share a more distant common ancestor in the form of grandparents, who are two generations back. The phylogenetic trees constructed by biologists can be seen as hugely scaled-up versions of family trees based on the same logic that the more related two things are, the closer they should be on the tree.

Unlike genealogists, however, biologists can't rely on people's memories or historical records such as birth certificates to reconstruct their phylogenies. Instead, phylogeneticists use the characteristics of different species to construct their trees. Early phylogenies were constructed on the basis of physical characteristics such as number of digits or the presence or absence of something like wings or fur. More recent phylogenies, including the phylogeny in figure 4.1, are based on genetic data. So humans and chimpanzees are placed closer together on the tree than are humans and gorillas because we share particular genetic traits with chimpanzees that are not present in gorillas (indeed, prior to genetic analyses, chimpanzees and gorillas were considered more closely related to each other than either was to humans, given their physical similarity; genetic analyses show instead that chimpanzees are more closely related to humans than to gorillas).

Shared characteristics (e.g., genes or physical traits) can be used to infer relatedness because of one of the basic principles of Darwinian evolution outlined in chapter 2: inheritance. Two closely related species are generally similar in their characteristics because they have both inherited those characteristics from a common ancestral species. The longer two species have been evolving along separate lineages, the more changes will have occurred (either random changes due to genetic drift or nonrandom changes due to selection), and the more dissimilar they will have become.

There is a problem with using similarity alone to infer relatedness, however. Inheritance is not the only reason that two species might share the same characteristic. They might have independently evolved the same characteristic in two separate and unrelated lineages. Think of the independent evolution of wings in the lineages leading to birds and to bats, or the independent evolution of fins in the ancestors of whales and fish. A phylogeny that was based entirely on similarity might incorrectly classify bats as birds, or whales as fish. As Darwin noted in *The Origin*, and as discussed in chapter 2, these independent evolutionary events result from convergent evolution, where two species have independently adapted to similar ecological niches.[3]

To address this problem, biologists have developed various formal methods for constructing phylogenetic trees that distinguish between shared characteristics that are similar due to descent (known as *homologies*) and shared characteristics that are shared due to convergent evolution (known as *homoplasies*). After distinguishing between these, phylogenetic trees can be built using only the former, which uniquely indicate true historical relatedness. One commonly used formal method for constructing phylogenies is known as *maximum parsimony*. This method is based on the general assumption in science that, all else being equal, simpler explanations are better than more complicated explanations. Here, this implies that the most likely phylogenetic tree is the one that explains the observed distribution of characteristics with the minimum number of evolutionary changes.

Figure 4.2 illustrates the logic of maximum parsimony.[4] The two trees in figure 4.2 both show possible evolutionary relationships between four species, 1–4. Each species is described in terms of four characters, indicated with four upper- or lowercase letters. Lowercase letters (a–d) are assumed to be ancestral characteristics, whereas uppercase letters (A–D) indicate derived characteristics. Derived characters represent evolutionary innovations that occurred subsequent to the ancestral version of the character. For example, the fins of whales can be described as derived compared to their hippopotamus-like ancestors, which had legs, with legs being the ancestral characters in this example. So species 4, which is *abcd*, is the most evolutionarily unchanged species, containing all four ancestral character states. Species 2 has undergone the most evolutionary change since all of the species shared a common ancestor, having all four derived character states

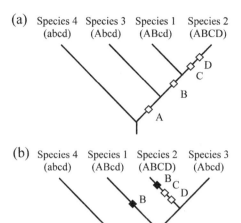

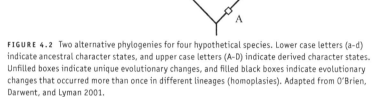

FIGURE 4.2 Two alternative phylogenies for four hypothetical species. Lower case letters (a-d) indicate ancestral character states, and upper case letters (A-D) indicate derived character states. Unfilled boxes indicate unique evolutionary changes, and filled black boxes indicate evolutionary changes that occurred more than once in different lineages (homoplasies). Adapted from O'Brien, Darwent, and Lyman 2001.

(*ABCD*). Species 1 (*ABcd*) and Species 3 (*Abcd*) contain a mix of ancestral and derived characters.

Figure 4.2a shows the most parsimonious tree possible for these four species. Species 4 branches off from the root of the tree, that is, the last common ancestor of all four species. Unfilled boxes indicate evolutionary changes that have occurred as the other species have branched off from this last common ancestor. So species 3 branched off from the common ancestor that it shares with species 4 after the ancestral character state *a* became A. Species 1 branched off after *b* became B, while species 2 branched off after both *c* became C and *d* became D.

The phylogenetic tree shown in figure 4.2b, on the other hand, incorporates an instance of convergent evolution (or homoplasy), with *b* becoming B in two separate lineages, one leading to species 1 and the other leading to species 2. These are marked with filled black boxes. This results in a different tree to the one in figure 4.2a, with species 1 and 3 in different positions. On the assumption of parsimony, however, this tree is considered less likely to accurately depict the evolutionary history of these species than the tree in figure 4.2a. The most parsimonious tree is therefore the one that correctly explains the observed variation in characteristics with the fewest number of independent evolutionary changes, or homoplasies. Phylogenetic methods are designed to produce the tree with the fewest number of homoplasies. The degree to which a particular tree fulfils this requirement can be assessed using what is called the consistency index (CI), defined as the total number of characters that is being considered divided by the number of changes in character states in the tree. A CI of 1 indicates a perfect tree with no homoplasies. The tree in figure 4.2a is an example of such a tree: there are four characters (A, B, C, and D) and four character state changes (the four unfilled boxes in the figure), so CI = 4/4 = 1. Lower CI values indicate less accurate trees. For example, the tree in figure 4.2b has five character state changes for the same four characters, giving CI = 4/5 = 0.8. Several other measures are also used, such as the retention index (RI), which controls for the number of species and number of characters in a tree. This is particularly useful when comparing different data sets, as we will see later.

This basic overview of phylogenetic methods as used in biology to reconstruct the evolutionary history of species is intended to illustrate the logic behind focusing on homologies rather than homoplasies, and of the principle of maximum parsimony. The construction of trees is now performed using sophisticated computer programs that can automatically calculate the most likely tree from large numbers of species and characters. Since gene-sequencing techniques have become more widely available, phylogenies have been built using genetic data in addition to, or instead of, morphological characters. Consequently, more sophisticated techniques than the maximum parsimony method outlined above have been developed, such as maximum likelihood or Bayesian inference methods, which contain more explicit assumptions about rates and patterns of molecular evolution, such as different probabilities that one nucleotide will be replaced by another nucleotide.[5]

Using Phylogenetic Methods to Reconstruct Past Cultural Evolution. Just as biologists use phylogenetic methods to reconstruct evolutionary relationships between species, in recent years several groups of cultural evolution researchers have shown that phylogenetic methods can also be usefully applied to cultural phenomena to reconstruct evolutionary relationships between different culturally transmitted artifacts, behavioral practices, and languages. The reason that phylogenetic methods can be applied to cultural data is that, like species, cultural traits undergo descent with modification: they are transmitted from individual to individual and generation to generation via social learning mechanisms such as imitation, thus forming lineages of similar traits.

The application of phylogenetic methods in archaeology has been spearheaded by Michael O'Brien and Lee Lyman from the University of Missouri-Columbia. In a series of papers and books, O'Brien and Lyman have argued, and indeed demonstrated, that phylogenetic methods offer archaeologists a valuable tool for reconstructing the evolutionary history of material artifacts.[6] They have focused on projectile points, which are stone artifacts that were commonly used by prehistoric hunters as the pointed tips of darts, spears, or arrows used to hunt animals for food. Projectile points can be found right across North America, having first appeared around 11,500 years ago. While each point was manufactured in a similar way, involving the chipping away of flakes from a larger piece of rock to form a symmetrical pointed shape, there is also much variation in point designs across North America. Points vary in their width, thickness, and length, as well as the shape of the point and the shape of the base. For example, some points have two small notches cut out of the base, while others have small nodules, or "ears," sticking out from the base, both of which make it easier for the points to be attached to an arrow or spear shaft. In order to deal with this variation, archaeologists have traditionally classified points into several distinct types according to the region in which they are found and their general characteristics. Such types include Clovis, Cumberland, Dalton, and Folsom. Cumberland points, for example, are generally narrower and thicker than Clovis points, and unlike Clovis points have ears on their bases.

Archaeologists have long speculated about the historical relationships between different types of projectile points, arguing over which type appeared first and the correct historical sequence linking each type. Unfortunately radiocarbon dating methods are not accurate enough to provide such information, so archaeologists have traditionally based their historical scenarios on the similarity between different points, with similar points assumed to be more closely related. As we have seen, this is a good starting point: just as similar species are likely to be closely related because they descended more recently from a common ancestor, so too similar points are likely to be closely related because they recently descended from a common ancestor. Yet this is not enough. We also need to use formal methods to distinguish between similarities due to descent (homologies) and similarities due to convergent evolution (homoplasies), and minimize the number of homoplasies in our hypothesized historical sequence.

O'Brien and Lyman, along with fellow archaeologist John Darwent, therefore used phylogenetic methods to reconstruct the evolutionary history of North American projectile points.[7] O'Brien et al. were explicit that the application of phylogenetic methods is only possible if one makes the assumption that artifacts undergo true evolutionary change, that is, the process of descent with modification that Darwin outlined in *The Origin of Species*. So just as lineages of species show continuity in their forms because of the inheritance of genetic information, so too lineages of artifacts show continuity in their forms because the knowledge and skills required to make those artifacts are culturally transmitted from individual to individual in successive generations of prehistoric hunter-gatherers. And just as changes accumulate in different biological lineages due to random genetic mutations or adaptation to different environments, causing two species to become more dissimilar the more time has elapsed since they diverged from a common ancestor, so too lineages of artifacts accumulate changes due to random innovations or cultural adaptation to different environments, causing two artifacts to become more dissimilar the more time has elapsed since they diverged from a common ancestor.

O'Brien et al. first defined eight characters that they thought captured the essential variation in projectile points, equivalent to the physical or genetic characters that are used to construct biological phylogenies. Each of these eight characters could take one of several discrete values. For example, *base shape* could take one of four values: "arc-shaped," "normal curve," "triangular," or "folsomoid" (the last term describing a concave base); while *length-width ratio* was categorized into one of six ranges: 1.00–1.99, 2.00–2.99, 3.00–3.99, and so on, up to ≥ 6. O'Brien et al. then determined the combined character traits of 621 points from across the southeastern United States. Of these traits, 17 combinations occurred in at least four points in the sample. These 17 combinations, containing 83 points in total, were taken as classes, or common types of similar points (interestingly, these empirically derived classes did not always coincide with the types that archaeologists had traditionally used to classify points, such as Clovis, Dalton, or Folsom, illustrating how quantitative analysis can reduce subjective bias). A phylogenetic tree was then constructed for these 17 classes in the way described above, parsimoniously assuming the minimum number of independent changes in character traits during projectile point cultural evolution.

The result was the tree shown in figure 4.3. The root of the tree is a point that was thought, on a priori grounds, to be ancestral to the other 16 points, which are shown branching out from this ancestral point. As in figure 4.2, open boxes indicate a single change in a character

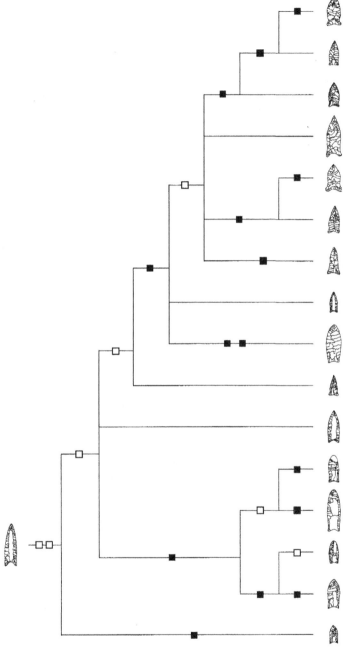

FIGURE 4.3 A cultural phylogeny for Palaeoindian projectile points from southeastern United States. Unfilled boxes indicate unique evolutionary changes, and filled black boxes indicate evolutionary changes that occurred more than once in different lineages (homoplasies). Adapted from O'Brien, Darwent, and Lyman 2001.

state, where this single change occurred only once across the entire tree. Filled boxes indicate single changes that occurred more than once in different lineages, indicating homoplasies. In total, there were 22 changes: 7 unique changes and 15 homoplasies. This tree has a consistency index of 0.59, which is comparable to many biological trees.

O'Brien et al. therefore demonstrated that phylogenetic methods provide a powerful, quantitative method for reconstructing the evolutionary relationships between different archaeological artifacts. Whereas archaeologists have long speculated about the historical relationships between different artifact types, phylogenetic methods provide a much more rigorous and precise means of identifying the most likely historical tree based on explicit assumptions (e.g., maximum parsimony). Of course, other researchers might quibble with the particular characters or classification system that O'Brien et al. chose, or the assumptions that they made when constructing the tree. But because phylogenetic methods are formal and quantitative, with explicit assumptions and algorithms that can be replicated, those researchers can build their own trees based on their own (explicit) assumptions and with alternative data. This is far more productive than informal, verbal arguments over different historical scenarios.

Testing Functional Hypotheses Using Phylogenetic Methods: Galton's Problem.
Imagine that you are an alien anthropologist from another planet surreptitiously studying our species. You are particularly interested in the many similarities and differences between the different groups of humans. One difference that you notice is in the average wealth of different groups. In some societies people live in large, heated (or air-conditioned) houses, they rarely die from illnesses, and they always have more than enough to eat and drink. In other societies people have little to eat and drink, they live in small, ramshackle huts, and their children often die from one of several diseases. In trying to explain these differences, you notice that many of the males in the rich societies wear colored ties around their necks, whereas few, if any, of the males in the poor societies wear these ties. Intrigued, you look closer: within each society, those males who wear neckties are more likely to have large houses and plenty to eat than males who are tieless. In your report back to the chief alien scientist, you confidently conclude that neckties are an important source of wealth in the human species, somehow generating large houses and food (through some unknown mechanism that you will leave for the alien psychologists and alien microeconomists to figure out).

Obviously this conclusion is incorrect. The reason it is incorrect is that it neglects history. Wealthy societies (and people) are not wealthy because of neckties. The necktie is just an arbitrary dress custom that happened to have been popular in Britain during the industrial revolution of the late 1800s. The technological advances during the industrial revolution made Britain wealthy, not the necktie, and as Britain's influence spread throughout the world via the British Empire the tie hitch-hiked along with other British customs and technology. In time, the custom of wearing a tie became associated with wealthy businessmen, such that even societies that have never been under the direct influence of Britain, such as Japan, have adopted the tie as business dress.

The problem of spurious correlations between traits due to history was recognized as long ago as 1889 by Darwin's cousin, Francis Galton.[8] In response to a long-winded discussion by anthropologist E. B. Tylor of correlations across societies in various customs and practices, Galton retorted that any functional explanation for why two traits are correlated across a number of societies is vulnerable to the possibility that those societies may not be independent, because they may share a common history. So the reason why traits occur together may simply be because an earlier ancestral society happened to have both of those traits, and they have been passed down the generations together despite having no direct, functional link. This problem—that societies cannot be assumed to be independent due to shared ancestry—has become known in anthropology as "Galton's problem."

Biologists face exactly the same problem. Why? Because like anthropologists, they are studying an evolutionary system of descent with modification. An example involves species of cichlid fish, which are small, tropical freshwater fish found in the many lakes of East Africa. Cichlids species exhibit variation in parental care along two dimensions in particular.[9] First, species can be either *nest guarders*, where eggs are deposited in a nest that is guarded by one or both of the parents, or *mouth brooders*, where eggs are incubated in the mouth of one of the parents. Second, this care can be provided by the mother, by the father, or by both parents. More cichlid species are mouth brooders than are nest guarders. And female-only care is more common than biparental care, which in turn is more common than male-only care. But which of these combinations of traits came first, and which evolved later? Are any particular combinations more likely to evolve than others, and does the presence of one trait favor the emergence of another trait? For example, we might predict on functional grounds that uniparental care is more likely to evolve in mouth brooders than in nest guarders, because mouth brooding increases the parents' mobility and makes it more likely that one of the parents will leave. Indeed, this seems to be the case: while 89 percent of mouth brooders show uniparental care (vs. biparental care), only 22 percent of nest guarders show uniparental care. Simply counting the number of species that exhibit each combination of nest guarding/mouth brooding and uniparental/biparental care in this way, however, is vulnerable to Galton's problem. We do not know whether this high frequency of uniparental mouth brooders is because uniparental care and mouth brooding have coevolved several times, or whether they simply all happen to have descended from a uniparental, mouth-brooding ancestor.

To solve this problem, biologists Nicholas Goodwin, Sigal Balshine-Earn, and John Reynolds constructed a phylogenetic tree of 174 genera of East African cichlids based on morphological and genetic data.[10] They then mapped onto this phylogeny details of whether each species was mouth brooding or nest guarding, and whether they were male-only, female-only, or biparental carers. The resulting tree showed that mouth brooding likely evolved from nest guarding on 10–14 separate occasions, far more than previously thought, while mouth brooding rarely reversed back to nest guarding. Similarly, biparental care was found to be ancestral to uniparental care, and this uniparental care was predominantly female-only, with the latter evolving on 21–30 independent occasions. The analysis of Goodwin et al., therefore, shows that the ancestral form of parental care in cichlids is biparental nest guarding, with female-only mouth brooding evolving from that ancestral combination on several independent occasions. This suggests a functional reason for such a transition rather than an accident of history. The aforementioned increased mobility of mouth brooders might be one such functional explanation.

In 1994 anthropologist Ruth Mace and biologist Mark Pagel suggested that social scientists can use phylogenetic methods to test similar hypotheses about cross-cultural variation.[11] As we have already seen with the case of projectile points, phylogenetic methods can be used to reconstruct the evolutionary history of a set of traits. Mace and Pagel, however, argued that we can go beyond simply reconstructing evolutionary history and actually test functional hypotheses concerning why cultural traits occur together in distinct, nonrandom patterns. An excellent example is provided by Ruth Mace and fellow anthropologist Clare Holden, who examined cultural variation between different societies in sub-Saharan Africa.[12] Some of these societies are pastoralist, which means that they keep large domesticated animals such as cows.

Others are horticultural, which means that they do not keep livestock and instead grow crops on small plots of land. Societies also vary in the way in which they inherit wealth within families: some inherit wealth (as well as political power, group membership, property, etc.) along the female line, from a mother to her children. These are known as matrilineal societies. Others inherit wealth down the male line, from a father to his children. These societies are patrilineal. (Groups may also feature a mix of matriliny and patriliny, but for simplicity I will ignore this here.) Cultural anthropologists have long observed a link between these two traits across African societies: those that keep livestock tend to be patrilineal, while horticultural societies tend to be matrilineal. For example, David Aberle found in a 1961 study that just 8 percent of pastoralist societies worldwide were matrilineal, while 30 percent of horticultural societies were matrilineal.[13] This suggests some functional link between patriliny and pastoralism and/or between matriliny and horticulture.

As Holden and Mace pointed out, however, Aberle's analysis is vulnerable to Galton's problem: there may be a spurious correlation between patriliny and pastoralism on the one hand and matriliny and horticulture on the other, because all contemporary societies happen to descend from either a patrilineal, pastoralist ancestral society or a matrilineal, horticulturalist ancestral society, with the association across multiple groups simply an accident of history. To correct this problem, Holden and Mace constructed a phylogenetic tree of 68 sub-Saharan African societies based on linguistic data. That is, societies that share similar languages are grouped together on the tree, based on the assumption that languages change relatively slowly and are transmitted relatively faithfully within societies. They then classified each society on the tree as either cattle keeping or not cattle keeping, and as matrilineal or patrilineal. The resulting tree showed that closely related clusters of societies that all shared a recent common ancestor were also likely to share the same combination of subsistence and inheritance rule. In other words, each society cannot be viewed as independent: clusters of societies are similar in their cultural traits because they inherited them from a common ancestor. However, there was evidence of several independent shifts from matriliny to patriliny or vice versa, and from cattle keeping to not–cattle keeping and vice versa. A statistical method known as maximum likelihood showed that these events were linked: a change in one trait was associated with a change in the other more than would be expected due to chance. It was also shown that changes in certain directions were more likely than others. Cattle-

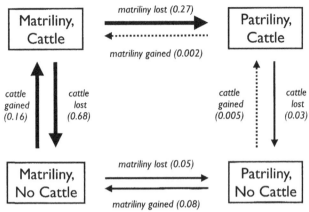

FIGURE 4.4 Phylogenetic analysis of cattle-keeping and inheritance rules in 68 sub-Saharan African societies. Numbers in parentheses and thickness of arrows indicate the probability of transition from one combination to another (higher numbers and thicker arrows indicate higher probabilities). Adapted from Holden and Mace 2003.

keeping matrilineal societies were most likely to either become patrilineal and cattle-keeping, or to stay matrilineal and lose their cattle. In other words, matriliny and cattle keeping was an unstable combination. Once a cattle-keeping society became patrilineal, however, it was unlikely to change in either trait. These transitions are shown in more detail in figure 4.4.

Holden and Mace argued that this evolutionary history can be explained because cattle are more useful to sons than daughters, and so favor a shift to patrilineal inheritance. In many African societies, grooms pay a bridewealth to the bride's family in order to marry. Large herds of cattle allow a man to offer a larger bridewealth, making him more likely to marry. Therefore the practice of keeping cattle makes a shift to patrilineal inheritance more likely. A further phylogenetic analysis conducted by Laura Fortunato, Clare Holden, and Ruth Mace explored the origin of the bridewealth system itself.[14] Bridewealth contrasts with the dowry system, in which the bride's family, rather than the groom's family, provides the wealth to the newly married couple. Most traditional societies worldwide have a bridewealth system, with far fewer having the dowry system. This has led some anthropologists to propose that bridewealth is the older of the two systems, with dowry emerging so recently that it has yet to spread widely.[15] Fortunato et al.'s phylogenetic analysis, however, showed that dowry is more likely to be the ancestral state, with bridewealth having evolved independently on at least four occasions. Here we have a clear example of how phyloge-

netic methods can significantly improve our understanding of historical cultural phenomena relative to traditional nonevolutionary, non-
phylogenetic methods.

But Is Cultural Evolution Treelike? The application of phylogenetic methods to cultural evolution by researchers such as O'Brien, Darwent, Lyman, Mace, Holden, and Fortunato has not gone without challenge. It
is frequently argued that, whereas biological evolution is treelike due
to the branching nature of speciation, cultural evolution is not very
treelike.[16] Ideas, customs, practices, and technology, it is argued, often
diffuse across cultural lineages due to horizontal transmission, making
these lineages blend together.[17] For example, words may diffuse from
one language to another (think of French words that are used in English, such as "impasse" or "sabotage"), an inventor might combine two
or more separate inventions to produce a new one (such as the joining
of various existing blades in a Swiss Army Knife), or a scientist might
integrate two separate theories (such as when James Clerk Maxwell
and other nineteenth-century physicists fused the separate theories of
electricity and magnetism into a unified theory of electromagnetism).
The non-treelike structure of cultural macroevolution was first mooted
by the cultural anthropologist Alfred Kroeber in the early twentieth
century, who viewed cultural evolution less like a tree and more like
a tangled bush, with no distinct lineages.[18] And because phylogenetic
methods were developed by biologists to identify evolutionary trees
in biological data sets, Kroeber's assumption has been used to argue
that these methods are inappropriate for cultural data sets. Here is the
biologist Stephen Jay Gould:

> Biological evolution is a bad analogue for cultural change . . .
> Biological evolution is a system of constant divergence without
> subsequent joining of branches. Lineages, once distinct, are
> separate forever. In human history, transmission across lin-
> eages is, perhaps, the major source of cultural change.[19]

This criticism is another variant of the criticisms of cultural evolution
encountered in chapter 2, where an apparent difference between biological and cultural evolution (e.g., regarding particulate vs. blending
inheritance, or Lamarckian vs. non-Lamarckian inheritance) is used
to reject cultural evolution. As for those earlier examples, the difference between biological and cultural evolution is far less clear-cut here
than is often assumed. The distinction between a branching, diver-

gent biological evolution and a blending, convergent cultural evolution is something of a distortion of both biology and culture. Although biological evolution was once thought to be treelike, recent decades have witnessed a major rethinking of this assumption. Geneticists have found that horizontal gene transfer is common in both bacteria and plants, wherein genetic material is transmitted across species boundaries by viruses.[20] Indeed, one analysis found so much crossing of species boundaries in bacteria due to horizontal gene transfer that rather than a tree of life, their evolutionary history can better be described as a ring of life.[21] So although cultural evolution might not resemble the branching, treelike vertebrate evolution that we humans are most familiar with, it may resemble quite closely a more blending invertebrate evolution.

The assumption that cultural evolution is blending rather than branching, originated by Kroeber and perpetuated by Gould and others, can also be challenged. The few empirical tests of this claim have revealed that branching may be a more common pattern for cultural evolution than often assumed. Anthropologists Jamie Tehrani and Mark Collard tested the role of branching versus blending in the patterns found on nineteenth-century rugs made by Turkmen women from five ethnic groups in Turkmenistan, Iran, and Afghanistan.[22] These patterns feature representations of animals such as birds, objects such as arrows, and abstract shapes such as stars, all of which vary across different ethnic groups. Tehrani and Collard reasoned that if patterns were transmitted primarily within groups, for example, via vertical transmission from mothers to daughters, then these patterns should result in a phylogenetic tree with few if any homoplasies, that is, changes due to independent invention or diffusion across lineages/groups. If, on the other hand, cross-lineage blending is common, then the phylogenetic tree should contain lots of homoplasies. To determine this, they used the consistency index (CI) measure, which as noted above is a measure of the number of homoplasies in a tree. Recall that a CI of 1.0 indicates a perfect tree with no homoplasies, with the CI getting smaller as the data become less treelike. They found a rather high CI of 0.68, showing that while there were a substantial number of homoplasies, the history of textile pattern evolution was predominantly one of distinct, branching lineages.

A subsequent study by Collard, Tehrani, and Stephen Shennan expanded this initial analysis to other data sets, both cultural and biological.[23] They reasoned that if biological and cultural evolution really are fundamentally different processes, the former branching and the latter blending, as suggested by Kroeber and Gould, then there should be a systematic difference in the tree-likeness of the biological and the cultural data sets. To test this prediction, Collard et al. collected twenty-one biological data sets that contained genetic, morphological, and behavioral data from a diverse range of taxa, including lizards, birds, hominids, bees, and primates. They also collected twenty-one cultural data sets, including Tehrani and Collard's Turkmen rug patterns, O'Brien et al.'s North American projectile points, other material artifacts such as Neolithic pottery decorations, plus nonmaterial data sets regarding food taboos, religious beliefs, and puberty rites. For each data set, Collard et al. calculated the number of homoplasies as described above, although this time using the retention index (RI), which controls for differences in the number of species and characters and is particularly useful when comparing data sets, as was done here. Like CI, an RI of 1 indicates no homoplasies and a perfectly treelike evolutionary pattern, with lower RI values increasingly less treelike. The results showed that the biological data sets and the cultural data sets had remarkably similar average RIs of 0.61 and 0.59, respectively. Assuming that the biological data sets are primarily generated through branching speciation, this analysis suggests that the cultural data sets, too, have been shaped by a similar branching process.

What microevolutionary mechanisms might be responsible for maintaining a branching, treelike pattern in cultural evolution? As critics have pointed out, ideas, beliefs, technology, words, and so on undoubtedly *can* spread from group to group, yet for the cultural data sets considered by Collard et al., this does not seem to have happened, or at least has not significantly reduced the treelike pattern. Anthropologist William Durham has suggested that branching is maintained in cultural evolution because of "transmission isolating mechanisms," or "TRIMs" for short, which act as barriers to the cultural transmission of information between groups.[24] TRIMs parallel the reproductive isolating mechanisms that prevent the transmission of genetic information across species boundaries, such as differences in chromosome numbers that prevent the successful fusion of gametes or physical barriers such as mountain ranges or rivers. What might constitute a TRIM in cultural evolution? Language is probably a good candidate, given that people who speak different languages may not be able to communicate ideas, beliefs, and knowledge effectively, if at all. Ethnocentrism may be another potent TRIM. Ethnocentrism describes the widespread tendency for people to identify with members of their own groups (the ingroup) and avoid, derogate, or act aggressively toward members of other groups (outgroups). Ethnocentrism has been documented by anthropologists in virtually every society ever studied, as well as under controlled conditions in the psychology lab.[25] Ethnic boundaries, then, may not only define but also create different social groups by preventing anything being transmitted across them.

The role that TRIMs play was explored by Tehrani and Collard in the textile pattern data.[26] Tehrani interviewed Iranian tribal women living in southwestern Iran, asking them from whom they learned weaving techniques and the specific patterns that they used. The women reported that they learned weaving techniques exclusively from their mothers, indicating vertical cultural transmission. This is consistent with the treelike pattern detected in the phylogenetic analysis. The textile patterns, on the other hand, showed a mix of vertical and horizontal transmission, as patterns learned from the women's mothers were supplemented with patterns learned from other members of their community. Crucially, however, this horizontal transmission was predominantly restricted to within communities. Social norms prevented women from traveling to other villages unaccompanied by men, and intertribal contact between weavers was rare. Moreover, women typically married within their own tribe, again preventing intertribal interaction. These norms therefore constitute strong TRIMs and may explain the high degree of fit to a treelike pattern observed for Turkmen textiles in the aforementioned analysis by Tehrani and Collard.

TRIMs are not ubiquitous, however. A phylogenetic analysis by archaeologists Peter Jordan and Stephen Shennan of late nineteenth- and early twentieth-century basketry designs of the indigenous populations of California found a low CI of around 0.35, suggesting that substantial cultural transmission across linguistic and ethnic group boundaries has greatly reduced any treelike pattern for this particular technology.[27] And it should be remembered that most of these studies that apply phylogenetic methods to cultural phenomena involve preindustrial societies, in which TRIMs such as ethnic boundaries may be particularly pronounced. Postindustrial societies are, superficially at least, characterized by much greater intergroup transmission than traditional societies, given the consequences of mass communication technology such as television and the internet. As a result, modern technological evolution can probably seldom be described as a branching process, although this has yet to be empirically addressed.

Drift and Demography in Cultural Macroevolution

Phylogenetic methods are not the only tools borrowed by cultural evolution researchers from biologists to study patterns and trends in cultural macroevolution. In chapter 3, we saw how some cultural evolution researchers have also borrowed models of *genetic drift* from population genetics to explain certain patterns of cultural change. Genetic (or "neutral") drift describes how random processes such as sampling error in small populations can generate evolutionary change despite the lack of any selection for particular alleles. We drew an analogy with the lottery: even though each number in a lottery theoretically has the same probability of being drawn each week, in reality some numbers are drawn more often than other numbers simply by chance. In the same way, selectively neutral alleles can increase in frequency or disappear from small populations of organisms simply by accident, such as when the sole carrier of a rare allele happens to die young. Population geneticists such as Sewell Wright in the 1930s and later Motoo Kimura and others have formalized these processes in mathematical models, yielding key insights into the conditions under which biologists can expect to observe genetic drift, and the kind of patterns that biologists would expect to see in natural populations if drift has been acting. For example, models predict (and subsequent laboratory experiments have confirmed) that, when drift is the only process acting, then (1) genetic variation gradually drops over time, as rare alleles are lost as described above and eventually just a single allele remains; (2) different alleles will become fixed in different populations, because of the random nature of drift; and (3) drift occurs faster in smaller populations, because smaller populations are more vulnerable to accidents of sampling.[28] These models provide specific predictions for biologists studying organisms in the wild. For example, a biologist who observed low within-group genetic diversity (point 1) and high between-group diversity (point 2) in their study species might conclude that drift is responsible for such a pattern.

Drift in the Archaeological Record. Cultural drift describes the analogous case where all cultural traits are equal in their fitness (their intrinsic probability of being copied and transmitted) yet accidents of sampling generate predictable patterns of cultural variation. Beginning with a landmark paper by archaeologist Fraser Neiman in 1995, a growing number of archaeologists have used the principle of cultural drift to explain patterns and trends in the archaeological record.[29] Neiman reasoned that many of the phenomena that archaeologists are interested in might be good candidates for having been influenced by drift. Certain characteristics of artifacts, such as decorative patterns on pottery, do not appear to have a clear functional purpose, and so may not be subject to cultural selection. Furthermore, human groups during prehistory have typically been small, raising the possibility of sampling effects. And remember that only a subset of a group, such as adult females, will have made the artifacts that archaeologists recover, further reducing the population size (this smaller subset is known as the "effective population size" to distinguish it from the absolute population size).

To test this inference, Neiman constructed a simple mathematical model of cultural drift based on similar models of genetic drift developed by population geneticists. In the model, individuals within a small population (e.g., fifty individuals) are assumed to copy the cultural trait of another member of the population entirely at random, with no intrinsic differences in the attractiveness or effectiveness of different traits. There is also a small probability that each individual will engage in innovation, either the de novo invention of a new trait or the copying of a novel trait from outside this particular population (e.g., a neighboring group of people). Using this model, Neiman showed that if cultural drift is operating on a collection of artifacts, then two quantitative predictions can be made. First, the larger the effective population size, the more cultural diversity there should be. This is because larger populations are less vulnerable to the chance extinction of particular cultural traits. And second, the higher the innovation rate, the more diversity is also to be expected. This is because innovation introduces new variation into the population. So if drift is acting, cultural diversity should increase with both population size and innovation rate.

Neiman then drew a link between within-group diversity and between-group diversity and how the two are predicted to be related under the cultural drift model. Higher rates of innovation result in higher within-group diversity. One form of innovation is the introduction of new traits from neighboring groups via intergroup cultural transmission. From a between-group perspective, however, high rates of intergroup transmission will reduce between-group diversity, as the same cultural traits spread across all groups. So high innovation rates, in the form of intergroup transmission, lead to both high within-group diversity and low between-group diversity. Conversely, low innovation rates produce homogenous groups that are different from one another.

Either way, within-group diversity and between-group diversity should be inversely correlated, that is, the higher one is, the lower the other should be.

Neiman tested this prediction—that within-group diversity and between-group diversity should be inversely correlated—in an actual archaeological data set: ceramic pottery from southern Illinois from the Woodland period from around 200 B.C. to A.D. 800. Neiman chose a particular feature of cooking pots, the decoration found around the outside of the rim. Twenty-six different decorative styles or patterns have been documented for the Woodland period, including the use of patterned fabric, the attachment of cords around the rim, and the stamping of different patterns into the pot. As none of these decorations appear to be obviously functional, they are good candidates for being neutral traits subject to cultural drift. Supporting the prediction, Neiman showed that for ceramic decorations from thirty-five separate archaeological sites, within-site diversity was indeed inversely correlated with between-site diversity. Sites that had high within-site diversity also had low between-site diversity, presumably due to high rates of intergroup transmission, while sites that had low within-site diversity also had high between-site diversity, presumably because they had low rates of intergroup transmission.

Neiman was also able to draw inferences about the changing influence of intergroup transmission over time. The Woodland period can be divided into three parts: Early (before 200 B.C.), Middle (200 B.C.–A.D. 400) and Late (A.D. 400–800). Neiman showed that both within-group and between-group diversity changed during these three periods: whereas the Early and Late Woodland periods featured low within-group and high between-group diversity, indicative of low intergroup transmission, the Middle Woodland period featured the reverse pattern of high within-group and low between-group diversity, indicative of high intergroup transmission. This conflicts with archaeologists' traditional understanding of Woodland social dynamics, in which intergroup contact and transmission were assumed to have steadily increased throughout the period. Here we have a clear case in which simple evolutionary models have provided a novel insight into archaeological change relative to traditional nonevolutionary theories.

Although Neiman demonstrated that the patterns of variation in ceramic decoration for this particular region and this particular time period were consistent with the cultural drift model, other analyses with other artifact types and from other regions and time periods have found no such match. Stephen Shennan and James Wilkinson, for example, tested the predictions of the cultural drift model in a much older sample of Neolithic (5300–4850 B.C.) ceramics found in western Germany.[30] Like Neiman, Shennan and Wilkinson chose a trait that a priori might be predicted to be neutral: the decorative bands that were incised on the sides of cooking pots. Thirty-five patterns have been documented. For example, some bands were made up of widely spaced parallel lines, others narrowly spaced parallel lines, others dotted lines. Recall that under the cultural drift model, the cultural diversity of artifacts found within a site should be proportional to the innovation rate and the group size, with more diversity expected for higher innovation rates and larger group sizes. Shennan and Wilkinson were fortunate enough to have good enough data for two Neolithic sites to be able to calculate all three of these measures directly: artifact diversity, measured directly from each site as the variation in relative frequencies of different band types; innovation rate, defined as the number of new band types per total number of pots; and population size, defined as the total number of different motifs documented.

When Shennan and Wilkinson inserted these into the equations predicted under the cultural drift model, however, they did not fit the predicted relationships. Diversity was *not* proportional to the product of innovation rate and population size. In fact, for most of the Neolithic period, there was far *more* artifact diversity than expected. Shennan and Wilkinson therefore concluded that, instead of being subject to cultural drift, pottery decorations during this period were subject to an anticonformist bias: potters were preferentially copying novel or rare decorative patterns. Although it is very difficult to say with any certainty why Neolithic potters would have favored novel patterns given the lack of written records from the period, Shennan and Wilkinson note that the anticonformist bias appeared to coincide with a leveling off in the number of households found in the region, suggesting that it may have served to "establish distinct local identities once the area had more or less filled up."[31] In other words, different households distinguished themselves by intentionally selecting rare, unique decorative designs. This might even be another example of a TRIM acting to keep cultural lineages distinct and cultural evolution treelike (assuming the rare traits were passed down subsequent generations within the same household).

Like the case of the increase in popularity of Dalmatians following the release of the Disney film *101 Dalmatians*, this study demonstrates the value of having a definitive null hypothesis—cultural drift—against which to identify nonrandom processes such as conformity in the case of dog breeds and anticonformity in the case of Neolithic pottery decorations.

Using Handaxes to Track Early Human Dispersal. Most of the examples of past cultural change given above have been concerned with the last few thousand years of human history. Humans—or the group of species collectively known as hominins—have been around for a lot longer than this, however. In recent years paleoanthropologists (who study early hominins), like archaeologists, have been using evolutionary models to explain early hominin cultural change. Fossil evidence suggests that hominins first appeared in eastern Africa around two million years ago, initially in the form of *Homo habilis* and *Homo ergaster* and subsequently *Homo erectus. Homo sapiens* only appeared relatively recently, around 200,000 years ago. One of the defining characteristics of these early hominin species is the construction and use of stone tools. A common and widespread type of stone tool was the handaxe, which was made by chipping flakes off a larger piece of rock to produce a broadly symmetrical shape with a sharp edge for cutting. This sharp edge could then be used to cut up the carcasses of hunted or scavenged animals. Handaxes appear to have been extremely useful to our hominin ancestors. After they appeared in east Africa around 1.6 million years ago, they remained the dominant tool of choice for early hominins until *Homo sapiens* appeared. They also remained largely unchanged in their basic design as hominins dispersed out of Africa and into eastern and southern Asia and Europe. Indeed, some paleontologists have suggested that the handaxe was one of the main reasons why hominins dispersed so far and wide over a relatively short period of time.[32]

The handaxe is also one of the earliest examples of culturally transmitted human technology. In order to persist over several hundred thousand years, they must have been transmitted from individual to individual, generation to generation via social learning mechanisms such as imitation or perhaps even direct teaching. This raises the possibility of applying cultural evolution models to handaxe data, just as archaeologists have applied cultural evolution models such as neutral drift to more recent artifacts such as projectile points and textile decorations.

Paleoanthropologists Stephen Lycett and Noreen von Cramon-Taubadel have recently done just this.[33] As we saw previously, one of the key insights to come from biological models of genetic drift is that genetic diversity scales with population size: small populations are more likely to lose rare genes through chance sampling effects (e.g., when the sole carrier of a rare gene happens to die before they can pass on that gene), and so have lower genetic variation than larger populations. Biologists have extended this basic principle to the case where populations disperse across a large geographical region. Typically, when species disperse, they undergo a series of "population bottlenecks," where the size of the founding colony in a new region is significantly smaller than the established population from which the colony originated. This is because dispersal is often dangerous, exposing the population to new and unpredictable predators and unfamiliar food sources. Because each of these bottlenecks features a reduction in population size, each one also reduces genetic variation according to the aforementioned principle of genetic drift.

This process of repeated population bottlenecks has been shown to characterize the dispersal of hominins out of Africa. DNA analyses of modern humans show that African populations have the greatest genetic diversity, and that genetic diversity steadily declines the further one moves away from east Africa (in order of decreasing genetic diversity: the Middle East, then Southwest Asia and Europe, then Southeast Asia, then Oceania, and finally the Americas[34]). Indeed, 85 percent of the variation in genetic diversity of modern human populations can be predicted from their geographical distance from East Africa. Lycett and von Cramon-Taubadel reasoned that the same principles that apply to genetically transmitted neutral alleles might also apply to culturally transmitted handaxes. After all, just as genes can be lost from small populations due to sampling effects, so too cultural traits, such as methods of constructing handaxes or mental templates for different handaxe designs, are more likely to be lost in smaller populations as there are fewer demonstrators available to learn from.

So Lycett and von Cramon-Taubadel measured the diversity in the width and length of handaxes found at ten Paleolithic sites along the presumed most likely dispersal route of early hominins, from an east African origin to the Middle East and then along two alternative routes, one into Europe and the other into southern Asia. As predicted by the repeated bottleneck model, the further a site was from east Africa, the less diverse its handaxes were. In quantitative terms, a full 50 percent of the variance in handaxe diversity could be explained in terms of geographical distance from east Africa. While not quite as high as the corresponding figure of 85 percent for genetic diversity, this is still a substantial amount. And when Lycett and von Cramon-Taubadel switched the presumed origin of the dispersal to either England or India, the match between handaxe diversity and geographical distance disappeared.

Lycett and von Cramon-Taubadel's study therefore demonstrates a striking parallel between genetic and cultural evolution: just as repeated past population bottlenecks reduce genetic diversity due to the increased chances of losing rare alleles, so too repeated bottlenecks reduce cultural diversity due to the loss of potential demonstrators from whom to learn. This is not the only study to show that demography (i.e., the size, structure, and distribution of populations) can affect past cultural macroevolution. A similar but perhaps more dramatic case of the loss of prehistoric technology due to reduced population size was documented by anthropologist Joseph Henrich for Tasmania.[35] Since becoming separated from mainland Australian populations around 10,000 years ago, prehistoric Tasmanians lost various technological traits, including bone tools, winter clothing, fishing spears, and boomerangs. Henrich argues that this is because of the reduced size of the isolated Tasmanian population, which increased the chances of losing the knowledge and skills required to make and use such complex technological artifacts. Conversely, a recent extension of Henrich's demographic model by biologists and anthropologists Adam Powell, Stephen Shennan, and Mark Thomas found that the first appearance of various complex technologies and practices in the paleontological record, such as cave paintings and body decorations, hunting tools such as spear throwers and the bow and arrow, and musical instruments, can all be predicted by population size.[36] Only when populations are large enough to counteract the negative effects of drift and bottlenecking can such behaviors be sustained without being lost by chance sampling effects. In sum, demography affects culture just as it affects genes, and the same quantitative drift models can be used to show this in both cases.

Conclusions: Evolutionary Insights into Culture's Distant Past

Archaeologists and paleoanthropologists face a huge challenge in making sense of our species' distant past, given the ambiguity and incompleteness of the material record left behind by our ancestors. Cultural anthropologists, too, confront a daunting task in trying to explain the striking cross-cultural variation in a multitude of practices and customs documented between societies. Yet biologists face similar problems interpreting a fossil record that is just as fragmentary and ambiguous, and explaining a species diversity that is just as rich. They have done this primarily through the use of quantitative tools such as phylogenetic methods and neutral drift models tested against observed historical and comparative data. In this chapter we have seen how a group of anthropologists and archaeologists are beginning to apply the same evolutionary tools to cultural data sets. The reason that such methods can be applied to cultural phenomena is that culture evolves: it is a process of descent with modification, just like the genetic evolution of species. Yet this is not some sterile academic exercise in demonstrating that a method from one domain happens to work in another. In several cases we have seen how these evolutionary methods have yielded novel insights that surpass the limits of traditional, nonevolutionary social science methods to explain something important about actual, real-life cultural change, from O'Brien et al.'s reconstruction of projectile point evolution, to Holden and Mace's phylogenetic test of functional hypotheses concerning cattle keeping and wealth inheritance without falling prey to Galton's problem, to Neiman, Shennan, and Wilkinson's demonstrations that certain characteristics of prehistoric artifacts are (or are not) copied randomly, to Lycett and von Cramon-Taubadel's finding that Paleolithic handaxe diversity is affected by demographic bottlenecks. The next chapter continues this exploration of patterns and trends in cultural macroevolution as applied to language and written history.

5 Cultural Macroevolution II: Language and History

Phylogenetic methods as a means of reconstructing evolutionary relationships are not limited to material artifacts like projectile points. They can also be used to reconstruct the historical relationships between the many diverse languages that have emerged over the last several thousand years. Indeed, there are so many striking parallels between linguistic and genetic evolution that language may be particularly amenable to evolutionary analysis.[1] Words and grammatical rules appear to be transmitted with a fidelity close to that of genes: there is a rather high probability that you speak the same language as your parents, and that they spoke the same language as their parents, and maybe even back a couple more generations. Consequently, compared to, say, scientific knowledge or clothes fashions, languages change very slowly, perhaps at a similar rate to many species. Yet historical linguists have generally been reluctant to embrace the phylogenetic methods used by evolutionary biologists to quantify and ultimately explain language change. In this chapter we will see how phylogenetic methods can resolve several hitherto outstanding problems in historical linguistics, from the age of the Indo-European language family to the reason why Austronesian languages spread so rapidly across the Pacific. We will then turn from spoken to written language, examining how phylogenetic methods can be used to reconstruct the historical relationships between the handwritten manuscripts that were copied from scribe to scribe before the invention of the printing press. Finally, we will examine how quantitative models adapted from population ecology have been used to explain the rise and fall of empires during recent human history.

Language Evolution: Descending the Tower of Babel

According to the book of Genesis, all of humanity originally spoke the same language. Then they built an enormous tower in Babylon—the Tower of Babel—as a way of ensuring that all of humanity would remain united, rather than becoming scattered across the world in mutually unintelligible groups that each spoke a different language. God, annoyed at this flagrant display of hubris, scattered the people across the world into mutually unintelligible groups that each spoke a different language.

Of course, no present-day linguist accepts this explanation for the diversity that we see in the languages of the world. Instead, it has long been established that languages are related by descent, with one language giving rise to new languages as groups become separated by geography or conflict, and changes accumulate in each separated language over time. And it has not gone unnoticed that this process of descent with modification bears a strong resemblance to the biological evolution of species. In fact, the idea that language change can be viewed as a branching evolutionary process predates the writing of *The Origin of Species*.[2] Sir William Jones in the late 1700s was the first to suggest that Sanskrit, Latin, and ancient Greek all share a common ancestor, thus forming the Indo-European language family. Jones's idea that languages are historically related by descent was expanded and popularized by philologists in the 1830s who began to identify specific similarities in word forms and grammatical rules between different languages. In the 1850s, the first Indo-European language trees were published by comparative philologists such as August Schleicher. Darwin could not have failed to have been influenced by such trees when writing *The Origin*. Indeed, one of the foremost philologists in Britain was Darwin's cousin and brother-in-law Hensleigh Wedgwood, who founded the Philological Society of London and helped to prepare the forerunner of the *Oxford English Dictionary*.

Immediately upon publication of *The Origin* linguists recognized the parallels between language change and species change. Schleicher wrote a pamphlet entitled *Die Darwinsche Theorie und die Sprachwissenschaft* (Darwinian Theory and Linguistic Science) just a few years after *The Origin* appeared. And in his 1871 book *The Descent of Man*, Darwin himself drew explicit analogies between linguistic and biological evolution:

> The formation of different languages and of distinct species, and the proofs that both have been developed through a gradual process, are curiously parallel . . . We find in distinct languages striking homologies due to community of descent, and analogies due to a similar process of formation . . . The frequent presence of rudiments, both in languages and in species, is still more remarkable . . . Dominant languages and dialects spread widely, and lead to the gradual extinction of other tongues. A language, like a species, when once extinct, never reappears . . . We see variability in every tongue, and new words are continually cropping up; but as there is a limit to the powers of the memory, single words, like whole languages, gradually become extinct . . . The survival or preservation of certain favoured words in the struggle for existence is natural selection.[3]

Modern comparative or historical linguistics has built on these foundations to further reconstruct the origins of language families. The main tool of historical linguistics is the comparative method.[4] The linguistic comparative method is based on the same logic as phylogenetic analysis: similar languages are more likely to be related to one another than dissimilar languages, and these similarities can be used to reconstruct the history of language families. For example, the synonymous English, Latin, and German words *father, pater*, and *Vater*, or *fish, piscis*, and *Fisch*, are too similar to have arisen by chance independent invention and indicate that English, Latin, and German share a relatively recent common ancestor.

But while the underlying logic is the same, the linguistic comparative method is more subjective than the rigorous statistical and phylogenetic methods developed by biologists. Typically, language trees are reconstructed based on the linguist's intuitions about what kinds of changes were more likely, and in what directions. And as linguists April McMahon and Robert McMahon point out, this is problematic because there is no widely agreed upon set of rules for the comparative method.[5] As a result, different linguists come up with different historical relationships; and with no objective criteria or statistical tests for measuring relatedness, there is no way to decide which historical tree is best supported by the data.

Phylogenetic methods provide just such a quantitative solution to this problem. Biologists construct trees not by subjectively deciding which species resemble each other more closely, but by using rigorous statistical techniques such as maximum parsimony, maximum likelihood, or Bayesian methods to quantify the likelihood that different trees accurately resemble actual evolutionary history according to explicit and objective assumptions and algorithms. This is not to say that phylogenetic methods will always produce a single, definite tree with 100 percent accuracy. Far from it. There is always a large degree of uncertainty. The point is that this uncertainty can be quantified and consequently minimized in a way that is not possible with traditional linguistic tree-building methods. So a group of cultural evolution researchers has begun to use phylogenetic methods to address questions about language evolution that linguists have failed to satisfactorily answer concerning the origin of language groups, the sequences in which different languages emerged, the absolute dates for the splitting of different languages, and the rate of change of different languages during different periods.[6] Here are some examples.

Riding the Express Train from Taiwan to Hawaii. In chapter 3 we saw how new genetic evidence suggests that agriculture spread through Europe from the Middle East via demic diffusion, as farming populations replaced indigenous nonfarming hunter-gatherers, rather than as a result of cultural diffusion, in which farming practices are copied by indigenous populations with no movement of people. This is not the only region in which agriculture is thought to have caused a mass migration, however. Jared Diamond and Peter Bellwood have recently argued that several mass migrations occurred as a result of the independent invention of agriculture in several regions of the world, and in each case farming populations rapidly spread and replaced nonfarming hunter-gatherers. These rapid expansions, they argue, have strongly shaped cultural, genetic, and linguistic diversity across the world. For example, as well as the Middle East, another mass migration appears to have occurred in Southeast Asia, when rice was domesticated about 9,000 years ago around the Yangtze River in China. Just as wheat-growing farmers spread out from the Middle East, so too rice-growing farmers spread from mainland China out through Taiwan to colonize the islands of the Pacific, from the Philippines out as far as New Zealand and Hawaii. This expansion of farmers was remarkably fast, taking just 2,000 years to reach and colonize islands over 10,000 km away from the Taiwanese takeoff point. Indeed, it was so fast that it has become known as the "express-train" model of Austronesian expansion. Just as in Europe, these East Asian farmers replaced the existing hunter-gatherers of the region as they spread, bringing not only their farming methods but also their language. Therefore, the similar languages spoken by myriad groups across Austronesia can be explained by this rapid and relatively recent expansion of farmers.[7]

This express-train sequence of Austronesian expansion has not gone unchallenged, however. Other anthropologists have suggested that Austronesian languages originated not with Taiwanese farmers but in eastern Indonesia long before agriculture spread to the region. Others have argued that, due to frequent intergroup transmission, it is impossible to accurately reconstruct the history of Austronesian languages, mirroring the criticism of phylogenetic methods considered earlier.[8]

Russell Gray and Fiona Jordan added some rigor to these debates by testing the express-train model using phylogenetic methods.[9] They constructed a phylogenetic tree from the basic vocabulary of seventy-seven Austronesian languages, with languages that share more cognates (similar words with the same meaning) assumed to be more closely related. Then they constructed another tree based on geographical proximity that might be expected from the express-train model. So Taiwanese languages were assumed to be oldest, Indonesian and Papua New Guinean languages more recent, and Hawaiian and New Zealand languages the most recent, matching the proposed migration route. The two trees showed a strong statistical match, supporting the express-train model. In showing that the Taiwanese languages are likely to be the oldest, and therefore the original, Austronesian languages, Gray and Jordan's analysis constitutes evidence against the alternative Indonesian-origin model. This shows how phylogenetic methods can be used to reconstruct patterns of linguistic expansion, thus explaining the present distribution of languages in the world.

Indo-European Language Family Origins. Another phylogenetic study by Russell Gray, this time with Quentin Atkinson, examined the origins of the Indo-European language family. As previously mentioned, this large group of several hundred related languages is spoken across Europe, Iran, and India. Much debate within linguistics has concerned the exact date at which the common ancestor of these languages occurred. The linguistic comparative method cannot provide details of absolute ages, only relative similarity. Another method in linguistics that is used to measure the age of languages is known as glottochronology. This method measures the percentage of cognates that different languages share. Assuming a constant rate of word replacement, linguists can then estimate the time since the languages diverged, given that similarity should correlate with time since splitting. In this sense it is much like radiocarbon dating, which uses the constant rate of radioactive decay to estimate the age of plant and animal remains. However, glottochronology has been severely criticized because the assumption of constant language change is unrealistic: there is evidence (reviewed below) that languages undergo rapid bursts of change followed by periods of stasis. As a result, linguists have little way of determining the absolute age of languages. In the case of the Indo-European language family, one linguist complains that its age "could be anything—4,000 years BP or 40,000 years BP are both perfectly possible (as is any date in between)."[10] This uncertainty has led to several competing hypotheses. One places the origin at around 5,000–6,000 years BP with the spread of Kurgan horsemen from the Ural Mountain region in what is now Kazakhstan. Another places the origin much earlier at around 8,000–9,500 years BP as agriculture spread from Anatolia.[11]

Again, phylogenetic methods borrowed from biology offer a solution to this problem. Gray and Atkinson constructed a phylogenetic tree of 87 Indo-European languages based on almost 2,500 cognates.[12] This resulted in a tree with a retention index of 0.76, indicating a strong treelike pattern (remember that RI ranges from 0 to 1, with 1 indicating a perfect tree with no borrowing across lineages). This tree resembled in many respects the historical relationships identified using traditional linguist methods, such as the linguistic comparative method. For example, Germanic languages (e.g., German, Dutch, and English) were grouped together on one branch of the tree, Italic languages (e.g., Latin, Italian, and Sardinian) formed another group, while another group comprised the Celtic languages (e.g., Welsh, Gaelic, and Irish). Once they had this tree, Gray and Atkinson imposed onto it the known dates of fourteen historical events. Unlike the Austronesian languages, the Indo-European languages have left many written records of known age. For example, ancient inscriptions from the fifth century AD written in Irish indicate that the Irish language diverged from other Celtic languages such as Welsh sometime before this date. Once the tree was rooted with these historical dates, the age of the entire Indo-European family could be estimated without requiring the assumption that languages change at constant rates. The resulting estimate of 7,800 to 9,800 years BP matched the estimated origin of agriculture in Anatolia based on radiocarbon analyses of archaeological remains. Thus the Anatolian agriculture hypothesis was supported over the Kurgan horsemen hypothesis.

Punctuation Marks in Language Evolution. It was noted earlier that one reason why glottochronology was flawed was because languages cannot be assumed to change at constant rates. Recent work by Quentin Atkinson, Mark Pagel, and colleagues has examined the rate of language evolution in more detail.[13] Specifically, they wanted to know whether language evolution is typically gradual and changes at a constant rate, or whether it occurs in brief bursts of change interspersed with longer periods of stasis. The latter pattern of rapid change and long stasis is known in biology by the term "punctuated equilibria" and characterizes certain parts of the fossil record. For example, most modern animal groups, including arthropods, mollusks, and echinoderms (starfish, sea urchins, and sea cucumbers) appeared around 543 million years ago during a geologically brief but evolutionarily turbulent period of about 30 million years known as the "Cambrian explosion."

So is language evolution also characterized by punctuated equilibria? More specifically, do we see clusters of new languages occurring together over time interspersed with periods of stasis? To find out, Atkinson et al. built phylogenetic trees of the three major language families that we have already met: the Bantu languages of sub-Saharan Africa, the Indo-European family, and the Austronesian languages. Rather than the simple parsimony-based methods examined in the previous chapter for generating trees, which only map splitting events along the branches of the tree, Atkinson et al. used more sophisticated Bayesian simulation methods for constructing their trees. This not only identifies splitting events but also provides an estimate of the amount of lexical change that has occurred in between splitting events. This is indicated on a tree by the length of the branches: the longer the branch, the more change (i.e., replacement of words) has occurred. Atkinson et al. reasoned that if language evolution is constant, then the length of each branch from the root to the tips should be independent of the number of splitting events along that branch. In other words, the appearance of new languages would have no effect on the rate at which words change. If, on the other hand, language evolution is punctuated, then longer branches should contain more splitting events than shorter branches. In other words, the appearance of new languages would increase the rate at which words change.

Atkinson et al.'s analysis showed that language evolution was better described as punctuated than constant. Indeed, a substantial amount of linguistic variation emerged during splitting events: as much as 31 percent for the Bantu languages. Why would the splitting of languages increase the rate of linguistic change? It could be for the same reason that punctuated equilibria are thought to occur in the fossil record: adaptive radiations. When a species colonizes a novel environment, the new and empty niches often stimulate divergence of that species into several new species with distinct adaptations. Similar adaptive radiations of languages may have occurred when new environments were colonized, such as the rapid agriculture-driven spread of Austronesian languages predicted by the express-train model. Atkinson et al. also suggest that social pressures may lead to punctuated bursts. For example, following US independence, a conscious effort was made to differentiate American English from British English. In his *American Dictionary of the English Language* of 1789, for example, Noah Webster wrote that "as an independent nation, our honor requires us to have a system of our own, in language as well as government."[14] Perhaps the collapse of empires, from the British to the Roman, stimulates bursts of language evolution in this way.

Use It or Lose It. A final study explored rates of linguistic change at the level of individual words, rather than entire languages. Linguists have long known that different words appear to change at different rates. Some words are likely to change in their form or meaning often, whereas other words are very unlikely to change. These rates of change translate into similarities and differences between languages, because words that seldom change tend to be shared across many related languages. For example, the English word "water," the German word "wasser," the Swedish word "vatten," and the Gothic word "wato" resemble one another because this word has changed little since English, German, Swedish, and Gothic all shared a common ancestor. Words that change more rapidly, however, are unlikely to be shared across languages because they have changed since those languages split. For example, the English word "tail," the German word "schwanz," and the French word "queue" all refer to the same thing but have undergone considerable change since these languages shared a common ancestor. What causes these different rates of change?

Mark Pagel, Quentin Atkinson, and Andrew Meade proposed that a major factor is the frequency with which words are used in everyday speech.[15] Words that are used often, such as "water," are less likely to change than words that are rarely used. They tested this hypothesis by first estimating the rate of change of 200 word meanings across 87 Indo-European languages, controlling for phylogenetic relationships between those languages. These rates ranged from very slowly changing words, such as "one," "two," or "night," which changed 0–1 times during the roughly 10,000-year history of the Indo-European language family, to very rapidly changing words such as "dirty," "turn," or "guts," which changed up to nine times in the same period. Pagel et al. then obtained word use frequencies for English, Spanish, Russian, and Greek from samples of magazines, newspapers, and books, as well as transcriptions of spoken language. As predicted, they found that the more often a word is used, the less likely it is to change. Remarkably, around 50 percent of the variation in rates of word change can be explained by usage frequency. Pagel et al. suggest two explanations for this strong relationship. First, commonly used words may be less vulnerable to mutation due to errors in recall. If you use a word every day, you are more likely to remember what it means and how to say and spell it than words that you seldom use. Second, commonly used words might be maintained due to conformity. Hearing lots of people frequently using a word in a particular way would encourage conformity to that common way of using, saying, or spelling it. Less frequently used words would be less subject to conformist pressure, because by definition they are rare. Here we can see, then, how quantitative phylogenetic methods are beginning to go beyond the mere description of macroevolutionary patterns (e.g., treeness or rates of change) and toward an exploration of the microevolutionary mechanisms that underlie, and thus explain, those patterns (e.g., conformity).

Manuscript Evolution

The phylogenetic analyses discussed so far are all primarily concerned with spoken language. Although written texts were used by Atkinson et al. to date the Indo-European tree and by Pagel et al. to calculate the frequency of word use in different languages, these studies had the ultimate goal of reconstructing the evolutionary history of a language in its spoken form. Written language can also be considered in its own right. Indeed, we might intuitively expect writing to better resemble high-fidelity genetic inheritance than spoken language. Consider a story such as a folktale that is passed down from generation to generation. If this transmission is purely spoken, we would expect many changes, errors, and distortions due to the vagaries of human memory. You have probably experienced this when you have heard a family member, partner, or even yourself tell the same anecdote repeatedly to different audiences: the date might change, bits might be exaggerated, finer details might be omitted. And this is on top of any mishearings, misunderstanding, or misinterpretation on the part of the listeners.[16] Writing, in contrast, provides much higher fidelity cultural transmission. Writing down information eliminates the need to store it in memory and therefore eliminates all of the associated biases and distortions that come with human memory.

With the invention of the printing press, the accuracy with which written text is reproduced is near-perfect. Before widespread use of mechanized printing presses, however, the transmission of written texts was performed by scribes who copied out by hand important or popular books. Although the popular image of a scribe is a monk transcribing the bible and other religious texts, many scribes were well-paid professionals employed by the wealthy upper classes to reproduce literary works such as Chaucer's fourteenth-century work *The Canterbury Tales* for their entertainment. Although transcription allowed far greater copying fidelity than oral retellings, it was still not perfect. Scribes working under candlelight would have made occasional errors, such as the omission of the odd word or the accidental repetition of a word or sentence. Some may also have intentionally corrected or, to their mind, improved a manuscript by modifying it in some way. And as texts were copied, and those copies were in turn copied by subsequent scribes, and those copies of copies themselves copied, these errors would have accumulated over time, just as genetic changes accumulate over successive biological generations.

Noting this parallel between genetic and textual transmission, a team of researchers including Christopher Howe and Adrian Barbrook from Cambridge University have used phylogenetic methods to reconstruct the evolutionary history of transcribed manuscripts.[17] The logic and method is much the same as for the spoken languages considered previously: the greater the number of differences between different manuscripts, the more distantly related they are assumed to be. And while manuscript scholars, like linguists, have been aware of this for many years and have constructed historical trees ("stemmata") of manuscripts without the use of methods borrowed from biology, these attempts have been both informal and subjective, and limited by the sheer volume of information that is contained in the multiple existing copies of a particular text. Just as in linguistics, phylogenetic methods offer manuscript scholars a powerful, quantitative tool for reconstructing manuscript evolution from large amounts of data and without the problems of subjective comparisons.

One study by Barbrook et al. examined the cultural evolution of Chaucer's *The Canterbury Tales*. Forty-three surviving fifteenth-century manuscripts of "The Wife of Bath's Prologue" from the *Tales* were analyzed, in which the titular wife tells of her five colorful marriages and the lessons she has learned from each. Eight hundred and fifty lines were chosen from the prologue, and differences across each of the forty-three copies were coded. Two kinds of phylogenetic methods were applied to the data. As well as the parsimony-based phylogenetic tree methods outlined in chapter 4, Barbrook et al. also used an alternative "split decomposition" method. The latter does not assume a priori that the data being analyzed necessarily exhibit a treelike history. As noted above, this may be the case for biological organisms such as bacteria or plants that frequently exchange genetic information horizontally. And as Barbrook et al. note, it may also be the case for culturally transmitted traits such as manuscripts, as scribes may have borrowed parts from more than one source text when copying out a manuscript.

Their phylogenetic analysis revealed six groups of closely related manuscripts, with each group descending from a single and distinct common ancestor. Reassuringly, this tree broadly recreated the historical relationships that manuscript scholars had identified previously using informal comparisons between manuscripts. A manuscript labeled *Hg*, for example, which appeared near the base of the phylogeny, is commonly considered by textual scholars to be the closest to Chaucer's original copy. But there were also novel findings. For example, this ancestral manuscript *Hg* was closely related to several other manuscripts that have typically been ignored by manuscript scholars, suggesting that a closer look at these manuscripts may be warranted.

One of the striking things to emerge from these analyses is that the changes that occur in manuscripts bear extremely close parallels to the changes that occur in the genetic code during genetic replication. Words or sentences were found to be omitted from manuscripts in the same way that one or more nucleotides can be omitted during genetic replication (known to geneticists as "deletions"). Conversely, words can be added to the manuscript, paralleling the insertion of nucleotides to the genetic code ("additions"). Words can be substituted for a different word, paralleling "point mutations" in which one nucleotide is replaced with another. Moreover, point mutations can be "silent mutations," where the new nucleotide codes for the same amino acid as the replaced nucleotide and so has no effect on the resultant protein, or "missense mutations," where the new nucleotide codes for a different amino acid, resulting in a different protein (or no protein at all). So too word substitutions can either change the meaning of the sentence or fail to change the meaning. Finally, a form of recombination was observed, where a scribe appears to have taken half the prologue from one copy and the other half from a different copy. So Barbrook et al. found that this scribe's version could legitimately be placed at entirely different points in the phylogeny depending on which half was used in the analysis. Other manuscripts show more extreme examples of this, in which a sentence or a whole section from an entirely different work was inserted into a text. This resembles horizontal gene transfer, in which genes cross species boundaries.

Barbrook et al. have therefore shown that phylogenetic methods can be applied not only to spoken languages but also to specific texts. Indeed, phylogenetic methods developed by biologists might be particularly useful for the latter, given that the cultural transmission of written texts is of similarly high fidelity to genetic inheritance and features many of the same kinds of changes, such as insertions, deletions, and substitutions. Barbrook et al.'s use of phylogenetic methods that do not assume a treelike structure may be more appropriate for certain cultural data sets. The resulting phylogenetic tree, while broadly resembling the historical relationships that manuscript scholars have suggested by informally comparing different manuscripts without quantitative tools, revealed novel relationships that have not been previously identified, and in a fraction of the time.

Population Ecology Meets History: The Rise and Fall of Empires

As well as studying the specific histories of individual manuscripts, historians are also interested in the larger-scale changes that are evident during human history, such as the periodic rise and fall of great empires over the course of centuries. Why, for example, did the Roman Empire rise up, occupy at its peak the majority of Europe, North Africa, and the Middle East, and then collapse in the fifth century AD? Historians typically explain such events by producing narratives of specific historical events based on contemporary written accounts. For example, the decline of the Roman Empire has been explained variously as due to the rise of the Sassanid Persian Empire in the east and various Germanic tribes such as the Visigoths in the north, the interaction with whom (including the sacking of Rome by the Visigoths in the early fifth century AD) led to increased military spending and, eventually, economic decline. Another commonly cited event is the assassination of the general Flavius Aetius, who was credited with successfully defending the Roman Empire from attacks from Attila the Hun and others. Thus historical trends (e.g., the fall of the Roman Empire) are explained in terms of a narrative of specific, prior events (e.g., the Visigoth invasion, the assassination of Aetius).[18]

Historical narratives such as these are often absorbing and meticulously researched. However, like the linguists' comparative method and manuscript scholars' stemmata, explanations of cultural change in history are typically limited by their informality and subjectivity. Purely verbal explanations cannot yield specific, quantitative predictions that can then be tested against historical data. And without clear criteria for testing alternative theories, historians often end up endlessly arguing back and forth with no way to determine which theory best explains a particular historical trend.

Recently, ecologist and historian Peter Turchin has argued that history as a field could benefit hugely from the use of dynamical, quantitative models such as those used in a branch of biology known as population ecology.[19] Just as historians seek to explain the growth and decline of empires over time, population ecologists often seek to explain the growth and decline of populations of naturally occurring organisms over time. Before examining how Turchin has applied such models to historical trends, it is useful to see how they are used in ecology.

Dynamical Models in Population Ecology. Ecologists typically explain biological growth and decline in terms of simple mathematical functions. Consider, for example, figure 5.1a, which shows two mathematically derived growth rates in a hypothetical population of individuals over time: exponential and logistic.[20] Exponential growth (the dotted line) is where the population increases over time and the rate of increase itself increases. So the growth rate starts out slow and gets increasingly fast as time goes by. Specifically, the growth rate is proportional to the number of individuals in the population, with the constant of proportionality, r, determining how quickly the rate of increase increases.

Exponential growth might describe the growth rate of any population of reproducing organisms, such as bacteria undergoing cell division, where each individual gives rise to two (or more) offspring. The growth rate increases because more and more individuals are reproducing as time goes by: one bacterium divides into two, those two each divide into two giving four, those four give rise to eight, and so on. After just twenty generations (which does not take very long for bacteria),

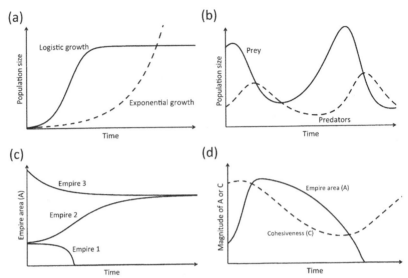

FIGURE 5.1 Population dynamics predicted by mathematical evolutionary models. (*a*) First-order models of biological growth: exponential growth increases population size indefinitely, whereas logistic growth increases population size up to some stable carrying capacity. (*b*) A second-order model of biological growth, where predator and prey population sizes fluctuate in response to each other. (*c*) A first-order model of empire dynamics where empire sizes converge on stable equilibria. (*d*) A second-order model of empire dynamics where empire size fluctuates in response to social cohesiveness. Adapted from Turchin 2003.

there will be 524,288 bacteria; after ten more generations there will be almost 537 million.

Real populations of organisms, however, cannot grow indefinitely in the way described by the exponential growth function. They are limited by the availability of resources and living space, for example. In other words, an exponential function with just a single parameter r is not sufficient to describe the way that actual biological populations change over time. A more realistic growth rate is the logistic function shown in figure 5.1a. Initially the population grows as it did before at an exponential rate according to the growth rate r. This time, however, the population reaches a maximum size and stays at that maximum. This maximum population size is known as the carrying capacity, k.

While the logistic model is more realistic than the exponential model, it is still very simple. More complex dynamics can arise as a result of interactions between more than one population, often of different species. It has long been known that the population size of prey species fluctuates in response to the population size of predator species, and vice versa, with regular cycles or oscillations observed over time. The reasons for this are intuitively obvious: the more predators there are, the more prey they will eat, and so the prey population gets smaller. Then, the fewer prey there are, the less the predators have to eat, and so predator populations get smaller due to starvation. Fewer predators mean less prey eaten, so prey populations get larger, leading to an increase in predator populations, and so on. Figure 5.1b shows how population ecologists have modeled predator-prey dynamics using what are known as the Lotka-Volterra equations. In figure 5.1b, the solid line representing the number of prey can be seen to fluctuate in response to the number of predators, represented with the dotted line, and vice versa. The Lotka-Volterra equations contain four parameters: the growth rate of the prey population in the absence of predators, the reduction in prey population growth as a result of predation, the growth rate of predator populations due to consumption of prey, and the exponential decline in predator numbers in the absence of prey. Just these four parameters, as well as simple assumptions about how they act and interact (e.g., the growth rate of the prey population is assumed to be exponential, for the reasons explained above), can generate the oscillatory population dynamics shown in figure 5.1b, and variations on the Lotka-Volterra model can reasonably accurately characterize the dynamics of many real-life biological populations.

From Ecology to Human History. Turchin has argued that the same kind of quantitative models can be usefully applied to the dynamics observed in human history.[21] In essence, the same kind of tools that ecologists use to understand the growth and decline of bacterial populations can be used by historians to understand the growth and decline of empires. Of course, the details underlying the dynamics of bacterial populations and human societies are undoubtedly very different. Yet this does not mean that evolutionary tools, in this case dynamical models, cannot be applied to cultural phenomena. It simply means that they must be modified to take the differences into account. This echoes the point made at the end of chapter 2 that while cultural evolution and biological evolution are both Darwinian at an abstract level (i.e., they both exhibit variation, competition, and inheritance), the details of each may be very different (e.g., particulate biological inheritance vs. nonparticulate cultural inheritance). And in many cases, these details can be obtained from existing research in the social sciences that has not necessarily been carried out within a cultural evolutionary framework.

So Turchin has fused existing, informal theories from history, sociology, and social psychology concerning individual-level social interactions with formal, quantitative models from population ecology. First, Turchin identified the research question that he wants to answer: how can we explain the gradual rise and fall of empires in Europe during the period from 0 to AD 1900? Written records from this period show fairly lengthy growth and decline rates for most empires. For thirty-one empires, Turchin calculates an average rise of just under a century (defined as the time it took for the empire to increase in size from 20 percent to 80 percent of its maximum area), followed by an approximately century-long peak (defined as the time between the end of the rise and the start of the fall) and another century-long period of decline (defined as the time from 80 percent to 20 percent of its maximum area). So, to restate the question more precisely, how do we explain the gradual (i.e., lasting several human generations) rise and fall of numerous successive empires in Europe during the period 0– AD 1900?

As a starting point, Turchin examined existing historical explanations for the rise and fall of empires. One that he focuses on in particular is Randall Collins's geopolitical theory.[22] Collins proposed that increases and decreases in an empire's area (A) can be explained by three factors and their interaction. First, empires get larger as a result of war success (W) because they conquer more territories. Second, larger empires have access to more resources (R), which in turn increase the empire's war success (W) and consequently its area (A). Third, larger empires also generate more logistical loads (L) in terms of army running costs, policing of citizens, transporting resources across the empire, and so on. Higher logistical loads (L) are assumed to reduce war success (W), because, for example, there is less money for weapons, and hungry armies do not fight as well as well-fed armies. This idea of "imperial overstretch"—where empires suffer increased running costs as they increase in size—is typical of many existing historical theories for empire decline.

Turchin translated all of these variables and their relationships into a quantitative mathematical model, allowing a formal test of Collins's theory. For example, the above assumptions specify that A is directly proportional to W (as war success increases, empire area increases), as determined by a parameter that translates war success into area. For ease of exposition I will not go into the mathematical details here, but figure 5.1c shows the growth/decline of three empires according to Turchin's model of Collins's geopolitical theory.[23] For each of these three empires the equations and parameters are identical; the only difference is the initial starting point. This starting point makes a big difference. Empire 1 starts at a small initial size, and as a result has too few resources (R) to expand. Consequently, empire 1 soon collapses (i.e., A falls to 0). Empire 2, on the other hand, starts off slightly larger, above the threshold at which resources act to increase war success and consequently increase empire area further. We can see, however, that empire 2 does not expand indefinitely. It eventually reaches a stable equilibrium size where the costs imposed by logistic loads exactly balance the benefits from increased war success (via resources). Empire 3 reaches the same equilibrium, but from a starting area above the equilibrium.

These kind of dynamics, however, do not resemble the gradual rise and fall of empires that historians have documented. In the geopolitical model, empires either collapse and disappear (like empire 1) or converge on a stable equilibrium area (like empires 2 and 3). They do not cycle or oscillate. Indeed, Turchin argued that the kind of model proposed by Collins is incapable of creating oscillatory dynamics of the kind exhibited by human societies. Collins's model is what is known as a first-order model: it contains a single unknown variable, A, called a "state" variable, and this state variable changes in response to other variables, in this case W, R, and L. First-order models include the exponential and logistic models already encountered in figure 5.1a. The logistic model, for example, tracks changes in the state variable "population size" in response to the growth rate r and carrying capacity k. Like Collins's model in figure 5.1c, these do not oscillate, they increase indefinitely or converge on a stable equilibrium.

Instead, Turchin argues that we need to describe historical dynamics in terms of a second-order model. Second-order models contain two state variables. The predator-prey model shown in figure 5.1b is an example of a second-order model, in that it tracks both the number of predators and the number of prey. One cannot predict the number of prey without knowing the number of predators, and vice versa. And as shown in figure 5.1b, second-order models *can* result in cyclic rises and falls over time, such as the illustrated predator-prey cycles, suggesting that they are more appropriate for the cyclic historical dynamics of empires.

To recap, then, Turchin has translated a nonquantitative theory of the rise and fall of empires (Collins's geopolitical theory) into a quantitative mathematical model of the kind used by population ecologists, used this model to show that Collins's theory cannot, in fact, generate the kind of population cycles characteristic of historical empires, and used insights from population ecology to point to what a better theory might look like, specifically, one that contains two state variables rather than just one.

The Missing Variable: Social Cohesiveness. What might this other state variable be? Turchin suggests that another factor that might affect the rise and fall of empires is the social cohesiveness of that empire. The cohesiveness of a social group, he argues, can be measured in terms of the degree to which people identify themselves as members of that group and consequently the degree to which they are willing to defend their group against other groups. Drawing on an earlier, informal theory of historical dynamics proposed in the fourteenth century by Arab scholar Ibn Khaldun, often considered to be one of the forefathers of modern sociology, Turchin proposed the following theory.[24] First, in small-scale societies, cohesiveness increases because collective action is often the key to survival, such as in the case of communal defense against a common enemy or the building of a communal well or bridge. Once cohesiveness has reached a critical point, the society is functioning so well that it begins to expand and successfully invade neighboring societies that are smaller and/or have lower cohesiveness. This is now an empire. However, when the empire grows too large, cohesiveness begins to decline as collective action is no longer necessary for survival. Instead, competition begins to occur within the empire between different elite factions. Eventually, cohesiveness is so low that the empire breaks up or is invaded by new, highly cohesive groups that have emerged in the frontier regions of the empire, where cohesiveness is lowest. This theory is a specific version of a general theory of *cultural group selection*, proposed by Boyd and Richerson among others, in which cohesive, cooperative groups outcompete less cohesive, less cooperative groups.[25]

Social cohesiveness might seem to be a vague, intangible concept. However, much evidence exists in social psychology and, more recently, experimental economics to suggest that ingroup identity and ingroup cooperation can be measured and has real-world consequences. Numerous experiments in social psychology demonstrate that people readily identify with, and preferentially cooperate within, their ingroup, even when that ingroup is arbitrarily defined.[26] These results are reinforced by experimental economists' findings that people in every society ever studied show some sense of fairness in tasks such as the ultimatum game, donating more money to a partner than they should do if they were behaving entirely selfishly, as we saw in chapter 1. We also saw in chapter 1 how different groups vary in their civic duty, such as the degree to which they give to charity or vote. So not only can cohesiveness be measured, but there is also evidence that it can vary across social groups.

Turchin proposed that social cohesiveness is a second state variable that might explain why empires gradually rise and fall over several centuries. Unlike logistical loads, which impact empire size relatively quickly on the order of weeks and months, he argued that cohesiveness takes several centuries to increase and decrease. To test this hypothesis, Turchin constructed a second-order model containing functions for both empire area (A) and cohesiveness (C). As before, A was defined in terms of war success, resources, and logistical loads. This time, however, war success and resources were dependent not only on A but also on cohesiveness (C): greater cohesiveness increases both war success and resources, as people are more willing to work together to defend the empire, conquer other territories, and exploit collective resources. A second function determined the value of C, which is assumed to be highest at frontier regions and lowest in the center of the empire. Small empires will be surrounded on all sides by other empires and be mostly made up of frontier regions, and so have high cohesiveness. Larger empires will have a larger internal nonfrontier area and so have lower cohesiveness. The resulting dynamics are shown in figure 5.1d for a single empire, showing both its area (A) and cohesiveness (C). The change in empire area shown in figure 5.1d resembles the actual rise and fall of empires much better than the geopolitical theory shown in figure 5.1c. We can see how the initially small empire increases in size due to its high cohesiveness, followed by a gradual decline in area as cohesiveness also drops. By the time cohesiveness starts to rise again (due to the small size of the shrinking empire) it is too late, because a positive feedback cycle has kicked in whereby small area reduces resources, which reduces area even faster. This overwhelms any positive effect of increased C. Turchin also constructed a more elaborate spatially explicit model in which multiple empires compete over land in a two-dimensional spatial grid, and which recreated the gradual rise and fall of several different empires over time.[27]

Turchin's study demonstrates how evolutionary models adapted from population ecology can be valuable tools in understanding historical dynamics. Translating informal, verbal theories into quantitative mathematical models reveals inadequacies that are not apparent otherwise and points to potentially more valid theories. These models can then be tested empirically with further historical data. For example, a novel prediction to come from Turchin's cohesiveness theory is that empires should originate predominantly from frontier regions where cohesiveness is highest. Sure enough, Turchin found that of fifty geographical regions in Europe analyzed during the period 0–AD 1900, the majority of regions were either frontier regions and gave rise to an empire (eleven regions) or were not frontier regions and did not give rise to an empire (thirty-four regions).[28] Just one nonfrontier region gave rise to an empire, and just four frontier regions failed to produce an empire. This association between frontier status and empire emergence was highly statistically significant.

Objections to Cultural Evolutionary Analyses of History

It is important to recognize that the research described in this chapter and the previous one is in the most part entirely compatible with traditional, nonevolutionary research in the social sciences and humanities. Indeed, in many cases social scientists have come up with informal methods, such as the linguists' comparative method or the manuscript scholars' stemmata, that are implicitly based on the same logic and assumptions as those that evolutionary biologists work with. And many of the findings obtained using evolutionary methods match well with what traditional scholars have already found, such as the broad topology of the Indo-European language family, the link between patriliny and cattle, or the likely identity of the oldest *Canterbury Tales* manuscript.

However, the real value of biologically derived phylogenetic methods and dynamical models lies in their rigor. Whereas linguists and manuscript scholars build their historical trees based on intuition, biologists and cultural phylogeneticists use quantitative statistical methods such as maximum likelihood or Bayesian inference to generate trees using explicit and exact criteria and with a known degree of statistical certainty. While cultural anthropologists draw comparisons across societies in order to explain systematic patterns of cultural variation (at least until social constructionism made cross-cultural comparisons unpopular), these comparisons are vulnerable to Galton's problem unless phylogenetic methods are used to distinguish between similarities due to descent and similarities due to independent convergence. And while historians propose informal theories to explain historical trends, such as Collins's geopolitical theory of empire decline, such theories can only be adequately tested using quantitative, population-based evolutionary models, which showed this particular theory to be incapable of explaining actual historical dynamics.

Despite the value of evolutionary methods, and the potential complementarity with existing social science research, I suspect that the majority of archaeologists, anthropologists, linguists, and historians will remain skeptical of such methods. Two common objections are that culture is too complex to be analyzed using simple evolutionary models, and that specific cultural phenomena (e.g., languages, empires) cannot be meaningfully compared with one another.

Objection 1: Culture Is Too Complex for Simple Evolutionary Models. Many social scientists often argue that cultural change is too complex to be reduced to the simple mathematical models described above, such as neutral drift or population dynamical models. Here is a typical response to cultural evolutionary models from a historian, Joseph Fracchia, writing with biologist Richard Lewontin:

> Cultural evolutionary theories are carefully constructed, logically consistent, and very neat . . . But this formulaic treatment is fully inappropriate to the labyrinthine pathways, the contingent complexity, the many nuances, and general messiness of history.[29]

This is a misunderstanding of the rationale behind using simple models. It is not being argued that human culture really can be described entirely in terms of just a handful of simple variables and processes. Rather, the reduction involved is methodological: faced with an enormously complex phenomenon such as culture, the most productive approach to understanding that phenomenon is to divide it up into small pieces and try to explain them in a piecemeal style, much like a jigsaw puzzle solver might assemble only small sections of a much larger and elaborate puzzle at a time. Only simple models can yield quantitative, testable predictions (e.g., "within-site diversity is inversely correlated with between-site diversity" or "the length of each branch on a phylogenetic language tree is independent of the number of splitting events along that branch") that can be shown to be either statistically supported or not; and if not, we simply build and test an alternative model. This approach of using simple, quantitative models has been hugely successful in biology as a means of explaining biological evolution, which is arguably just as complex as cultural evolution. And what is the alternative to simple models? We could continue to argue over verbal theories based on subjective assumptions, which might end up at the correct explanation, but might not (and even if they did, it would take a lot longer than quantitative models). Or we could admit that human culture is too complex to ever understand fully, which is a rather pessimistic and intellectually sterile sentiment.

Objection 2: Cultural Phenomena Are Unique and Particular. A second common objection from social scientists is that artifacts, languages, societies, manuscripts, and empires cannot be meaningfully compared with one another in the manner described above. This is typically argued by cultural anthropologists, who have generally abandoned attempts to compare different societies in favor of attempting to explain each society in its own terms, and historians, who, as noted previously, typically explain historical phenomena in terms of specific antecedent events (e.g., the assassination of Aetius, which precipitated the fall of the Roman Empire) rather than general processes (although there are exceptions, such as Collins's geopolitical theory). For example, Fracchia and Lewontin complain that

> [w]hether they forcibly subsume disparate historical phenomena under a transhistorical explanatory principle or write off as mere contingencies historically significant events that cannot be so subsumed, cultural evolutionary theories cannot answer the many crucial questions pertaining to the particularity, the uniqueness, of all historical phenomena.[30]

Again, this is a confusion of the rationale behind generalizing across more than one society or more than one historical period. The aim is not to *replace* the study of specific historical events or societies with general microevolutionary processes. On the contrary, without details of specific societies or time periods, there is no data with which to test the validity of the general evolutionary processes. Nor is it to deny that there are important differences between societies and time periods. Of course there are. But there are also similarities, and identifying these similarities, and explaining them with simple principles (such as Turchin's cohesiveness factor) surely *adds* to the study of specific cases rather than detracts from them.

In fact, the systematic comparison of different individuals, populations, species, and genera is an indispensible tool of the modern biologist, and a powerful means of testing causal hypotheses. The simple reason is that a single species is just a single data point, and a single data point is of little use when testing causal hypotheses. We saw this in the case of Goodwin et al.'s cross-species phylogenetic analysis of cichlids, where they showed that female-only mouth brooding evolved from biparental nest guarding for functional reasons (rather than being an accident of history). Holden and Mace showed that the same phylogenetic methods can be used to test functional explanations of cross-cultural patterns, such as the association between patrilineal inheritance and the adoption of cattle. They would not have been able to do this without comparing different societies, given that a single society, like a single species, is just a single data point.

This reluctance to compare across societies in the social sciences is partly an understandable reaction against the racist nineteenth-century theories of Spencerian cultural "evolution" espoused by Tylor, Morgan, and others, as discussed in chapter 2. The comparisons that these early anthropologists made were typically unfavorable to non-Western societies, describing them as inferior ancestral versions of Western societies. To reiterate, this is emphatically not implied by the cultural evolutionary theory that is presented in this book, nor any of the research discussed herein. Darwinian evolution does not place societies along a ladder of increasing complexity, and moral judgments simply do not follow from modern evolutionary theory, biological or cultural. So while cultural anthropologists are right to be wary of cross-cultural comparisons derived from outmoded and politically motivated Spencerian evolutionary theories, in rejecting any kind of cross-cultural comparisons they are throwing out the baby with the bathwater, and missing out on a valuable method for testing hypotheses concerning cultural phenomena.

Conclusions: Linking Micro- and Macro-

The research described in this and the previous chapter shows how cultural evolution researchers are using various methods borrowed from evolutionary biology—phylogenetic methods, drift models, dynamical models from population ecology—to reconstruct past patterns and trends in cultural macroevolution, from regional diversity in Paleolithic handaxes to the rise and fall of the Roman Empire. More importantly, in several cases studies have gone beyond the mere description of macroevolutionary patterns and toward explanations of these patterns in terms of the specific microevolutionary processes that we encountered in chapter 3. So, for example, debates over the treeness of cultural macroevolution are informed by an understanding of the microevolutionary transmission pathways that might generate tree-like patterns, such as whether transmission is vertical or horizontal, or the role of cultural migration across groups. Drift models link the microevolutionary process of random copying of functionally neutral traits to population-level macroevolutionary patterns, such as inversely correlated between- and within-group artifact diversity. Conformity (a form of frequency-dependent cultural selection) may explain the preservation of frequently used words throughout history. In the following two chapters we will see how experimental methods from psychology and ethnographic methods from cultural anthropology are being used to make further links between cultural microevolution and cultural macroevolution.

6

Evolutionary Experiments: Cultural Evolution in the Lab

For a long time, the study of cultural evolution remained a highly theoretical exercise involving the construction of mathematical models such as those discussed in chapter 3. In recent years, however, a growing number of cultural evolution researchers have begun to use experiments to test the assumptions and predictions of those cultural evolution models under controlled conditions in the laboratory. Although psychologists are typically responsible for conducting laboratory experiments in the social and behavioral sciences, the interdisciplinary nature of cultural evolution is encouraging linguists, economists, archaeologists, and historians to get in on the act as well. Before examining some of these studies in detail, it is useful to highlight the benefits of experiments in the study of evolution. Because these benefits apply not only to cultural but also biological evolution, let's start with an examination of how experiments have helped to uncover the causes of biological evolution.

Simulating Biological Evolution in the Lab

For over a decade, evolutionary biologist Richard Lenski has been watching the bacteria *E. coli* evolve in his lab at Michigan State University. From a single genetically identical colony founded in February 1998, Lenski and his team have slowly bred over 45,000 generations of the bacteria.[1] This has allowed Lenski and his colleagues to study an assortment of the fundamental processes of biological evolution, such as adaptation, mutation, selection, and extinction, with a level of detail and control that is impossible to achieve under natural conditions in the field. Bacteria such as *E. coli* are ideally suited to such experiments: they are small and don't take up too much space, they reproduce quickly (imagine the time it would take to breed 45,000 generations of elephants), they require only a simple environment (a petri dish and some nutrients), and they reproduce asexually so that genetically identical clones can be easily bred.

They can also be frozen. Every five hundred generations a sample of the colony is frozen at –80°C and kept in "suspended animation." This allows Lenski and colleagues to directly measure the relative fitness of a particular generation of the colony compared to the original founder colony. This is done by mixing the current generation with an equal number of thawed-out founder colony members and comparing the number of each type a day later (they are identified using a selectively neutral genetic marker that makes each strain a different color). If the recent generation has increased in fitness due to the accumulation of beneficial mutations, then it should outcompete and outreproduce the original ancestral colony, and the extent of this outreproduction can be precisely measured.

Such precise measurements of fitness are extremely difficult to obtain for naturally occurring populations in the wild at a single point in time, let alone repeated measurements in the same population at regular time periods through history. The laboratory experiments therefore generate unprecedentedly accurate data on evolutionary-driven fitness changes over time. Lenski's studies have revealed that when a genetically identical colony is placed in a novel environment (e.g., from a glucose to a maltose solution), fitness tends to increase rapidly at first, before plateauing to a constant level. In one lineage, for example, the average fitness gain in the first 5,000 generations after an environmental change was ten times greater than the average fitness gain between generations 15,000 and 20,000.

Another key benefit of laboratory experiments is the ability to "re-run" evolutionary history multiple times. Because *E. coli* reproduce asexually, Lenski's team can produce several genetically identical colonies, put them in the same environment and see whether the same evolutionary trends occur in each parallel lineage. This addresses a fundamental issue regarding whether biological evolution is deterministic or whether it is subject to the chance contingencies of history. Barring the invention of a time machine, biologists cannot re-run actual evolution on earth; experiments are the only way to address such questions. Lenski's experiments suggest that evolutionary trends are to some degree repeated, but with small historical deviations. So twelve replicate populations of E. coli all showed a similar pattern of change in fitness over time, with a rapid initial increase followed by an eventual leveling off. But different lineages converged on slightly different fitness values, with some slightly fitter than others.

A final benefit of experiments is the ability to manipulate variables. One such variable is colony size. Lenski found that the more E. coli there were in the colony, the faster was the increase in fitness. At very small colony sizes, little increase in fitness occurred at all. This suggests that colony size is an important determinant of adaptation. To explain these findings, Lenski invokes the notion of an *adaptive landscape*, a concept first introduced by population geneticist Sewell Wright in the 1930s.[2] Wright imagined evolution as occurring on a three-dimensional landscape with each coordinate in the landscape representing a different combination of genes, and the height of the landscape representing the fitness of that particular combination. Genotypes with high fitness form adaptive *peaks* in the landscape, while genotypes with low fitness form adaptive *valleys*. Mutation and drift move organisms around this landscape randomly, while selection pushes organisms up to regions of higher fitness as beneficial mutations are accumulated. Wright's key point, though, was that such landscapes rarely have a single peak that can be easily reached. Real adaptive landscapes feature many peaks of varying height/fitness, representing alternative solutions to similar adaptive problems. Because biological evolution is short-sighted and lacks foresight or planning, if a population gets stuck on a low fitness peak then it will not be able to traverse the surrounding adaptive valleys to find a higher peak elsewhere in the landscape.

How does this adaptive landscape idea help to explain Lenski's E. coli experimental findings? When placed in a new environment, chances are that the E. coli found themselves in a low fitness adaptive valley. The rapid increase in fitness occurs as selection drives the population uphill to the top of an adaptive peak. Once there, little further increase in fitness occurs, because any changes will move the population off the peak and reduce fitness. And due to the random nature of the initial genetic mutations, different replicate colonies may converge on different adaptive peaks of varying height, therefore explaining the small differences in final fitness. Finally, larger colonies with more individual *E. coli* are more likely to, by chance, discover a high fitness peak, because there are more individuals in which beneficial mutations can occur.

Lenski's studies show how laboratory experiments can be used to explore the microevolutionary mechanisms (e.g., selection, mutation, drift) that underlie macroevolutionary patterns and trends (e.g., adaptation, historical contingency). Experiments offer unique advantages over field studies, such as the high degree of control over the environment, the isolation and manipulation of specific variables (e.g., colony size), and the ability to re-run history multiple times. Such control and manipulation is not possible with field studies for practical and ethical reasons, while paleontologists cannot re-run evolutionary history to see whether trends in the fossil record are subject to chance historical contingency. And experiments have advantages over mathematical models given that they use real organisms which behave in more realistic ways than hypothetical entities in models. Lenski's experiments are just one example of a rich tradition in biology of using laboratory experiments to simulate biological evolution. We have already seen in previous chapters examples of this tradition in the form of Mendel's pea plant experiments, Weismann's mouse-tail-cutting experiments, and Luria and Delbrück's directed mutation experiments, all constituting major contributions to evolutionary biology.

From E. Coli to Culture

In the same way that biologists simulate biological evolution in the lab, so too cultural evolution researchers have begun to simulate cultural evolution in the lab. In a typical cultural evolution experiment, cultural traits (e.g., skills, words, ideas, customs) are passed along chains of participants or within small groups of participants. Any changes that occur in those traits can then be precisely measured over time. Exactly the same benefits exist for cultural evolution experiments as for biological evolution experiments: researchers can conduct experiments under controlled conditions in the lab without distractions or confounding factors, they can accurately record data, they can manipulate variables to test specific hypotheses, and they can re-run history to replicate evolutionary trends.[3] Of course, experimental psychologists have conducted laboratory experiments for decades. However, rarely is this work explicitly conducted within a cultural evolutionary framework. As a result mainstream psychology experiments seldom address such issues as long-term changes over multiple (cultural) generations or whether those changes are adaptive relative to individual (asocial) learning.

Experiments also come with drawbacks, however. What one gains in control and manipulation ("internal validity") one loses in realism ("external validity"). Participants doing simple tasks for an hour or so under artificial conditions may not behave in the same way as they would in real life. And even if they did, some of the topics that interest cultural evolution researchers, such as hunter-gatherer traditions and prehistoric manuscript evolution, involve people who are very different to the typical experimental participant, who is usually North American, English-speaking, university-educated, middle-class, and fairly well-off. Another issue is whether an hour-long experiment can meaningfully capture cultural change that has occurred over hundreds or thousands of years.[4]

The solution to these problems lies in interdisciplinarity, which is a key facet of cultural evolution research. When used on their own, experiments have little value, telling us not much more than how Western undergraduate students behave in psychology labs. When informed by findings from archaeology, anthropology, history, and sociology, however, experiments can be rooted in real-life cultural phenomena. When experimental data match actual historical and geographical patterns and trends, then we can be more confident that the experiments are capturing some aspect of the empirical record. Experiments then allow more rigorous tests of hypotheses than the purely observational or historical methods of archaeologists, historians, anthropologists, and sociologists. Anthropologists cannot randomly assign hunter-gatherers to live in different villages that all vary in some key factor. Archaeologists and historians cannot re-run history multiple times to see whether observed trends are meaningful or simply due to chance. Experimentalists *can* do this. And the results of the experiments can often then be tested back in the real world by other social scientists, which generate new findings that can be probed with further experiments, and so on. Hopefully, this cycle results in increasingly accurate explanations of cultural phenomena.

So with these points in mind, the following sections outline several recent experiments that have simulated various aspects of cultural evolution in the lab, from archaeological artifacts, to gossip, to entire languages.

The Transmission Chain Method. In the episode of *The Simpsons* called "The PTA Disbands," the teachers' union goes on strike in response to Principal Skinner's woefully inadequate school facilities, including newspaper-filled school dinners and textbooks that include William Shatner's TekWar. Bart, trying to foment this dispute in order to keep the school closed, starts a false rumor at one end of a crowded union demonstration that he "heard Skinner say the teachers will crack any minute." By the time the message has passed from person to person through the crowd, it emerges as "Skinner says the teachers will crack any minute purple monkey dishwasher." The leader of the strike, teacher Edna Krabappel, is incensed at what she thinks is Skinner's misplaced confidence, but is especially offended at "that 'purple monkey dishwasher' remark."

This *Simpsons* sketch is a parody of the party game Telephone (also known as Broken Telephone or, in the UK, Chinese Whispers), where a message is passed along a chain of people. Usually, by the time the message gets to the last person in the chain it is typically so distorted that it is amusingly unrecognizable from the original message (an expectation that is confounded for comic effect by the writers of *The Simpsons*). As well as being parodied on *The Simpsons*, a more scientific version of the Telephone game has been used by psychologists for decades to study cultural transmission, in the form of what is known as the *transmission chain method*. In the psychologists' version, some carefully prepared stimulus material, such as a written story, is presented to the first participant in the chain. The stimulus is then removed and the participant writes out the original from memory. The resulting written recall of the first participant is then given to the second participant in the chain to read; it is again withdrawn and the second participant writes this out from memory. Their output is given to the third participant, and so on down the chain. The experimenter then analyses the content of each step (or "cultural generation") in the chain in order to measure systematic distortions and biases in cultural evolution.

The transmission chain method is ideally suited to identifying both *content biases* and *guided variation*. As noted in chapter 3, content biases occur when some kinds of information are more likely to be acquired, remembered, and transmitted than other kinds of information: its content determines its evolutionary success. The transmission chain method can test for the existence of different content biases by passing various kinds of information along chains of participants and measuring what kind of information gets transmitted best. Guided variation, on the other hand, occurs when people modify information that they have acquired before passing it on to someone else. Again, such modifications can be measured using the transmission chain method by tracking novel distortions or modifications that occur along the chain.

The transmission chain method was introduced into experimental psychology as a scientific method in the 1930s by pioneering Cambridge University social psychologist Sir Frederic Bartlett. In his book *Remembering*, Bartlett reported findings from several transmission chain studies that used various stories and pictures.[5] The classic textbook example of Bartlett's work involves a Native American folktale called "The War of the Ghosts." This story tells of a Native American man who accompanies some ghosts to fight people from another village. The man is wounded and dies the following morning. When Bartlett passed this story along chains of British undergraduates, he found that the supernatural elements that were unfamiliar to his participants were lost or distorted. For example, just before the man died, the original story reports that "something black came out of his mouth." This (to British college students, at least) odd detail was either lost altogether or distorted to become consistent with the students' preexisting beliefs, such as that the man's "soul passed out from his mouth."[6]

The findings from Bartlett's studies and several subsequent transmission chain studies simply confirmed the informal findings of countless party games of Telephone: that human cultural transmission is far from accurate, and that information is frequently lost and distorted in systematic ways. Random elements (such as "purple monkey dishwasher") are not added to existing faithfully transmitted messages; instead, messages are transformed according to preexisting expectations and prejudices. Contrast this with genetic inheritance, which has far higher fidelity and is far less susceptible to error and distortion, and where random elements may well be added to the end of existing DNA sequences. The findings of transmission chain studies, then, suggest that content biases and guided variation may play potentially important roles in human cultural evolution.

As cognitive psychology, with its focus on the individual, became the dominant paradigm within experimental psychology during the mid- to late twentieth century, the transmission chain method fell from favor among most psychologists. This is unfortunate. Cultural evolutionary models show that what might be very small selection biases in a single cultural generation can have dramatic effects when repeated over several cultural generations. Such effects can only be observed using the multiple-generation transmission chain method. In recent years several researchers working within a cultural evolutionary framework have revived Bartlett's method, using it to obtain evidence for several content biases and forms of guided variation.

From Golf to Gossip. In late November 2009, the US media went into Tiger Woods frenzy. At first this was over a bizarre driving accident outside his house following an alleged argument with his wife. Then more than a dozen women came forward claiming to have had affairs with Woods over the previous several years, resulting in Woods apologizing to his family for his "transgressions." The stories about Woods's many extramarital affairs made headline news in many newspapers, magazines, and TV news programs around the world. And this didn't just reflect the low-brow mindset of newspaper and TV news editors, it was driven by genuine public interest. According to Google Trends, internet searches for "Tiger Woods" increased twelvefold in November 2009 compared to the previous ten months of 2009.[7]

But why are people apparently so intensely interested in the marital infidelities of a golfer? Surely knowledge of the intimate details of Tiger Woods's personal life is of little or no practical value to the millions of internet searchers who have never met him and are unlikely to ever meet him in the future. And his marital problems surely have no bearing on his golfing performance, at least not until the media frenzy started and he was forced to announce a temporary break from the game. Countless similar stories hit the headlines every week about the marital infidelities and personal troubles of sportspeople, movie stars, and other celebrities, while at the same time stories about things that actually will affect people's lives, such as climate change, receive scant attention. Around the same time as the Tiger Woods story broke, an international summit on climate change was held in Copenhagen, which was widely viewed as the largest multinational effort to address the problem to date. It garnered little interest, only causing a 2.5-fold increase in internet searches for the term "climate change."

But rather than simply dismissing such phenomena as a curious oddity or a marker of the declining values of modern society, perhaps this socially oriented mass media reflects something deeper about human culture. Indeed, this preoccupation with social interactions and social relationships is consistent with what is known as the "social brain" hypothesis proposed by primatologists Nicholas Humphrey, Andrew Whiten, Richard Byrne, and Robin Dunbar.[8] The social brain hypothesis holds that the large brains of primates, including and especially humans, evolved to deal not primarily with ecological problems such as finding food or using tools, but rather to solve social problems.

We are good at the ecological tasks, too, but it seems to be the so-cial problems that have driven brain size. Social interactions give rise to a range of particularly challenging problems, such as coordinating actions with others, successfully communicating intentions, forming coalitions and alliances, keeping track of other individuals' coalitions and alliances, deception, trying not to be deceived by others, and so on, all of which demand quite sophisticated cognitive abilities. And social problems are intrinsically more challenging than nonsocial eco-logical problems because they involve other individuals of the same species who are capable of the same kind of complex social reasoning as you are: it's much easier to be outwitted by another person than by a fruit tree, for example. Evidence for the social brain hypothesis comes from studies that show strong correlations, across primate species, be-tween brain size and various measures of social behavior such as group size, time spent interacting, frequency of deception, and frequency of social play. There is no correlation, on the other hand, between brain size and measures of nonsocial behavior, such as range size, tool use, and diet.[9]

So in terms of the cultural evolution biases introduced in chapter 3, we might predict that there exists a content bias in cultural evolution for acquiring information about social interactions and social relation-ships, given that social brains should be particularly good at processing social information and remembering social facts. We can call this a *social bias* for short. In a study that I conducted with Andrew Whiten and Robin Dunbar, this prediction was tested experimentally using the transmission chain method.[10] To test for a social bias, we passed four stories along several chains of student participants: a "social gos-sip" story about a student having an affair with her professor, a "so-cial nongossip" story about a person in the street asking strangers for directions to a swimming pool, a "nonsocial individual" story about a student who is late for a lecture, and a "nonsocial physical" story about forest fires increasing carbon dioxide levels in the atmosphere, thus contributing to global warming. All four stories were given to the first person in the transmission chain, and then taken away. They then wrote out the stories from memory. What they recalled was given to the second person in the chain, who read it and recalled it in the same way. The second person's recall was given to the third person, and so on down the chain. Essentially the experiment simulates repeated instances of cultural selection in the lab: each person is exposed to a range of stories varying in their "socialness," some of which may be re-called better than others (i.e., selected). Ten separate chains were run in total, and results were averaged across each chain in order to increase the reliability of the findings.

As predicted, the two social stories were transmitted better than the two nonsocial stories by every one of the several chains that we tested. The level of recall was measured by counting the number of "propositions" in each variant of the story. Propositions can be thought of as "units of meaning" that cognitive psychologists have shown are reasonably good at representing the underlying information within a written text. Whereas the four original stories (social gossip, social nongossip, nonsocial individual, and nonsocial physical) each contained 14 propositions, after four cultural generations the two social stories contained approximately 5.5 propositions each (39 percent of the original), whereas the two nonsocial stories contained about 2 propositions (14 percent) each. This appeared to be a content bias rather than guided variation because little distortion of the nonsocial stories was observed.

These results support the existence of a content bias in cultural evolution that favors social information over equivalent nonsocial information. A key word here is "equivalent," however. Not all social information will always be more attractive than all nonsocial information: the information that an out-of-control forest fire is approaching your house will probably be of more interest to you at that particular moment than the information that your neighbor is cheating on her husband. But all other things being equal, we appear to be intrinsically motivated to acquire and pass on social information due to our social brains. This is perhaps why celebrity gossip spreads so easily, yet important factual information (e.g., about climate change) is so hard to transmit.

A Trip to the Minimally Counterintuitive Museum. One of the potential content biases discussed in chapter 3 was a minimally counterintuitive bias. Anthropologists Pascal Boyer and Scott Atran have suggested that concepts that violate a small number of folk intuitions about how the world works are particularly memorable.[11] Ghosts, for example, violate certain intuitive rules of folk physics (e.g., they can pass through walls) but they conform to other intuitive rules of folk psychology (e.g., they seek revenge). Such minimally counterintuitive concepts, it is proposed, are more likely to be remembered than ordinary, intuitive concepts, or even highly unusual concepts that nevertheless still conform to our folk intuitions. Consequently, supernatural beliefs such as ghosts or gods spread easily and are prevalent in every society ever studied.

This theory sounds plausible, but the central assumption that minimally counterintuitive concepts are remembered, and consequently transmitted, better than both ordinary and unusual concepts needs to be tested directly. We might also be interested in whether this is actually a content bias or whether guided variation is at work. If the former, then people should be more likely to recall and transmit minimally counterintuitive concepts without modifying those concepts in any way. The latter, guided variation, would be operating if people modify ordinary or unusual concepts that they acquire from others to make them minimally counterintuitive (but not excessively counterintuitive).

To address such questions, cognitive anthropologists Justin Barrett and Melanie Nyhof conducted a transmission chain experiment in which different concepts were passed along parallel chains of participants.[12] The first participant in each chain read a sci-fi story about an intergalactic ambassador's visit to an alien planet. According to the story, in order to find out about the different things on the planet, the ambassador visits the planet's version of the Smithsonian, where a network of museums and zoos contains exhibits of various beings, animals, and objects. The rest of the story described these beings, animals, and objects. Different versions of the story transmitted along different chains contained different kinds of beings, animals, and objects: they were either minimally counterintuitive (e.g., "a species that will never die of natural causes and cannot be killed"), common (e.g., "a species that will die if it doesn't get enough nourishment or if it is severely damaged") or unusual (e.g., "a species that does not die easily of natural causes and is hard to kill"). The researchers then tracked the relative accuracy with which each type of information was transmitted, as well as whether any parts of the story were systematically distorted.

Barrett and Nyhof's results confirmed the prediction that minimally counterintuitive concepts are more likely to survive during transmission than common and unusual concepts. The original story contained six items from each category. After it passed through three cultural generations, the story contained on average 2.72 minimally counterintuitive items, 1.29 unusual items, and just 0.89 common items: a clear advantage for minimally counterintuitive concepts. Of more interest, this advantage for minimally counterintuitive concepts appears to be driven by guided variation rather than content bias. The numbers above included any minimally counterintuitive, unusual, or common items whether they were in the original or not. Restricting the analysis to just the proportion of the original six items of each category, Barrett and Nyhof found that almost as many unusual items survived (1.89) as did minimally counterintuitive items (2.11), a difference that was not statistically significant (although both were significantly greater than the 0.89 common items recalled). The reason that there were more minimally counterintuitive items in the final generation was because unusual items were frequently transformed into minimally counterintuitive items (while the reverse, minimally counterintuitive into unusual, seldom occurred, and common items were simply lost). This transformation resembles guided variation acting instead of, or in addition to, content biases that favor already existing minimally counterintuitive information.

As noted in chapter 3, guided variation can be a powerful driver of cultural evolution, often more powerful than cultural selection, of which content biases are an example. Barrett and Nyhof's finding that minimally counterintuitive concepts are favored not only by content biases but also by guided variation might therefore explain the seemingly widespread prevalence of supernatural and religious concepts around the world, as documented by generations of ethnographers.

Evolving Alien Languages in the Lab. Linguists are also beginning to use experiments to simulate language evolution in the lab. A recent transmission chain study conducted by Simon Kirby, Hannah Cornish, and Kenny Smith, all linguists at the University of Edinburgh, showed that an entirely new language with several key features of real languages can be evolved from scratch in the lab.[13] Like Barrett and Nyhof, Kirby et al. asked their participants to imagine that they were an intergalactic traveler. Rather than identifying alien life forms and objects, this time the participants were tasked with learning an alien language. During an initial learning phase the participants were exposed to a series of objects along with the alien's names for those objects. Objects varied in their color (black, blue, or red), shape (triangle, circle, or square) and motion (horizontal, bouncing, or spiraling), and labels were nonsense words such as "kihemiwi." For the first participant in the chain, each combination of color, shape, and motion was given a unique label: kihemiwi, for example, described a bouncing red square. Once the participants had seen several label-object pairings, the aliens made them take an alien language test: they were shown objects without any labels and had to remember what the alien label for that object was. The resulting object-label pairs (whether they correctly matched the original input or not) then served as the training pairs for the next participant in the chain. The second participants' object-word pairs were then given to the third participant to learn the alien language, and so on down the chain. Four separate chains were run, and results averaged across the chains. Crucially, none of the participants knew that they were a part of a chain, they were simply told to label the objects as accurately as possible. Any changes in the language, therefore, could not be attributed to participants intentionally shaping their labels to make them easy to understand by the next participant.

Kirby et al. found that after ten cultural generations the error rate in naming dropped significantly. For example, whereas the first generation correctly named only about 25 percent of the original labels, the tenth generation correctly reproduced almost all of the pairings made by the previous (ninth) generation. Effectively, the language gradually adapted to become more effective in communicating the labels for the objects. How did this dramatic adaptation occur? Kirby et al. explained it in terms of what linguists call *underspecification of meaning.* Whereas the first generation had a unique label for each one of the 27 combinations of color, shape and motion, in later generations a single label came to represent several different combinations. For example, by the eighth generation of one chain, all horizontally moving objects were labeled "tuge," all spiraling objects were labeled "poi," and bouncing objects were labeled either "tupim" (for bouncing squares), "miniku" (for bouncing circles), or "tupin" (for bouncing triangles). So what were originally 27 labels became just 5, making the language much easier to remember and hence reproduce along the chain.

While this was an interesting finding, Kirby et al. recognized that a key aspect of real human languages was missing: its *expressivity,* or its ability to distinguish between different objects. In the example above, for instance, it is impossible to distinguish between differently shaped or colored objects that moved horizontally, because all horizontally moving objects were called "tuge." So in a second experiment Kirby et al. filtered the set of object-label pairs that each participant was trained on: if any label referred to more than one object, then all but one of those meanings was removed. Although this is an artificial intervention, it captures the real-life constraint that requires labels to refer to specific objects, that is, for language to be maximally expressive.

The result of this intervention was to reduce the transmission errors as before, but without a drop in the number of unique labels. Instead, structure emerged *within* each label, with each part of the label describing a different characteristic of the object. This is shown in table 6.1. The labels, which were originally not divided up by the participants, have been hyphenated in table 6.1 into three parts. Each of these parts

Table 6.1 Alien words referring to each object in the experiment conducted by Kirby, Cornish, and Smith (2008) as recorded after ten cultural generations

Motion	Color			Shape
	Black	Blue	Red	
Horizontal	n–ere–ki	l–ere–ki	renana	Square
	n–ehe–ki	l–aho–ki	r–ene–ki	Circle
	n–eke–ki	l–ake–ki	r–ahe–ki	Triangle
Bouncing	n–ere–plo	l–ane–plo	r–e–plo	Square
	n–eho–plo	l–aho–plo	r–eho–plo	Circle
	n–eki–plo	l–aki–plo	r–aho–plo	Triangle
Spiraling	n–e–pilu	l–ane–pilu	r–e–pilu	Square
	n–eho–pilu	l–aho–pilu	r–eho–pilu	Circle
	n–eki–pilu	l–aki–pilu	r–aho–pilu	Triangle

refers to a different object attribute. The initial letter "n," for example, has become a marker indicating the color black, with "l" indicating blue and "r" indicating red. The final few letters indicate motion ("ki" = horizontal, "plo" = bouncing, "pilu" = spiraling), with the middle part of the label indicating shape with less regularity. A single irregular label "renana" indicates a horizontally moving red square. Other than this irregularity, however, we can see the emergence during transmission of morphemes, or units of meaning, which are observed in natural languages. This constitutes a key defining property of natural language, *compositionality*, where larger units of meaning are made up of smaller constituent parts that, in combination, determine the meaning of the whole unit.

What Kirby et al. did in this experiment was to show that languages can evolve over time to become easier to learn and easier to transmit. Just like natural languages, their artificial language was fully communicative in that it allowed the accurate transmission of information from one individual to another. It did this by becoming increasingly easy to learn: essentially, the language adapted to fit the cognitive abilities of its users. And this occurred in a way similar to how natural languages form: by becoming structured into underspecified units of meaning that referred to categories (e.g., "red") that generalized across objects rather than referring to specific objects. In natural languages, nouns (other than proper names) similarly refer to a general class of objects rather than a single object. "Dog," for example, refers to all dogs, not just Fido. The same applies to regular grammatical elements. The suffix "-ed," for example, indicates past tense for all regular English verbs, not just one.

This finding potentially challenges traditional nativist views of language structure. Nativist theories, often associated with the linguist Noam Chomsky, tend to assume that language is the result of a genetically specified ("innate") language-specific mental faculty that pre-encodes the structure of language. Language is therefore easy to learn because we all share the same hardwired universal language faculty. Kirby et al., on the other hand, have shown that language does not have to be fixed: it evolves as it is transmitted from individual to individual. So rather than requiring an innate and universal language faculty to explain the fact that all known languages share common features (e.g., compositionality), Kirby et al.'s results suggest that such features might instead be the product of cultural evolution as languages adapt to more general, nonlanguage-specific cognitive processes.[14] This emergence of structure occurred with no overall design or intentionality on the part of the participants, who were unaware that they were part of a transmission chain, and so could not have been intentionally shaping their output to make them maximally understandable. While this does not prove that intentionality never plays any meaningful role in cultural evolution, it suggests that it is not always necessary, at least for language evolution.

The Endless Battle of the Sexes. Economists have also begun to use the transmission chain method to simulate the long-term, multiple-generation consequences of economic decisions. Traditional theoretical models in economics often assume that individuals are rational actors. These rational actors independently calculate the costs and benefits of different behaviors and then reasonably accurately choose the behavior that maximizes their monetary payoff or welfare. An increasing number of behavioral economists, however, are challenging this view of economic actors as rational and asocial.[15] In particular, it is increasingly being recognized that people often do things not because they have calculated that the payoff of a particular choice is optimal, but simply because other people are doing it. In other words, people (or collections of people in organizations) follow cultural traditions.

Economists Andrew Schotter and Barry Sopher have recently adapted the transmission chain method to study culturally transmitted behavioral traditions in the lab.[16] Like other experimental research in economics, they used a highly simplified game played between two participants that is intended to capture a basic aspect of economic decisions. The game that they used is commonly known as the Battle of the Sexes game, so named because of its original framing as a dilemma between a husband and a wife as to where to go one evening: either to a baseball game or to the opera. Because economists like to put numbers on everything, it is assumed that each party's satisfaction can be represented on a scale from 0 to 100 percent. Both the husband and the wife prefer to be together rather than apart, so if they both go to different events then both have a satisfaction of 0 percent. However, they disagree on where to go: the husband prefers to go to the baseball game, while the wife prefers to go to the opera (the game was formulated in the 1950s, so please excuse the gender stereotypes). If they both go to the baseball game, the husband's satisfaction is 100 percent and the wife's is 50 percent. If they both go to the opera, then the wife's satisfaction is 100 percent and the husband's is 50 percent. This situation creates a dilemma: either the husband is happier or the wife is happier; they can never be equally satisfied. In modeling terms there are two pure equilibria: one where both parties go to the baseball game, and another where both go to the opera. So even though the game favors coordination (i.e., both parties doing the same thing), there is no solution to the game where both parties are optimally and equally rewarded. This kind of "unfair coordination game" captures a situation that many organizations probably find themselves in frequently: being forced to cooperate with another firm (e.g., suppliers of materials or components, or distributors of products) where there is some inequity in that relationship.

Schotter and Sopher were interested in whether traditions emerge in the Battle of the Sexes game, and in particular, what kind of cultural transmission processes might be responsible for traditions. Whereas usually the game is played a single time between two players, Schotter and Sopher introduced a cultural dimension by having multiple generations of pairs of participants play the game. Each pair played the game only once, but they could both receive information from previous generations. This information came in two forms: *history* and *advice*. The former comprised the past choices (option 1 or option 2) made by every previous generation of players. Advice, on the other hand, came from the previous generation only, and consisted of a personal recommendation to choose one of the two options and a written message explaining why they should choose that option. Eighty-one generations (i.e., 81 pairs of players) were run in total.

Schotter and Sopher observed distinct traditions emerge over the course of the experiment. Long periods could be seen where both players chose the same option, interspersed with short periods of chaos marked by a lack of coordination. Interestingly, this pattern of stasis and change resembles the punctuated equilibria documented in biological evolution via the fossil record and also, as we saw in chapter 5, language evolution. But generally, what this result shows is that, despite there being no theoretical equilibrium that both players should converge on, people do in fact tend to coordinate their actions in the Battle of the Sexes game.

To get some idea of the microevolutionary processes that were responsible for these stable cultural traditions, Schotter and Sopher took advantage of the fact that experiments allow researchers to manipulate variables and run alternative experimental conditions. As well as the baseline condition mentioned above that allowed players to see both history and advice during the entire 81 generations, they also ran two additional conditions. The "no-history" condition started off with both history and advice, but after 52 generations access to the choice history was removed. The "no-advice" condition also started off with both history and advice, but after 52 generations the option to provide advice was removed. By systematically removing either history or advice and comparing the resulting coordination (or lack of coordination) to the history-plus-advice baseline, Schotter and Sopher could measure the role of each in generating cultural traditions.

Removing access to history had little effect on the appearance of traditions. In the baseline condition, 58 percent of generations showed coordination (i.e., both players chose the same option). Removing history reduced this only slightly to 49 percent. Removing advice, however, reduced the frequency of coordination to just 29 percent. So direct, personal advice received from a single previous player seemed to be far more important in maintaining cultural traditions than passively viewing the history of all previous players' choices. This flies in the face of traditional economic theory, which would assume instead that the past history of all previous players' behavior should be far more useful in estimating the optimal choice than advice from a single previous participant. The former is an unbiased behavioral record of a large sample of individuals; the latter is a subjective message based on barely any more information than is available to the participant receiving the advice. The two take-home messages here, then, are that culture, in the form of advice from other people, can significantly alter people's behavior and significantly impact upon economic systems, and that cultural evolution experiments are vital in revealing these effects, which are not predicted by traditional (noncultural) economic theories.

Rewriting Manuscript Evolution. In the previous chapter we saw how cultural evolution researchers are using phylogenetic methods to reconstruct the evolutionary history of manuscripts such as *The Canterbury Tales.* The fact that these manuscript phylogenies closely resemble the stemmata constructed informally by manuscript scholars increases our confidence that phylogenetic methods can accurately capture real historical relationships. Yet there is still some degree of uncertainty: without the ability to go back and directly observe each medieval scribe copying each version of the manuscript, we cannot be 100 percent sure that phylogenetic methods really work. Obviously this time travel is impossible, but an alternative way of testing the validity of phylogenetic methods as applied to culturally transmitted texts is to use experiments. The basic idea is this: first, a manuscript is copied from person to person in the lab, and the actual historical relationships are recorded. Then, phylogenetic methods are applied to the resulting manuscripts. This phylogenetic reconstruction can then be compared to the known history. If it fits, then researchers can be confident that phylogenetic methods can accurately reconstruct manuscript evolution. And if the fit is not perfect, they can try to see exactly why it is not perfect and potentially improve the methods to take this into account.

This approach was taken by Matthew Spencer, Elizabeth Davidson, Adrian Barbrook, and Christopher Howe of the University of Cambridge.[17] The text used was a medieval German poem that was similar to those manuscripts actually studied by historians. This text was passed through a group of participant "scribes," each of whom copied out the previous version of the manuscript as accurately as they could. Note that unlike the transmission chain studies discussed above, the scribes in this study could see the previous generation's text while they were writing out their own. It is thus not so much a test of memory as a test of the ability to copy out a text verbatim, which is what the original medieval scribes would have been doing. And rather than a linear chain of scribes, Spencer et al. tried to recreate the somewhat haphazard historical relationships thought to characterize real manuscript evolution. So some manuscripts were copied by more than one scribe, giving two or more diverging branches. This is shown in figure 6.1a.

Just like real scribes, Spencer et al.'s participant scribes made systematic errors while they were copying: they substituted one word for

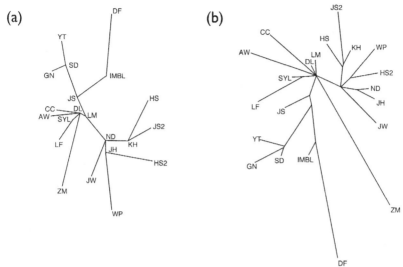

FIGURE 6.1 Two trees showing (*a*) actual historical relationships between manuscripts transmitted experimentally in the lab by Spencer et al. (2004), where historical relationships are known with 100 percent accuracy, and (*b*) historical relationships as reconstructed by Spencer et al. from the manuscripts only, using phylogenetic (neighbor-joining) methods. The length of the lines connecting the manuscripts are proportional to the amount of change that occurred, either actual amounts in (*a*) or estimated amounts in (*b*).

a similar word (e.g., "horse" instead of "hare"), they changed word divisions (e.g., "out-landish" instead of "outlandish") and they inserted or deleted small words (e.g., "of" and "a"). This is crucial, because phylogenetic methods depend on differences between manuscripts to estimate historical relationships, and these differences arise as a result of the accumulation of copying errors. Spencer et al. then applied various phylogenetic methods to the resulting experimental manuscripts, including maximum parsimony, which was discussed in chapter 4, and an alternative method called neighbor joining, which produces starlike networks in which multiple lineages can branch out from a single ancestor in different directions, and the length of the branch indicates the amount of evolutionary change that has occurred along that branch.

The phylogenetic methods reproduced the actual historical relationships between the manuscripts with a very high degree of accuracy, as shown in figure 6.1b (the tree shown was constructed using neighbor joining, although Spencer et al. report little difference between this method and maximum parsimony). Generally, those manuscripts that were copied from the same common ancestor are placed together on the same branches. However, the deviations also tell us something important. The mismatches between the real tree and the reconstructed tree tend to occur where manuscripts are placed at the tips of branches rather than where they actually belonged at a node between two or more branches. Take the original manuscript, for example, labeled in figure 6.1 as LM. Whereas this can be found in the center of the true tree, with all other manuscripts branching out from it, the reconstructed tree places LM near the center but branching off from an unknown common ancestor. This occurs several times: IMBL, JS, ND, and SYL are all correctly placed but are external tips rather than internal nodes. This systematic mismatch reflects the fact that phylogenetic methods were designed by biologists with biological evolution in mind: typically the data that biologists put into phylogenetic programs are all extant species, so they are by definition found at the tips of the trees. Manuscripts, on the other hand, are more like "living fossils": the manuscript that a fifteenth-century scribe copied might still exist today, so we have both steps in the evolutionary lineage, both ancestor and descendant. By taking this difference between biological and cultural data sets into account, future phylogenetic reconstructions of real manuscripts might be made more accurate. Generally, however, Spencer et al.'s experiment shows that phylogenetic methods can effectively reconstruct historical relationships between culturally transmitted manuscripts.

Virtual Arrowheads. Not all cultural evolution experiments have used the transmission chain design. Indeed, for many of the processes of cultural microevolution discussed in chapter 3, the transmission chain is unsuitable. Take model-based biases such as prestige bias, for example, in which people preferentially copy prestigious demonstrators. Such a preference cannot be tested using the transmission chain method because, by design, participants can only acquire information from one other participant, the previous person in the chain, rather than from a range of potential demonstrators who vary in prestige. An alternative method involves having a small group of participants repeatedly engage in some task, with the experimenter tracking cultural transmission within that group over successive generations. One experiment that used this group-based method simulated a distinct pattern of archaeological artifacts found in the Great Basin region of California and Nevada.

In chapter 4 we came across projectile points, which are stone arrowheads or spear tips that were used with bow-and-arrow or spear-throwing technology by prehistoric hunters across North America to kill animals for food. We saw there is extensive diversity in the shapes and sizes of these projectile points, the evolutionary history of which have been recently reconstructed by Michael O'Brien, John Darwent, and Lee Lyman using phylogenetic methods. Yet one question remains: why are projectile points so diverse? This is a question that was tackled for one small part of North America by archaeologists Robert Bettinger and Jelmer Eerkens of the University of California at Davis.[18] Bettinger and Eerkens were interested in a curious difference in the projectile points, specifically arrowheads, collected from two sites, one in central Nevada and the other in eastern California, and dated to around AD 300–600. In central Nevada, Bettinger and Eerkens found that arrowheads varied little in their dimensions, and only certain combinations of dimensions occurred. For example, some of the arrowheads were corner-notched, which means that they had hooklike notches in the base of the arrowhead that prevent them from coming loose when embedded into flesh. In the Nevadan region, arrowheads that were corner-notched and had narrow bases were almost always light. Shape and weight were therefore linked in this region, as were other attributes such as length, width, and thickness. In eastern California, on the other hand, there were no such links between different attributes. Corner-notched arrowheads that had narrow bases were no more likely to be light than to be heavy. Other attributes similarly showed no systematic links: some were thick and narrow, others were thick and wide; some were long and heavy, others were long and light. In summary, the two regions differed in the variability of their arrowheads: Nevadan arrowheads were uniform because of tight links between dimensions, whereas Californian arrowheads were much more diverse with no discernable links between the dimensions.

Bettinger and Eerkens ruled out any kind of ecological or external explanation for these between-site differences, given that the two regions do not appear to differ in the prey that were hunted or the materials used to make the arrowheads. Instead, Bettinger and Eerkens invoked an explanation in terms of cultural microevolution. They proposed that in California, where arrowhead designs were highly variable, arrowhead technology originally spread via guided variation. That is, hunters acquired arrowhead designs from other people, and then modified those designs according to individual trial-and-error learning. It is this latter individual learning component that, according to Bettinger and Eerkens, was responsible for the high diversity in this Californian region. As different people modify different attributes in different ways, diversity slowly builds up. One person might modify the width, another might modify the weight, and as a result width and weight will diverge independently.

In the Nevadan site, on the other hand, Bettinger and Eerkens proposed that arrowhead technology originally spread via prestige bias.[19] Recall from chapter 3 that prestige bias is where the cultural traits associated with highly prestigious or successful individuals are preferentially copied. If prehistoric hunters were engaging in prestige bias, then they would have copied the entire arrowhead design used by the most successful hunter in their group. And as everyone copies the same, most-successful hunter, then everyone in the group will end up with the same arrowhead design. The result: very uniform arrowheads in Nevada. In sum, Bettinger and Eerkens explained macroevolutionary (population-level) differences in arrowhead variation across two archaeological sites in terms of different microevolutionary processes: either guided variation, which increases diversity, or prestige bias, which reduces diversity.

As Bettinger and Eerkens note, however, "it is impossible to observe these transmission processes directly in the archaeological record."[20] Barring the invention of a time machine, we cannot see prehistoric hunters copying prestigious individuals, engaging in trial-and-error learning, or anything else. We can, as Bettinger and Eerkens showed, infer such behavior from macroevolutionary statistical patterns, but this is necessarily indirect: the same patterns might have been generated by entirely different processes. For this reason, archaeologist Michael O'Brien and I conducted an experimental simulation of the scenario proposed by Bettinger and Eerkens.[21] We created a computer game in which participants (University of Missouri college students) designed and used their own "virtual arrowheads." They entered the length, width, thickness, shape, and color of their arrowhead. They then tested its effectiveness by going on a virtual "hunt," after which they were told how many calories they had received. The aim of the game was to discover, over a series of hunts/generations, the optimal arrowhead design for that environment. This optimal design was preset by us, the experimenters, but hidden from the participants.

The experiment was divided into two phases.[22] The first phase simulated guided variation. Here, participants copied the arrowhead design of a previous participant and then engaged in several trials of individual trial-and-error learning, during which they tried out different values of height, width, thickness, shape, and color to try to find the optimal values. According to Bettinger and Eerkens, this phase should result in steadily greater diversity as different participants change different dimensions in different ways. The second phase simulated prestige bias. In the last few hunts of the session, participants were allowed to view and copy the arrowhead designs of other group members. To enable prestige bias, participants could see every other participant's accumulated score, in calories, up to that point, and therefore potentially copy the most successful group member. If everyone does this (except the most successful group member themselves, of course, who cannot copy him/herself), then diversity should drop as everyone in the group ends up with the same arrowhead design.

The results supported Bettinger and Eerkens's hypothesis. The first guided variation phase resulted in significantly more diverse arrowhead designs than the second prestige bias phase. This supports the link between guided variation and high diversity on the one hand, and prestige bias and low diversity on the other. We can be more confident, therefore, that the pattern of low diversity observed by Bettinger and Eerkens in prehistoric Nevada and high diversity in prehistoric California really were generated by prestige bias and guided variation, respectively. Of course this isn't definitive proof, because of all of the limitations of experiments (the artificiality of the laboratory setting, the differences between American college students and prehistoric hunter-gatherers, etc.), but we can at least be sure that the hypothesis works in principle and is consistent with human behavior.

Our experiment went further than simply recreating the past patterns and showing that they were in principle consistent with Bettinger and Eerkens's hypothesis. One weakness of Bettinger and Eerkens's hypothesis is that, if we assume that there is a single, best-possible arrowhead design, then given enough time and minimally intelligent arrowhead makers, guided variation will result in low diversity as well. This is because each hunter will independently arrive at this single best-possible arrowhead design. So under this assumption both guided variation and prestige bias would reduce diversity. An alternative possibility is that there was not, in fact, a single optimal arrowhead design. Recall Sewall Wright's concept of an adaptive landscape introduced earlier in the chapter, where there are multiple adaptive peaks of varying fitness. In our experiment we assumed that the same applied to arrowhead fitness: that there are several locally optimal arrowhead designs that have varying degrees of fitness. So guided variation drives different individuals to different peaks in the landscape, and once they are there they get stuck on those peaks. Because any minor deviation away from their local peak reduces their score, participants at the lower peaks will not be able to cross the adaptive valleys to reach the highest peak in the landscape. Some will be stuck on low peaks, others on high peaks, and a lucky few may have found the highest peak. So under this assumption of a multimodal adaptive landscape (i.e., one with lots of peaks), guided variation *does* maintain diversity in the group, because different people get stuck on different peaks. We can also explain the finding that prestige bias reduces diversity in terms of the adaptive landscape: when participants copied other group members during the second phase of the experiment, then they were in effect "jumping" from their low-fitness peak to a higher peak found by another group member (and who had, because they were on a high-fitness peak, amassed a higher score).[23] To test this further, I changed the adaptive landscape so that it had just a single peak.[24] As predicted, here guided variation resulted in lower diversity than when there were multiple peaks. What's more, prestige bias was adaptive only when fitness landscapes were multimodal. In unimodal fitness environments, individual learners managed easily to find the single adaptive peak.

So a new, refined conclusion is that Bettinger and Eerkens's hypothesis only works if prehistoric arrowhead evolution took place within a multimodal adaptive landscape. If there was a single optimal arrowhead design, then guided variation and prestige bias both make arrowhead designs uniform. And there is evidence that actual arrowhead fitness is indeed determined by a multimodal adaptive landscape. By firing replica arrowheads of varying dimensions at animal carcasses, archaeologists have found certain tradeoffs in arrowhead designs that may generate multiple locally optimal designs.[25] For example, long and thin arrowheads are easier to aim and more likely to penetrate an animal's skin, but less likely to kill the animal. Wide and thick arrowheads, on the other hand, are more difficult to aim and fire, but when they do hit they create larger wounds and the animal is more likely to die. So we have at least two peaks: a "long, thin, penetrative" peak and a "wide, thick, wounding" peak.

This last extension involving adaptive landscapes illustrates the value of experiments. It is impossible to determine what the adaptive landscape underlying arrowhead evolution that occurred over 1,500 years ago looked like. Indeed, it is difficult to determine adaptive landscapes for contemporary technological artifacts, let alone 1,500-year-old artifacts. Experiments allow us to precisely define and manipulate the adaptive landscapes underlying cultural evolution and test hypotheses in a way that is impossible with purely historical methods. As well as methodological benefits, the study also illustrates how specific evolutionary concepts, such as adaptive landscapes, can inform the study of cultural change.

Conclusions: The Benefits of Lab Experiments

The studies outlined above give a taster of how experiments are being used to simulate cultural evolution in the lab. Just as biologists use experimental simulations to explore the microevolutionary processes (selection, drift, mutation, adaptation, etc.) that underlie biological evolution, experiments have been used to explore equivalent micro-evolutionary processes that underlie cultural evolution. Transmission chain studies have identified a content bias for social information and shown that guided variation favors minimally counterintuitive concepts. Other experiments showed how language adapts to become more easily learned and transmitted, challenging nativist explanations for the universal structure of language, and that the possibility of giving advice generates stable traditions in an economic coordination game, which challenges rational actor theories of human decision making that predict that advice should have little effect. Experiments have also been used to validate phylogenetic analyses of manuscript evolution and point to ways of improving such methods. Finally, we saw how experiments have simulated prehistoric technological evolution, showing that regional patterns of prehistoric artifact variation are consistent with different microevolutionary processes (guided variation and prestige bias), but only under certain conditions (i.e., a multimodal adaptive landscape). Other studies not mentioned here have simulated other microevolutionary processes, such as conformity, intergroup cooperation and competition, migration, cultural drift, and social learning mechanisms.[26] In each of these cases, experiments have allowed researchers to test hypotheses in ways that are not possible using historical or observational methods alone: experimenters can re-run history multiple times, manipulate variables, and accurately record behavior.

7

Evolutionary Ethnography:
Cultural Evolution in the Field

While experiments offer a powerful means of testing hypotheses, they are open to the criticism that they lack external validity, that is, the extent to which the experiment captures the actual behavior of real people in their everyday lives. Even if someone engages in a particular behavior—prestige bias, say—in the lab, it does not mean that they would necessarily engage in prestige bias when faced with a similar task in their everyday lives. Timescale is another issue: an experiment that lasts a few hours at most cannot easily capture long-term processes such as parent-to-child vertical cultural transmission.

These problems can be reduced by complementing experiments with observational field studies of people's behavior in the real world, outside the lab. Although field studies suffer from a lack of internal validity, that is, the ability to test causal hypotheses by manipulating variables, randomly assigning people to different conditions, and replicating results, there is an obvious increase in external validity. By directly observing or measuring people's everyday behavior, we get around the problem that people may behave in an artificial manner in the lab because of a lack of incentives, prior norms about laboratory experiments, or anxiety. So in recent years a group of cultural evolution researchers has begun to test the predictions of cultural evolution models in the field. Before examining such efforts, it is instructive to see how field studies are used by biologists.

Studying Biological Evolution in the Field

Exactly the same trade-off between internally valid laboratory experiments and externally valid field studies can be found in biology. Laboratory experiments that simulate biological evolution in bacteria or fruit flies have undoubtedly provided invaluable insights into the genetic mechanisms that constitute biological inheritance, the basis of genetic mutation, the effects of different forms of selection, and so on. Yet these studies are similarly limited by the artificiality of laboratory conditions. Evolutionary responses to restricted laboratory conditions may not be the same as evolutionary responses in the wild, and experiments are usually limited to short-lived, easy-to-manage species such as fruit flies rather than, say, elephants or whales. Consequently, experimental methods are complemented by observational field studies of biological evolution as it occurs under natural conditions.

A classic example is Rosemary Grant and Peter Grant's field studies of Darwin's finches on the Galápagos Islands.[1] For the past thirty years, the Grants have been observing the evolutionary changes that have been occurring in several populations of finches. Each wild bird observed within a particular region is caught, ringed to allow individual identification, and its weight and size measured, before being released back into the wild. Observations are then made of each bird's behavior, and data are collected about aspects of the population's environment, such as the availability of food and number of predators. These data allow the Grants to test basic assumptions of theoretical population genetic models. For example, by comparing parents and their offspring, they showed that morphological characteristics such as beak length and beak width are highly heritable, with 80–90 percent of the variation in such characteristics attributable to genetic differences. Behavioral observations showed that finches with larger beaks can more effectively open larger, harder seeds than finches with smaller beaks. The Grants then showed that, during a severe drought on the islands in 1977 during which small seeds became scarce, finches with larger beaks could more effectively feed on the remaining large seeds and so were more likely to survive and reproduce than finches with small beaks. In other words, there was selection for large beaks. As a consequence of this selection pressure, the average beak size in the population increased by 4 percent by the end of the drought in 1978: a remarkably large change in just a single generation.

The Grants' study therefore demonstrated both that phenotypic traits are strongly heritable and that selection can be extremely strong. The strength of selection has been a contentious issue in the history of biology. As we saw in chapter 2, in the first few decades of the twentieth century naturalists thought that selection was too weak to generate significant evolutionary change, instead arguing that the Lamarckian inheritance of acquired characteristics must be responsible for most evolutionary change. While population genetic models showed that even small selection pressures can in theory generate significant change in a few generations, as did artificial selection experiments in the laboratory, the strength of selection in wild populations remained a contentious issue for some time. Just because selection can have significant effects in theoretical models or in the lab doesn't mean that it does in the wild. The Grants' studies provided actual estimates of the strength of selection acting on real populations of organisms and so informed this debate in a way that theoretical models and laboratory experiments never could.[2]

Studying Cultural Evolution in the Field

The Need for Cultural Field Studies. In the same way that biologists such as the Grants conduct field studies of biological evolution, so too there is a need for field studies of cultural evolution. Although mathematical models can illuminate the possible consequences of different cultural microevolutionary processes, models are only ever as good as their assumptions. Experiments add a certain degree of external validity in the form of studying actual human behavior, yet experiments are still artificial. A complete understanding of cultural evolution requires observational field studies that track people's real-life behavior over time. Such studies can potentially address key questions about cultural microevolution. For example, what is the relative influence of our parents (via vertical transmission), our teachers (via oblique transmission), and our peers (via horizontal transmission) in determining our cultural beliefs, attitudes, skills, and knowledge? Theoretical models demonstrate that these different pathways have different macroevolutionary consequences (e.g., vertical transmission can result in slower change than horizontal change), yet there are little data on the importance of each in actual cultural evolution. We also need estimates of the strength of cultural selection and guided variation in actual societies: are they as strong as natural selection? Is guided variation stronger than cultural selection, as suggested by theoretical models? These are just a small sample of questions that need to be tested in actual societies to complement theoretical models and laboratory experiments.

As discussed in chapter 1, the traditional method of studying culture in the field, ethnography, has undergone a crisis of confidence partly as a result of the recognition that the ethnographic method is intrinsically biased. The realization that the ethnographer brings to their research their own cultural biases has led many cultural anthropologists to abandon the idea that culture can ever be studied scientifically and objectively, and many are instead content to provide subjective descriptions ("thick descriptions") of other people's lives. Yet a group of cultural evolution researchers have taken an alternative path. They have used modern statistical techniques to update the ethnographic method and partially solve such problems as self-report bias, in order to answer key questions regarding how human culture evolves.[3]

Skill Acquisition in the Aka. As described in chapter 3, Cavalli-Sforza and Feldman's groundbreaking 1981 book *Cultural Transmission and Evolution* contained detailed mathematical models of different pathways of cultural transmission and their evolutionary consequences. These models showed that different transmission pathways have distinct consequences for rates of cultural change and patterns of variation between and within human groups. Vertical (parent-to-offspring) cultural transmission, for example, results in relatively slow cultural change because it is limited by the length of biological generations, and also creates large individual differences in culturally acquired behaviors, because each person acquires different information from their own parents. Horizontal cultural transmission, on the other hand, can potentially result in much more rapid change and more homogenous cultural groups, as novel technologies, words, or practices diffuse from person to person within a group and within a single biological generation.

These predictions from mathematical models can then be tested in the real world by examining to what extent people learn from their parents and from their peers, whether different traits (e.g., skills, words, rituals, beliefs) all follow the same transmission pathway, and whether observed transmission pathways fit with predicted rates of change and variation (e.g., whether vertically transmitted traits show the slowest rate of historical change). To test these predictions, anthropologist Barry Hewlett, along with Cavalli-Sforza, conducted a study of cultural transmission among the Aka people, a community of hunter-gatherers living in the tropical forests of the Central African Republic and the Republic of the Congo.[4] The Aka studied by Hewlett and Cavalli-Sforza lived in small villages of 25–30 people, each incorporating several families. The small size of these groups, along with the lack of formal education, lack of literacy, and limited communication with the outside world via the mass media and mass transit, make it easier to identify different transmission pathways than in larger, postindustrial societies.[5] Hewlett and Cavalli-Sforza interviewed 72 Aka people, asking them about fifty skills that were thought to be important in Aka society. These included hunting skills, such as techniques for chasing duikers (small antelopes) into nets and spearing them, food-gathering skills, such as successfully locating and identifying edible mushrooms, fruits, and nuts, infant-caring skills, such as whether and how long to carry or breastfeed infants, and dancing and singing skills, which were used in groupwide celebrations and rituals. For each of the fifty skills, the interviewee was asked whether they knew the skill, and, if so, from whom they acquired that skill.

The results indicated that vertical cultural transmission was the dominant mode of transmission in the Aka community. Overall, 81 percent of skills were reported to have been acquired from a parent. The next-largest influence was unrelated people from different villages, which was reported for 10 percent of skills. Other sources were negligible: 4 percent from grandparents, 1.5 percent from other family members, 1.5 percent from unrelated members of the same village, and 1 percent of skills were reported to have been invented by the respondent from scratch with no social influence.

This finding that vertical transmission was the most important transmission pathway suggests that cultural change in the Aka should be relatively slow. And indeed, hunter-gatherer societies such as the Aka are often called "traditional" societies by anthropologists because they appear to have changed little in lifestyle for thousands of years. Compare this to postindustrial societies, in which horizontal and oblique transmission likely play a much larger role in the form of mass education and mass media, and which feature rapid technological and social change. Indeed, developmental psychologist Judith Rich Harris has forcefully argued that horizontal transmission is the dominant mode of transmission in Western postindustrial societies and that little, if anything, is learned from parents.[6] We might also speculate that these different transmission pathways have resulted in different patterns of variation. While postindustrial societies are appearing, through globalization, to become increasingly homogenous with respect to language (e.g., English), technology (e.g., computers, mobile phones), and customs (e.g., business suits), traditional hunter-gatherer societies are still quite culturally diverse.

However, while vertical transmission was the dominant mode of transmission in the Aka for the majority of skills, it varied for different types of skills in interesting ways. For example, 89 percent of food-gathering skills were reported to have been learned from parents and only 4 percent from unrelated members of other villages. In contrast, far fewer dancing and singing skills were acquired from parents (52 percent) and far more from unrelated members of other villages (42 percent). This likely reflects the different functions of these two sets of skills. Food is crucial to survival, so if parents want their children to survive then they must teach them how to find and process food. And, for the Aka living during this time period, sources of food were unlikely to change over successive generations, so parents' knowledge is still relevant for their children to learn. Dancing and singing, on the other hand, are social norms that serve to foster social ties and maintain group cohesion. It is crucial, therefore, that each Aka knows the same dances and songs as members of other villages, explaining why far more of these skills than any other category are acquired from unrelated members of other villages. Dances and songs are also more likely to change over time given that they are not tied to any fixed external phenomenon, as is food-related knowledge.

Another exception to the dominance of vertical cultural transmission occurred in the category of "other hunting skills," of which 20 percent were acquired horizontally from unrelated members of other villages. Most of these skills related to novel technologies that had been invented after the respondents' parents had learned their hunting skills, making parents useless as sources of information. One example is the crossbow, a recent introduction to the Aka community that was in the process of replacing the bow and arrow as the primary method of hunting. Another concerns elephant hunting, a practice so difficult that adolescents often supplement the basic skills that they acquire from their fathers by observing an "ntuma," or "great elephant hunter," a potential instance of prestige bias. These examples indicate the flexibility of human cultural learning: where parents lack an obviously beneficial skill, people will readily switch from vertical to horizontal transmission.

Food Taboos in the Congo. A major problem with Hewlett and Cavalli-Sforza's study, and other studies that have similarly found that parents play a major role in cultural transmission,[7] is their reliance on self-reports. Asking people from whom they learned a particular skill does not necessarily result in an accurate answer. Social psychologists have repeatedly demonstrated that people often have extremely poor insight into the causes of their own behavior, while cognitive psychologists have found that people's recall is biased toward single, vivid events or explanations.[8] Moreover, many societies have social norms that state that one should obey and learn from one's parents, including the Aka. So perhaps the self-reports from the Aka that a skill was learned from a parent were exaggerated. If in reality a skill was acquired from several sources in addition to a parent, or was initially learned from a parent but then substantially modified through nonparental learning later in life, the parent may nevertheless be reported as the sole source of learning.

To get around the problem of self-reporting bias, anthropologist Robert Aunger devised a more indirect but potentially far more accurate method of measuring cultural transmission.[9] Aunger studied food taboos—rules governing what should or shouldn't be eaten—in a group of horticulturalists living in the Ituri Forest region of the Democratic Republic of Congo. Like Hewlett, Aunger used self-report methods, asking 248 members of several different villages from whom they acquired various food taboos. However, Aunger also inferred patterns of transmission from the similarity between different people's combinations of taboos. The assumption here is that transmission increases similarity: when individual A successfully acquires a taboo from individual B, then individual A and B will be more similar in their taboos than two individuals between whom transmission has not occurred. So if children have very similar taboos to their parents and dissimilar taboos to their peers, then Aunger might infer strong vertical transmission; if same-age peers are all very similar to one another and dissimilar to older or younger generations, then Aunger might infer strong horizontal transmission.[10]

The results of the self-report measure were strikingly similar to Hewlett and Cavalli-Sforza's finding: 76 percent of food taboos were reported to have been acquired from parents, 6 percent from grandparents, 15 percent from unrelated elders, and 3 percent from unrelated members of the same generation. Thus food taboos, like the skills reported for the Aka by Hewlett and Cavalli-Sforza, also seem to be predominantly vertically transmitted, at least according to self-report.

However, Aunger's similarity analysis suggested a somewhat more complex situation. Aunger identified two general types of food taboos, each of which showed a distinct pattern of transmission. Ancestral taboos prohibited the consumption of particular foods because they were believed to be incompatible with the bloodline of that individual's family. This typically concerned the male lineage, because this society was patrilineal (i.e., identity and wealth was transmitted from father to son). As an example, Aunger reports one respondent explaining that "Male children [in our family] can't eat boku [a type of catfish]; it bends them over [like an old person] and they die."[11] The similarity analysis showed that ancestral taboos such as these were most similar between fathers and their sons, with other family pairs (e.g., mother/ daughter, father/daughter, mother/son) less similar. This suggests that ancestral taboos were transmitted primarily from fathers to sons, a male-specific form of vertical transmission. As a result, ancestral taboos showed particularly high within-household homogeneity, and substantial between-household variation, as each family transmitted its own ancestral taboos along its male lineage.

The second set of taboos were what Aunger called homeopathic taboos. These primarily related to what foods pregnant women should eat in order to give birth to a healthy baby. As the name suggests, the logic behind homeopathic taboos was that if a pregnant woman ate the meat of a particular animal, then her baby would be born with some quality exhibited by that animal. For example, one of Aunger's respondents describes a homeopathic taboo as follows: "Kelikofu [a type of hornbill] is bad for parents of children to eat, for when a child is sick, it shakes just as the bird, when comes out of its hole [in a tree trunk], is cold and shakes." Homeopathic taboos showed the reverse pattern to ancestral taboos according to the similarity analysis, with similarities best explained by maternal transmission to both daughters and sons, along with some paternal transmission to daughters. This made mothers and sons most similar, because sons only received taboos from their mothers, followed by father-daughter and mother-daughter pairs, because daughters received taboos from both parents, with fathers and sons the least similar, because there was little father-to-son transmission. The result of this mother-dominated transmission was much greater similarity between different villages. This is because this society is patrilocal: women go to live with their husband's family, and so take their taboos with them to their new household. Over time, taboos spread across every household. Note that this is the opposite pattern to the one discussed in chapter 4 that was found by Jamie Tehrani and Mark Collard in their study of Iranian tribal textile pattern evolution.[12] Like homeopathic taboos, textile techniques and patterns were transmitted primarily from mothers to daughters, with patterns additionally spreading horizontally from unrelated women. However, in that case Tehrani and Collard found that female weavers did not marry out of their local tribes, and so textile patterns did not spread across social group boundaries, thus explaining the highly treelike phylogenetic pattern of textile evolution. We might predict that homeopathic food taboos in the Congo would show poor evidence of a treelike branching pattern if they were subject to phylogenetic analyses.

Finally, the similarity analysis showed that the strength of these different forms of vertical transmission was far weaker than suggested by the self-report data. Aunger identified three general life stages in the acquisition of food taboos in the people of the Ituri Forest. The first stage lasts until the age of ten and is one of ignorance of food taboos. Children have personal food preferences and have taboos imposed on them by parents but do not themselves possess socially normative food taboos. The second stage lasts from the age of ten until twenty years old, during which time food taboos are acquired primarily from one or both parents in the manner described above, differently for ancestral taboos and homeopathic taboos. The third stage continues throughout the rest of the person's life and consists of the less intense acquisition of food taboos from unrelated members of other households. As a result of this last stage, Aunger found greater variation within households than between households in the same village for adult informants, because adults were learning from members of other households via horizontal transmission. Because this third stage of horizontal transmission occurred after a more intense and explicit stage of vertical transmission during adolescence, when asked from whom they acquired food taboos, people tended to report parents to the exclusion of unrelated villagers. Yet the fact that villages were more homogenous than expected indicates that this forgotten stage of horizontal transmission had a significant effect on the cultural evolution of food taboos in this society.

Ethnobotanical Knowledge and Skills in the Tsimane'. Another cultural evolution–inspired ethnographic study, also based on similarity of responses rather than self-report, supports Aunger's conclusion that vertical transmission is not always the dominant force in cultural evolution. This study was conducted as part of a large multidisciplinary project, the Tsimane' Amazonian Panel Study (TAPS). The Tsimane' are a group of about 8,000 horticulturalists and hunter-gatherers living in the Amazonian rainforests of Bolivia, and in which cultural transmission is again primarily face-to-face rather than through formal education. The TAPS team, in this case led by cultural anthropologist Victoria Reyes García of the Universitat Autónoma de Barcelona, wanted to know how ethnobotanical knowledge and skills are transmitted among the Tsimane' people.[13] "Ethnobotanical" refers to a group's knowledge of the effects and uses of plant species that live in their region and the skills required to find, use, or process these plants for food or medicinal purposes. Ethnobotanical knowledge and skills are crucial for survival in the Amazonian rainforest. A Tsimane' mother's ethnobotanical knowledge, for example, is significantly associated with various measures of her child's health, such as immune response, growth rate, and subcutaneous fat stores.[14] So there is a large incentive for individuals to acquire accurate and comprehensive ethnobotanical knowledge and skills. But do Tsimane' people do this via vertical, oblique, or horizontal cultural transmission?

To answer this, Reyes García et al. surveyed the ethnobotanical competence of 270 Tsimane' informants, asking them to identify 15 randomly selected plants from a selection of local species (assessing ethnobotanical knowledge) and quizzing them on potential uses for another 12 local plants (assessing ethnobotanical skills). Multiple regression analysis was then used to determine the extent to which an individual's knowledge and skills could be predicted from (a) the knowledge and skills of their same-sex parent (indicating vertical transmission), (b) the knowledge and skills of the parental generation (indicating oblique transmission), and (c) the knowledge and skills of their same-age peers (indicating horizontal transmission).

The results showed that the cultural transmission of ethnobotanical competence among the Tsimane' is primarily oblique, to some extent vertical, and seldom horizontal. Within this general pattern there were slightly different results for knowledge and skills, and for men and women. First, vertical transmission was stronger in women than men for both knowledge and skills. Reyes García et al. suggest that this may reflect the Tsimane' sexual division of labor. Girls tend to spend most of their time performing household and agricultural tasks with their mothers as they are growing up, providing ample opportunity to acquire ethnobotanical competence vertically. Boys, on the other hand, are discouraged from going hunting with their fathers due to the dangers associated with hunting wild animals. They therefore spend less time with their fathers, and have less opportunity to learn from them. The second major finding was that skills were more likely to be acquired by vertical transmission than knowledge. Reyes García et al. suggest that this is because skills are more difficult to acquire, requiring repeated exposure and practice, compared to more easily acquired knowledge. Consequently, it may be easier to acquire knowledge from a range of sources through oblique transmission, while costly skills must be acquired from parents who are more accessible and more willing to spend time teaching their children. Finally, a similar age effect was observed to that found by Aunger, with vertical transmission stronger and oblique transmission weaker for younger (<25) individuals than older (>25) individuals.

Reyes García et al.'s study adds to others, including Hewlett's and Aunger's studies discussed above, that are providing an increasingly more accurate understanding of cultural transmission pathways in small-scale societies.[15] The initial conclusion that vertical transmission is the dominant pathway in small-scale societies is giving way to a more nuanced understanding of the role of parents in cultural evolution. Oblique and horizontal transmission have been found to be far more important than first thought, increasingly so as an individual gets older. This makes adaptive sense: one's parents are only a limited sample of just two individuals, and learning from the entire group allows the rapid acquisition of the accumulated cultural information of many more individuals, some of whom may well be more skilled or knowledgeable than one's parents. Horizontal transmission also allows for the acquisition of beneficial novel traits, such as crossbows, that one's parents never had the opportunity to master.

From the Forest to the Lab: Observing Scientists in Their Natural Habitat

There is no reason why ethnographic field studies of cultural evolution must be carried out in small-scale, nonindustrial societies. It may be easier to track the cultural transmission of particular skills and knowledge through such societies than in postindustrial, postglobalization societies such as the United States because of the former's lack of literacy, mass media, and formal education. However, just because a task is more difficult does not mean it should not be tackled. In fact, more than two decades ago one pioneering cultural evolution researcher, the philosopher of biology David L. Hull, carried out an ethnographic study of conceptual change among groups of scientists at various US universities.[16] While the Aka and Tsimane's natural habitat is the rainforest, the typical scientist's natural habitat is the lab.

Hull wished to test his theory that conceptual change in science is a cultural evolutionary process of the kind outlined in chapter 2. That is, scientific knowledge comprises a varying set of concepts or theories that differ in various ways. These concepts or theories are tested via the scientific method. That is, each theory entails a set of predictions, and these predictions are tested through observations or experiments. Those theories that have their predictions upheld can be said to have been selected, such that they are preferentially transmitted to the next generation of scientists in the form of published journal articles and citations in textbooks. Over time, theories that better explain aspects of the world tend to increase in frequency, resulting in more accurate scientific knowledge.

This kind of evolutionary model of scientific change has been suggested many times. Prominent philosopher of science Karl Popper, for example, remarked that "the growth of our knowledge is the result of a process closely resembling what Darwin called 'natural selection'; that is, the natural selection of hypotheses."[17] Uniquely, however, Hull wanted to actually test his evolutionary model empirically. So like traditional ethnographers, Hull went to live with his subjects, the scientists, with the aim of observing and documenting their practices and customs under naturalistic conditions. Being a philosopher of biology, Hull chose a group of scientists that he was familiar with: systematists. This is a general term applied to any biologist who seeks to categorize the diverse forms of life on earth. We have already come across systematics in previous chapters in the form of phylogenetics. Phylogenetics, or to give it its more specific label, *cladistics*, is a particular school within the more general field of systematics that uses evolutionary principles such as maximum parsimony to classify organisms on the basis of their evolutionary history. This is why such attention is paid to distinguishing between homologies (similarities due to common descent) and homoplasies (similarities due to independent evolution in separate lineages): because only the former should be used when classifying organisms. While cladistics is now the dominant method of classifying biological organisms, when Hull conducted his study in the 1970s it was only beginning to be developed. The dominant paradigm at that time was called *phenetics*. This approach classified organisms on the basis of similarity, as does cladistics, but it does not distinguish between ancestral and derived traits. So Hull picked a very opportune moment to conduct his ethnographic study: just as one conceptual framework, cladistics, was replacing another, phenetics (although he only knew this in hindsight). To document conceptual evolution among systematists, Hull spent time in the labs of several major researchers, both pheneticists and cladists. He interviewed the researchers and their lab members and sat in on lab meetings. He also elicited survey responses from the wider scientific community and gained access to every submission and every referee report to the major journal of the field, *Systematic Zoology*.

You may recall from chapter 1 that a similar ethnographic study of scientists at work was conducted by the sociologist Bruno Latour. Observing numerous instances of subjectivity, impartiality, and bias on the part of scientists, Latour concluded that science is far from the objective system of knowledge acquisition that he thought it should be, and instead is just a collection of socially constructed beliefs that have no grounding in reality. Partly as a result, cultural anthropology abandoned any attempt at the scientific study of human culture, embracing the social constructionist position that all knowledge is subjective. Hull reached a very different conclusion. While he observed many instances of subjectivity, bias, and impartiality on the part of the individual scientists that he studied, he argued that this was entirely consistent with both a cultural evolutionary theory of scientific change and with the objectivity of science as a whole. Hull proposed that just as biological organisms act in order to benefit their kin group and increase their inclusive genetic fitness, such as when a sterile worker bee collects food for other genetically related bees in the hive, so too scientists act in order to benefit their "conceptual inclusive fitness." That is, they act to spread the use of and the support for their particular conceptual framework (e.g., phenetics or cladistics) by conducting and publishing empirical studies, by arguing for their position in debates at conferences, and by spawning graduate students who inherit their ideas. And because science is rarely nowadays conducted by single, isolated individuals, we see the formation of groups of scientists who all share the same conceptual framework (e.g., the pheneticists and the cladists). Scientists within the same conceptual group cooperate with one another through collaboration and mutual citations, whereas different conceptual groups compete to become the dominant framework of that particular field. In other words, science is a process of conceptual group selection. As we have already seen, in the case observed by Hull, the cladists eventually won and became the dominant method for classifying organisms, with phenetics becoming obsolete.

This view of science paints scientists as rather self-interested creatures, only interested in furthering their own careers by making their own conceptual group dominant and crushing all others. Indeed, Hull's interviews and observations confirmed that the motivations of scientists were rarely such lofty goals as furthering humanity's understanding of the world or benefitting humankind, but rather to knock a rival off his or her perch. As Hull notes, "Time and again, scientists whom I interviewed described the powerful spur that "showing that son of a bitch" supplied to their own research."[18] Supporting these informal interview responses, Hull showed that editors and manuscript reviewers of *Systematic Zoology* were noticeably more supportive of manuscripts from scientists who shared their conceptual framework (phenetics or cladistics) than those of the opposing camp. Moreover, successful scientists in each group were those whom colleagues and students perceived as being the most strongly committed to their conceptual framework and the most willing to publicly and aggressively defend their framework/group. And using historical data, Hull showed that older, established scientists who had already subscribed to a particular conceptual framework were less likely to adopt a new framework than younger, more junior scientists who had not fully committed to a conceptual group, even in the face of superior evidence for that position. This confirms the old adage expressed by Max Planck that "a new scientific truth does not triumph by convincing its opponents and making them see the light, but rather because its opponents eventually die, and a new generation grows up that is familiar with it."[19]

This view of scientists as self-interested, biased, and egotistical bullies seems to chime with the social constructionists' criticisms that science is rarely if ever objective. Yet Hull notes that these proximate, self-interested motivations on the part of individual scientists coincide almost exactly with what one needs in order to ensure that scientific knowledge increases in accuracy. As Hull puts it, "science is organized so that self-interest promotes the greater good."[20] For example, scientists are rewarded for publishing their work by receiving credit for that work. This could be major credit in the form of having a theorem or field named after them (e.g., "Darwinian" evolution, "Newtonian" physics) or simply a citation in another journal article. If no credit were given, then there would be no incentive to publish and make results public. Darwin, after all, sat on the idea of evolution until Alfred Russel Wallace spurred him into publication out of fear of losing credit for his theory. And if results are not made public, then other scientists will not be aware of how well a theory is supported. They also cannot build on those findings, and scientific knowledge cannot accumulate over time. So the individual reward—credit from one's peers—results in increased scientific understanding—the "greater good."

And contrary to the social constructionists' assertions that scientific knowledge is entirely subjective, Hull repeatedly found that the selection criteria for scientific theories is, ultimately, whether it is supported empirically and objectively. This is illustrated by the often very severe punishment of scientific fraud. In 2005, for example, Korean stem cell researcher Hwang Woo-Suk was accused of, and later admitted to, fabricating the results of a series of high-profile experiments. As a result his career was effectively over. He lost his job at Seoul National University, he lost his government license to conduct research, and at the time of writing may even face a jail term. Scientific fraud is punished so severely, according to Hull, because it harms every other scientist in the field. Scientists rarely have time to replicate and check every other scientists' findings. Consequently, they often trust that other scientists' published findings are reliable, and they use those findings in their own research. When those findings are fabricated, then the other scientists are wasting their time and resources by basing their research on false premises. And again, this self-interested motivation of individual scientists—to punish and deter fabrication of data—simultaneously serves to increase the overall accuracy of scientific knowledge.

Hull's ethnographic study of scientists at work is not as methodologically rigorous as the other studies discussed earlier in this chapter. However, it is valuable in demonstrating that cultural evolutionary theory and methods apply to Western scientists just as well as to Congolese hunter-gatherers, by showing that scientific change can be understood as an evolutionary process in which scientists act to maximize their conceptual inclusive fitness just as organisms act to maximize their genetic inclusive fitness, and in countering the claims of social constructionists that science does not result in objective scientific knowledge.

Conclusions: The Benefits of Field Studies

As noted in chapter 1, ethnography has undergone something of a crisis of confidence in recent decades. The rise of social constructionism within cultural anthropology has led to the rejection by many ethnographers of the possibility that culture can be studied scientifically, and there is now little attempt to test specific, theory-driven hypotheses using rigorous, quantitative, statistical methods. Cultural evolutionary theory, on the other hand, provides a set of specific theoretical predictions that can guide ethnographic research, such as the prediction that vertical transmission should result in slowly changing traditions compared to horizontal transmission or that the norms of science should favor the selection of empirically supported concepts. These predictions demand quantitative answers and encourage the use of statistical methods such as multiple regression analysis of similarity measures in responses, rather than reliance on biased self-report.

Yet the ethnographic studies discussed above mostly focus on a very narrow topic in cultural evolution, that of transmission pathway. There is enormous opportunity here to quantitatively measure the many other cultural processes listed in table 3.1, such as the strength of content-biased cultural selection in causing the spread of novel ideas, beliefs, or technologies through small-scale societies, or measuring the strength of conformity in maintaining intergroup differences. And there is no reason why these predictions cannot be tested simultaneously in postindustrial societies. We saw an initial attempt to do this by Hull in his ethnographic study of Western scientists, which found that scientific change can be usefully analyzed as an evolutionary process. Sociologists, meanwhile, are increasingly using "small-world network" methods to quantify social structures in postindustrial societies, from internet and mobile phone networks to networks of collaborating scientists and even networks of terrorist cells.[21] Yet while these methods can accurately capture social networks at a single point in time, they are less effective at capturing the evolutionary dynamics that generated the networks in the first place and cause the networks to change over time.[22] Cultural evolutionary theory, on the other hand, explicitly deals with change over time and the causes of that change and may provide a means of synthesizing sociological and ethnographic methods.

8

Evolutionary Economics:
Cultural Evolution in the Marketplace

Cultural evolutionary concepts and methods can also be used to explain various aspects of economic change. Unlike some other branches of the social sciences, economics as a field has no problem with quantitative, mathematical models, and economists routinely construct complicated mathematical models of economic processes. These models concern both microeconomic phenomena, such as the interactions of individuals or firms within a market in response to different levels of supply and demand, and macroeconomic phenomena, such as changes in the GDP or unemployment rates of entire countries. Indeed, many of the methods that economists have developed have been so useful that biologists have used them to explain biological phenomena. As noted in chapter 2, Thomas Malthus's economic model of exponential population growth served as the basis of Darwin's key insight that animals face a constant and competitive "struggle for existence," while in the 1960s biologists such as John Maynard Smith used game theory, originally developed to model the strategic interactions of individuals within economic markets, to model the strategic interactions between individual organisms competing over mates or resources.

Yet there has been much less transference of ideas and methods the other way, from biology to economics. In recent years this has been slowly changing. Two emerging subfields that have used cultural evolution theory to inform our understanding of economic processes are evolutionary economics and behavioral economics. Evolutionary economics is concerned with modeling economic change as a Darwinian process in which firms are selected in the marketplace and behavioral routines are transmitted from individual to individual within firms. This contrasts with the traditional economic assumption that economies are in a constant state of equilibrium, and that individuals can always calculate the optimal long-term strategy to follow. Behavioral economics, meanwhile, has amassed growing evidence that human economic behavior is far more altruistic and far less self-regarding than is assumed by traditional economic models. This altruistic behavior, several researchers argue, is the result of a process of cultural group selection, where altruistic groups outcompete less altruistic groups. Although both subfields are generally identified with different researchers, there are strong connections between them, and both are united by the core principle that cultural change, in this case economic change, constitutes a Darwinian evolutionary process.

Evolutionary Economics: Challenging the Myth of Perfect Foresight

The history of evolutionary thinking in economics somewhat parallels that of other social sciences.[1] In the late nineteenth and early twentieth century, several economists sought to use Darwinian principles to explain economic phenomena, most notably Thorstein Veblen and Joseph Schumpeter. Following the Second World War, however, interest in evolutionary theory among mainstream economists virtually disappeared. It was not until 1982 that a formal evolutionary theory of economic change appeared, in the form of Richard Nelson and Sidney Winter's book *An Evolutionary Theory of Economic Change.*[2] In this book, Nelson and Winter outlined what they believed were serious shortcomings of mainstream economic theory and models before presenting an evolutionary theory of economic change that addresses these shortcomings. In particular, they argued that mainstream economics is unrealistically focused on static equilibria. A typical economic model specifies a set of decisions that a firm can carry out in response to a set of external conditions, such as supply and demand in the market, and internal conditions, such as stock levels, assuming that firms are attempting to maximize profits. Rigorous mathematical modeling techniques can be used to determine the static equilibrium, or stable state, of the economic system at which all economic forces balance out, such as when supply matches demand. While such equilibria describe real economic conditions reasonably well at a single point in time, Nelson and Winter argued that they are not so good at explaining changes in economic systems over time. Economic growth that is driven by technological or scientific change is particularly poorly described by static equilibria, given that computing or pharmaceutical technology, for example, exhibits rapid and unpredictable growth and change. As famously expressed in Moore's Law, computer processing power doubles approximately every two years, and firms that rely on computer technology must adapt to this technological change. Change this rapid does not easily translate into models featuring static equilibria.

A second problem with mainstream economic theory pointed out by Nelson and Winter is its assumption that people are perfectly rational. That is, people are assumed to be able to accurately evaluate every possible behavioral option available to them (e.g., what stocks to buy, what product to launch onto the market) and choose the option with the highest long-term payoff (e.g., in terms of sales or profit). This assumes quite a lot about people's cognitive abilities: that they are aware of every possible behavioral choice, that they can tally up all of the potential costs and benefits of each choice, and that they possess almost omniscient powers of foresight, able to predict long-term changes in markets. As Herbert Simon pointed out long ago, however, people are not this clever.[3] In Simon's terminology they possess *bounded rationality*, which means that they are reasonably rational but operate within certain constraints imposed by the limitations of human cognition and the sheer complexity of many economic choices (think about how even the most complicated mathematical models and computer simulations failed to predict the 2007 global recession). Furthermore, we have encountered much evidence in the previous chapters, including models, experiments, and field studies, that people often don't engage in individual learning at all, whether it is bounded or unbounded. Instead, they simply copy the behavior of others, which, after all, is often a cheap shortcut to acquiring adaptive behavior.[4]

Routines not Rationality. So Nelson and Winter outlined an evolutionary theory of economic change that, they argued, can more accurately capture the observed dynamics of real economic systems compared to orthodox static equilibrium models that assume unbounded rationality. The first element of their theory was what they called "routines," defined as well-learned and automatically executed sequences of behaviors carried out by workers or managers in a firm. As examples, Nelson and Winter list "well-specified technical routines for producing things, through procedures for hiring and firing, ordering new inventory, or stepping up production of items in high demand, to policies regarding investment, research and development (R&D), or advertising, and business strategies about product diversification and overseas investment."[5] Routines are transmitted to new workers when they arrive at a firm and are transmitted from managers to workers when new strategies are implemented. As such, routines constitute the inheritance mechanism in Nelson and Winter's theory (as encapsulated in the slogan "Routines as genes"), which as we saw in chapter 2 is an essential prerequisite of Darwinian evolution. They also embody a more accurate assumption regarding human behavior than the extreme rationality of traditional economic models. Rather than each individual economic actor independently calculating the optimal action to perform in a given situation, they assumed that people simply engage in tried-and-tested routines that they acquired or were taught by other members of the firm. Indeed, recall from chapter 6 Andrew Schotter and Barry Sopher's experimental finding that participants are strongly influenced in their behavior in an economic game by advice given to them by a previous participant. This advice can be seen as an example of a culturally transmitted routine. And whereas this advice allowed players to successfully coordinate their choices in the form of stable conventions, providing participants with the full behavioral history of every previous player of the game had virtually no effect. If people were rational maximizers, then they should have used this behavioral history to calculate the optimal choice. Instead they went with the (possibly biased and inaccurate) advice.

An economic theory built on culturally transmitted routines rather than individual rational calculation can explain hitherto puzzling aspects of economic change. An example is the failure of Polaroid to shift into the digital camera market in the late 1990s. By interviewing key Polaroid employees and analyzing financial records and internal research reports, Mary Tripsas and Giovanni Gavetti showed that this failure to adapt was due to managers applying existing routines to a novel situation where they were no longer appropriate.[6] Polaroid's problem was not technological: from the early 1980s the company had invested huge sums of money into researching digital camera technology, and by the early 1990s when the digital camera market was taking off they had a working prototype of a high-resolution megapixel camera that was superior to any existing camera on the market. Yet by 1998 Polaroid had a limited product range and a small share of the digital camera market. To explain this failure to capitalize on their initial technological advantage, Tripsas and Gavetti point to the Polaroid management's insistence on the "razorblade" business model. Traditionally, Polaroid had made money not from their cameras, which were sold at a loss, but from photographic film, which customers had to keep buying in order to use the camera (a business model also adopted by, as the name suggests, razorblade companies, who make their money on disposable blades rather than the razor itself). But digital cameras do not easily fit into the razorblade business model, because images can be stored digitally and require no film. While the people at Polaroid were trying to develop digital imaging technology that could work with the razorblade business model, other companies overtook them in the digital camera market. As late as 1997, the CEO of Polaroid stated in an interview that "[i]n the digital world we believe that hard copy is required . . . Unless there is a consumable component, the business model falls apart."[7] This cultural inertia reflected an unwillingness to abandon previously successful routines in response to a novel technology.

Firm Competition in the Marketplace. Routines provide the inheritance in Nelson and Winter's evolutionary theory of economic change, but, as outlined in chapter 2, Darwinian evolution also needs variation and competition. Variation comes in the form of new technological innovations that result from firms' research and development (R&D) efforts. Larger firms are assumed to be able to devote more resources to R&D, and so generate more novel variation, than smaller firms. Competition might occur at the level of routines, with more-effective routines replacing less-effective routines. More commonly, however, competition is modeled at the level of the firm, with firms containing inefficient or inappropriate routines making fewer profits than firms containing more efficient routines. This ultimately leads to less profitable firms going bust. In this sense Nelson and Winter's theory is an example of cultural group selection, where selection acts on groups of individuals (i.e., firms) causing entire groups to either increase in size or go extinct.

Putting these ideas concerning variation and competition together, economist Steven Klepper has put forward an evolutionary theory concerning how and why the number of firms in an industry changes over time.[8] Klepper's model starts with the appearance of some new technological or scientific innovation, which is potentially exploitable by firms. Yet because this innovation is unfamiliar and novel, firms are not aware of how best to exploit it (given their limited foresight). Many different firms appear, each one exploiting the innovation in a different way. Eventually one or more firms hit upon a product design that is particularly effective, or at least one that consumers become familiar with. This design comes to dominate the industry and firms that do not adopt this design go bust. Once product design has converged on this single dominant form, surviving firms can invest in R&D to develop the dominant design further. As a result, new companies that try to enter the market will be at a disadvantage compared to the incumbent firms, which form an oligopoly.

So Klepper's theory predicts a distinct industry life cycle: initially the number of firms rapidly increases until the dominant design is discovered, then the industry becomes dominated by a small number of established firms. Klepper and colleagues have shown that this life cycle can be observed in many real-life industries, from the automobile industry to television manufacturing.[9] The tire industry, for example, showed a steady increase in the number of firms in the initial 25 years since the first tires were produced for the first cars in 1896, peaking at 274 in 1922. At around this time the tire industry fixed on a particular "cord and balloon" design in which the tire rubber is supported by cords rather than fabric as it had been prior to 1922, and an internal balloon is used to maintain the tire's shape. Over the next fifteen years, the number of tire firms declined more than 80 percent, with just a handful of large firms remaining. By 1950, just four companies—Goodrich, Goodyear, the United States Rubber Company, and Firestone—accounted for almost 80 percent of the tire market, a situation that has not changed much to this day. And as predicted by Klepper's model, the older and larger a firm was, and the more it spent specifically on R&D, the more likely it was to survive this culling process. The aforementioned four largest firms in 1950, for example, had all entered the market in its first ten years of existence, by 1906.

Two further points are worth highlighting here. First, although the appearance of technological innovations in Klepper's model is treated exogenously (i.e., as external events not accounted for by processes within the model), such as the initial invention of the automobile tire or the development of the new cord and balloon design, we should not forget that such technological innovations are also the result of an evolutionary process. This was argued in chapter 7, where we encountered David Hull's theory that scientific change constitutes an evolutionary process in which concepts are transmitted from scientist to scientist and selection occurs as conceptual groups of scientists compete. Given that technological developments are partly driven by scientific progress, such as the chemical process of vulcanization leading to the development of more durable tires, we would expect technological change to also take the form of an evolutionary process. There is as well a large literature on technological evolution more specifically, as mentioned in the context of the accumulation of modifications in chapter 2.[10] So a full account of industry evolution would be one of coevolution between, on the one hand, science and technology as specified by Hull and others, and, on the other, firms within industries as specified by Nelson, Winter, Klepper, and others. Such a coevolutionary process has not, to my knowledge, been formally modeled or empirically studied but might provide valuable insights into both evolutionary processes.

Second, the pattern of industry evolution predicted and documented by Klepper—an increase in the number of firms in response to a novel technology followed by a rapid reduction in the number of firms—has an intriguing parallel in biological evolution, specifically the phenomenon of adaptive radiation. When a new environmental niche opens up, such as when a mass extinction event wipes out existing species in a region, or when a geological event such as a volcanic eruption creates a new and uninhabited island, there follows a rapid increase in the number and diversity of species that fill the newly created niches. But these adaptive radiations do not continue forever. At some point all available niches have been filled, and the number of species stabilizes. Exactly this process has been observed in the lab. Biologist Michael Brockhurst and colleagues have found that when bacteria are experimentally introduced into a new environment, adaptive radiation is more likely to occur if there are no resident bacteria already occupying the available niches.[11] When resident bacteria are already present, then the newly introduced bacteria are unlikely to diversify. This resembles Klepper's finding that companies are more likely to diversify and increase in number when entering a vacant market (e.g., the tire market at the start of the automobile industry) than when entering a filled market (e.g., the tire industry after 1923 following the convergence on the cord and balloon design).

Although still somewhat at the fringes of economics, Nelson and Winter's evolutionary theory of economic change is becoming increasingly influential (more so in Europe than the United States, interestingly). Empirical case studies illustrate the value of their evolutionary theory, such as cultural inertia within Polaroid caused by maladaptive, out-of-date routines, and the diversification-then-stabilization in the tire industry in response to a new technological niche. Traditional economic theory predicts that the Polaroid management should have exhibited rather more accurate foresight and switched from the old, inappropriate business model to a new, more appropriate business model. Under an evolutionary theory of the firm, the observed cultural inertia is unsurprising, given people's reliance on culturally transmitted routines. Similarly, if the managers of tire firms possessed perfect foresight then there should not have been so many failed firms in the automobile industry. According to an evolutionary theory, strong selection during an initial period when the environment has yet to be exploited is to be expected.

Behavioral Economics: Challenging the Myth of Pure Self-Interest

Another problem with the traditional economic model of human behavior is its assumption that people are entirely self-interested: that is, human behavior is guided solely by one's own economic payoff. This assumption has been challenged recently by a wealth of experimental and field studies that show that people are not ultimately self-interested. Most people seem to possess a strong sense of fairness, which in many cases results in unselfish behavior. Take the ultimatum game, for example, which was discussed in chapter 1. Recall that in the ultimatum game a proposer divides up a sum of money between themselves and a responder. This might be an entirely fair split of 50/50, or a selfish split, such as a 70/30 split in favor of the proposer. The responder can then choose to either accept the split, in which case both players get the specified amounts of money, or reject the offer, in which case neither player gets anything. A purely self-interested responder should accept any non-zero offer, given that any offer is better than nothing, which is what they get if they reject the offer. Proposers, knowing this, should therefore offer the smallest possible amount. Yet when Western undergraduates play the ultimatum game, the most common offer is a fair 50/50 split. This is because responders typically reject any offer less than 30 percent, and only reliably accept offers greater than 40 percent. Responders therefore appear to have an irrational sense of fairness: they are willing to forego a significant payoff (30 percent of an often quite large sum of actual money) if they think that the proposer is being unfair. As detailed in chapter 1, there is a substantial amount of cross-cultural variation in this finding, with some societies such as the Machiguenga of Peru exhibiting weaker fairness norms than Western undergraduates.[12] Yet despite this cross-cultural variation, no society ever studied exhibits purely self-interested behavior, as standard economic theory predicts they should.

This finding is not specific to the ultimatum game, however. A variety of other experimental setups, as well as actual labor markets, also shows that fairness concerns are a significant motivator of people's economic decision making.[13] For example, in the gift exchange game, an "employer" can offer a contract to a "worker" in which the employer agrees to pay the worker a fixed wage in return for a specified amount of effort in an experimental task. This contract is nonbinding, and workers receive the full preagreed wage no matter how much effort they put in. Employers receive a payoff proportional to the worker's effort minus their agreed wage, while workers receive a payoff proportional to the agreed wage minus their effort. A purely self-interested worker would take any nonzero wage and put zero effort in, giving them the maximum possible payoff (assuming that the game is played only once and participants are anonymous, which are the conditions of most actual gift exchange experiments). Employers, knowing this, should offer the minimum possible wage in order to minimize their losses. Yet real people don't behave in this way. The higher the offered wages are, the more effort the worker puts in. Again, a sense of fairness is at play here, motivating workers to honestly repay the wages offered to them in terms of effort even when this is unnecessary, and indeed reduces their payoff.

Such experimental findings are reinforced by field studies and real-life case studies. When workers feel that they are being treated unfairly, they protest by decreasing their work effort. One study found that tires produced at a plant where workers had been threatened with wage cuts and temporary contracts were of significantly lower quality than tires produced during the same period at the same company's other plants, which were unaffected by employment problems.[14] Another study found significantly more flight delays for an airline that had cut its pilots' wages simply in order to increase already-healthy company profits, compared to other airlines that cut pilot pay by the same amount but in order to avoid bankruptcy.[15] Finally, the introduction of a minimum wage has been shown to significantly, and irrationally, alter people's perceptions of a fair wage.[16] After it is introduced, a minimum wage is perceived by workers to be unfairly low, even if they were happy with the same wage level before the minimum wage was introduced. And when the minimum wage is removed, perceptions of a fair wage do not return to pre–minimum wage levels. They remain high, as if people's standards of fairness have been shifted. None of these findings are consistent with the assumption that people are purely self-interested. People are more cooperative than they should be, more concerned with what other people are receiving, and more motivated to punish selfish free riders than they should be if they were solely maximizing their own economic payoff. How can such a mismatch be explained?

One potential explanation centers on the theory of cultural group selection, as developed by anthropologists and economists including Robert Boyd, Ernst Fehr, Herbert Gintis, Joseph Henrich, and Peter Richerson.[17] These researchers argue that the tendencies to cooperate and punish free riders arose in our evolutionary past as a result of gene-culture coevolution. Specifically, cultural groups in which people cooperate with one another and punish selfish free riders would have, during human evolutionary history, outcompeted cultural groups that were less internally cooperative and allowed free riders to exploit collective rewards. This intergroup competition might be through direct conquest, because internally cooperative groups are more effective in intergroup warfare (e.g., members of cooperative groups are more likely to sacrifice themselves for the rest of the group and punish deserters or cowards). Or it might be through more indirect means, such as when people are more likely to migrate to groups that exhibit pro-social norms (e.g., providing welfare for the poor or sick). Whether direct or indirect, this cultural group selection may then have favored a set of genetically specified psychological dispositions such as those exhibited in the experiments and field studies discussed above, such as a tendency to cooperate with other members of one's group, and a sense of fairness that motivates people to punish selfish free riders. These genetically specified psychological dispositions would have then facilitated the cultural evolution of various large-scale cooperative institutions. At first, these large-scale institutions took the form of egalitarian hunter-gatherer societies. Then larger social groups emerged, such as the empires that were discussed in chapter 5. Indeed, Peter Turchin's theory of empire expansion and competition is an example of the general process of cultural group selection, where empires high in internal cohesiveness expand at the expense of empires that are less internally cohesive.[18]

Business firms may be a modern-day example of organizations that are made possible by culturally group selected cooperative tendencies.[19] Traditional economic theory (e.g., transaction cost theory) views business firms as a set of explicit rules that counteract people's intrinsic self-interest. Employment contracts that specify the minimal amount of required effort from an employee, for example, ensure that employees do not free ride. Yet we have already seen plenty of experimental and real-world evidence, such as the gift exchange game or the effect of minimum wages, that people are motivated not just by explicit contracts, but also by their sense of fairness and their unselfish, cooperative tendencies. Without the prosocial motives that have emerged as a result of cultural group selection, firms could not exist.

Economist Christian Cordes and colleagues have recently modeled the growth and contraction of firms using predictions derived from the cultural group selection hypothesis.[20] In their mathematical model, a firm exists that is composed of a number of workers. Workers are either cooperative, in which case they add profit to the firm by doing work, or selfish, in which case they contribute nothing to the firm's profits. All workers cost the firm wages. Two processes change the relative frequency of cooperative and selfish workers in the firm: genetically evolved psychological predispositions and prestige-biased cultural transmission. Regarding the former process, selfish psychological dispositions cause cooperative workers to become selfish: this represents the rational temptation to free ride. Cooperative psychological dispositions, on the other hand, cause selfish workers to become cooperative: this is the result of cultural group selection. Regarding the latter process, workers are assumed to copy the behavior of the entrepreneur who founded and leads the company (who is, by definition, "prestigious" within the organization). Entrepreneurs are assumed to be cooperative in their behavior. However, their influence depends on the size of the firm. It is more difficult for entrepreneurs to influence a large firm of hundreds or thousands of employees than a small firm with tens of employees. Every cultural generation, these two sets of processes act jointly on the frequency of cooperative and selfish employees in the firm. Firms grow when adding new employees increases profit and shrink when they are making a loss.

Cordes et al.'s model showed, first, that firms grow in size as prestige bias effectively transmits cooperative behavior from the entrepreneur to the employees. Once the firm reaches a certain size, however, the firm stops growing as the entrepreneur's influence cannot reach enough employees to make it cost-effective to grow further. Second, the higher the costs of selfish behavior relative to altruistic behavior, the smaller the firm size that can evolve. High costs of selfish behavior produce small firms of mostly cooperative workers motivated by their culturally group-selected altruistic dispositions. Low costs of selfish behavior allow firms to be larger but with a higher proportion of free riders. So Cordes et al.'s model suggests that firms initially grow in size due to cooperative behavior on the part of their members, before they reach a maximum size due to the temptation to free ride and the inability of leaders to invoke cooperation via direct social influence.

One implication of this model is that business managers can influence the cooperativeness of their firms by using prestige bias to invoke their employees' innate psychological dispositions to act cooperatively. Ultimately, this should result in higher profits, as employees voluntarily put more effort into their work. Indeed, a recent meta-analysis found a significant correlation between a firm's financial performance and its "social responsibility," such as the degree to which it fosters cooperation (rather than competition) between its employees.[21] Over time, a further process of cultural group selection may then act, as more internally cooperative firms outcompete less-cooperative firms in the marketplace.

Conclusions: Cultural Evolution Explains Economic Phenomena Better Than Standard Economic Theory

In this chapter we have seen how cultural evolutionary theory has been used to explain certain aspects of economic change that traditional economic theory cannot explain well. Cultural inertia prevents firms such as Polaroid from adopting new and better routines, while industries such as tire manufacturing exhibit a wasteful culling of firms that have not adequately exploited a new technology. Neither of these makes much sense under the standard economic assumption that people (and firms) can effectively and independently determine the most adaptive long-term strategy. Employees within firms also work harder than they should do if they were, as standard economic theory predicts, solely maximizing their own economic payoff. Instead, they are motivated by a sense of fairness and a tendency to cooperate even when there is no payoff for doing so. Such altruistic tendencies can be explained by a gene-culture coevolutionary theory based on the process of cultural group selection.

9 Culture in Nonhuman Species

Throughout the history of the social sciences, culture has typically been defined as something that only humans have. This can be seen in E. B. Tylor's famous 1871 definition of culture as "that complex whole which includes knowledge, beliefs, art, law, morals, custom, and any other capabilities and habits acquired by man as a member of society."[1] As should be apparent, the words "by man" indicate that Tylor was not thinking of nonhuman species when he came up with this definition. A. L. Kroeber, in his hugely influential 1948 cultural anthropology textbook, was even more explicit about this, writing that "we can approximate what culture is by saying it is that which the human species has and other social species lack."[2] Most subsequent definitions of culture adopted by cultural anthropologists have been derived from these sources, and the situation is not dissimilar in other branches of the social sciences.[3]

Defining culture as something that only humans have, however, is not a very scientifically productive thing to do. If culture is defined as something that only humans have, then this obviates the need to even look for similarities between the cultural capacities of humans and other species, which should surely be an empirical question. In fact, in the last few decades there has been an explosion in the study of nonhuman culture. This has been stimulated by a move away from the anthropocentric definitions of culture put forward by Tylor and Kroeber and toward the definition of culture given in chapter 1 as information that is acquired from other individuals via social transmission mechanisms such as imitation, teaching, or language. Not all of these exemplar social transmission mechanisms (e.g., language) are likely to apply to many, if any, nonhuman species. But if culture is defined in broad terms as socially transmitted information regardless of the specific transmission mechanism involved, then it is possible that culture, or some subset of the mechanisms that collectively constitute and allow human cultural evolution, are present in other species. Indeed, there is pretty solid evidence that this is the case. And the methods used to provide this evidence are in many cases exactly the same methods that have been described in the previous chapters as having been applied to human culture, such as ethnographic field observations, laboratory experiments, neutral drift models, and phylogenetic analyses.[4]

But why study nonhuman culture in the first place, and why should social scientists take any notice of such studies? There are at least two ways in which nonhuman studies can inform the study of human cultural evolution. The first is by telling us something about the biological evolutionary origin of the capacities for cultural evolution. The underlying capacities for cultural evolution surely did not spring from nowhere, and it is reasonable to assume that they evolved due to natural selection. And knowing what the selection pressures were that shaped these capacities might tell us something important about how they currently operate. If the anthropologists quoted above are correct and no other species is found to have any kind of cultural capacities, then we can infer that culture evolved de novo sometime in the last six million years since the human lineage split from our last common ancestor with chimpanzees, and that some aspect of Pliocene or Pleistocene environments was responsible for this appearance. If, on the other hand, we find one or more cultural capacities in all extant great ape species—chimpanzees, gorillas, orangutans, and humans—then we can infer that those capacities evolved much earlier, in the common ancestor shared by all these species.

This, however, assumes that descent is the only way in which two species can share traits. As we saw in chapter 4 in our discussion of phylogenetic analyses, it is also possible for traits to evolve in more than one lineage independently (making them homoplasies, rather than homologies). So we might find, for example, that a set of phylogenetically unrelated species exhibit the capacity for culture. This might tell us something about the conditions that favor the evolution of culture. If all of these species live in large groups, for example, then we might conclude that culture evolves in response to the demands of group living. Such a conclusion might have important implications for the kinds of processes we might expect to find in human cultural evolution, such as what kind of information should be favored by content biases. Only by carefully comparing the cultural capacities of different species can we answer these kinds of questions.

A second benefit of studies of nonhuman culture is a much sharper understanding of the different components that make up culture. This is somewhat counterintuitive: by broadening our definition of culture to include nonhuman species, we make our understanding of human culture more precise. This is because behavioral biologists and comparative psychologists studying nonhuman species cannot take it for granted that their subjects exhibit culture. They must demonstrate this empirically, and in so doing they carefully pick apart the precise mechanisms by which information is socially transmitted. Social scientists, on the other hand, can take it for granted that their subjects possess culture and so have not been required to study it in as detailed a fashion. For example, whereas social psychologists, cultural anthropologists, and sociologists have sometimes put forward somewhat vague theories about how people acquire information culturally, such as "socialization" or "enculturation," behavioral biologists have precisely defined and empirically identified a range of distinct social learning processes, such as imitation, emulation, stimulus enhancement, response facilitation, and observational conditioning. Yet there is no reason why this list should not also apply to human social learning. Moreover, cross-species comparisons have identified three different aspects of culture—one-to-one social learning, cultural traditions, and cumulative cultural evolution—that have distinct characteristics and appear to be underpinned by different underlying mechanisms. Yet they have often been conflated in humans, because we, unlike other species, have all three.

For these reasons, it is important that any science of cultural evolution acknowledges and is informed by studies of the cultural abilities of nonhuman species. The following sections outline the evidence for nonhuman culture as obtained from field and experimental studies and then discuss the implications of this evidence for the study of human cultural evolution.

Social Learning Is Widespread and Adaptive

Countless field and laboratory experiments have shown that numerous species have the capacity for social learning, defined in minimal terms as where one individual acquires information from a second individual nongenetically, as a result of exposure to the second individual's behavior.[5] For example, rats learn what is good to eat by sniffing the breath of other rats: when given a choice between food that they have previously smelled on the breath of another rat or novel food not previously encountered, rats prefer the former. Guppies learn how to get to food from other guppies: when given a choice between two routes to a food source, guppies prefer the route along which they had previously followed a larger shoal, even when the alternative route is shorter. Rhesus monkeys learn what to fear from other rhesus monkeys: laboratory-born monkeys only develop fear responses to snakes if they observe another monkey acting afraid in the presence of a snake. Female quails learn who to mate with from other females: when female quails are given a choice between mating with a male that they had previously seen mating with another female or with a male that they had not seen mating, they choose the former. Many species of songbird learn local song dialects from other songbirds: a male cowbird caught in one region and moved to another location sings the song of neighboring adult males rather than the song of its father. Octopuses learn to identify prey from other octopuses: an octopus that has seen another octopus attack a red ball prefers to attack red balls rather than white balls, and vice versa. Honeybees learn how to find food from other honeybees: upon returning to the hive, bees that have found a novel, high-quality source of food perform a waggle dance in which the direction of the dance indicates the direction of the food relative to the sun, and the duration of the dance indicates the distance of the food from the hive.

We should perhaps not be surprised that social learning is so widespread in the animal kingdom. Social learning provides a quick and cheap shortcut to the acquisition of adaptive information: what to eat and where to find it, who to mate with and how to attract those mates, what predators to avoid, and so on, without going through the time-consuming and potentially costly process of individual trial-and-error experimentation. Why run the risk of eating something poisonous if you can copy what other individuals are eating? If they're still alive, you can be reasonably sure that it's not too deadly. Mathematical models confirm the adaptive benefit of learning in cases where aspects of a species's environment change too rapidly for genetic evolution to track, such as the identity and location of food.[6] However, the social learning of information from one individual to another is only one aspect of culture, perhaps its most basic. Most social scientists would struggle to see the relevance of the above findings for human culture, which surely is far more complex than rats sniffing each other's breath or fish shoaling together. But how exactly is it different?

From Social Learning to Cultural Traditions

While one-to-one social learning is necessary for any kind of culture, a distinctive element of human culture is the presence of group-specific *traditions*. These occur when all or most of the members of one group exhibits one behavior, while all or most of the members of another group exhibits a different behavior, and these group-level differences can be explained in terms of social learning rather than as the product of genetic differences between the groups, or of individual learning in response to different external conditions. A familiar example among humans involves eating utensils: most people who live in East Asia use chopsticks, while most people living in the West use knives and forks. This is not a genetic difference—there are no genes for using chopsticks or forks—and nothing in the physical environments of East Asia and the West favors the use of the different utensils. Rather, the differences represent cultural traditions: people in East Asia use chopsticks because they acquired the tendency and skill to use chopsticks from other members of their societies, most likely their parents, while Westerners use knives and forks because they acquired knife-and-fork-use behavior from other Westerners. This group-specific aspect of culture is not necessarily the same as the one-to-one social learning outlined previously. In order for a behavior to become traditional, it must be transmitted not only from one individual to another, but across all members of a social group without any significant loss of fidelity. It must also persist for long enough such that distinct group-level cultural traditions can be clearly identified. This would likely be a minimum of one biological generation.

So do nonhuman species have cultural traditions? In a landmark paper published in 1999, a team of nine primatologists led by Andrew Whiten of the University of St. Andrews in Scotland provided evidence that different groups of chimpanzees living across Africa exhibit behavioral differences that, the researchers argued, are cultural in origin.[7] The researchers took what they called an ethnographic approach to the question of chimpanzee culture, in the sense that each of them had spent decades observing at close quarters the behavior of chimpanzees at their respective study sites across the breadth of Africa, from Uganda in the east to the Ivory Coast in the west. They then combined this with an ethnological, or "cross-cultural," comparison of chimpanzee behavior across these sites. The aim was to identify behaviors that fulfilled the researchers' criterion of being cultural in origin. Following the description of cultural traditions above, this criterion was that the behavior must be exhibited by all or most members of at least one group but absent in at least one other group, and where this presence or absence could not be explained by ecological differences (much like the chopstick/knife-and-fork example given above). As a result, Whiten et al. identified thirty-nine behaviors that fulfilled this criterion of being cultural in origin. For example, chimpanzees living in two west African sites, Bossou in Guinea and Tai Forest in the Ivory Coast, have been observed cracking open nuts by placing them on a large flat stone and hitting them with another smaller stone, essentially using the two stones as a hammer and an anvil. In contrast, chimpanzees at two east African sites in Tanzania, Gombe and Mahale, have never been observed cracking nuts in this way, despite the presence both of nuts and of stones suitable for use as hammers and anvils. Other behaviors identified as cultural in this way include fishing for termites and ants using sticks, using leaves to squash parasites, and what is known as hand clasping, a social custom where two chimps clasp one hand each above their heads and groom each other with their other hands.

Whiten et al.'s study received a great deal of attention in the scientific community. There quickly followed a series of studies claiming to show similar patterns of between-group cultural variation in other species, not only primates such as orangutans and capuchin monkeys but also other large-brained mammals such as dolphins and whales.[8] Some groups of bottlenose dolphins, for example, have been observed breaking off a piece of marine sponge, carrying it in their mouths and using it to probe for fish in the seabed. Other groups do not show this practice, leading to the suggestion that such group differences are cultural in origin. And the original chimpanzee culture study has gained support from experimental studies with captive chimpanzees that show that chimpanzee social learning is of sufficiently high fidelity to generate stable and persistent group differences, and phylogenetic analyses that show that the distribution of the thirty-nine putative cultural variants cannot be explained in terms of genetic differences between the chimpanzee groups.[9]

Cultural traditions have not only been demonstrated for large-brained mammals, however. In fact, it has been argued by some researchers that even better evidence for cultural traditions exists for fish and birds than for primates and cetaceans.[10] This is because the kinds of experimental manipulations that are necessary to conclusively demonstrate that behavioral variation is cultural rather than genetic or the result of individual learning are impractical or unethical to perform on primates and cetaceans. Take this experiment performed by Gene Helfman and Eric Schultz on French grunts, a small fish species that lives in the waters off the coast of the US Virgin Islands.[11] First, Helfman and Schultz took juveniles from one site and placed them in a new group. These transplanted juveniles adopted the same schooling sites and migratory routes as the existing residents of their new group rather than the schooling sites and migratory routes of their original group. This rules out genetic inheritance, given that the transplanted juveniles were unrelated to the residents of the new site. Second, control fish were transplanted to the same site but only after all of the residents had been removed. In this case, the transplanted juveniles did *not* adopt the same schooling sites and migratory routes as the previous residents had used. Instead, they adopted new sites and routes, and these sites and routes persisted longer than a generation. This rules out individual learning, which we might assume would have caused the transplanted juveniles to independently rediscover the same high-quality schooling sites and migratory routes that the residents had discovered. These experimental manipulations therefore demonstrate that choice of schooling site and migratory routes are socially learned cultural traditions.

Birdsong is another well-studied example of nonhuman cultural traditions. As noted above, many species of songbird have distinct song dialects that characterize different regions, just as human languages show regional dialects. Similar relocation experiments to those described above for fish have shown that juvenile male birds learn song dialects from adult males of their local group, ruling out genetic and individual learning explanations. Consequently, some researchers have explicitly described birdsong as a process of cultural evolution and have explained cultural variation in birdsong using the same neutral drift models that geneticists use to explain the distribution of functionally neutral genes and that cultural evolution researchers use to explain the distribution of functionally neutral cultural traits such as pottery decorations, as we saw in chapter 4. For example, Alejandro Lynch and Allan Baker have shown that within-group diversity in the song dialects of sixteen chaffinch populations from various islands in the North Atlantic, as well as mainland Spain and Morocco, is consistent with a neutral drift model in which song syllables (the smallest building blocks of songs) are assumed to be functionally equivalent and change according to the processes of random copying from individual to individual, random mutation due to copying errors in transmission, and the migration of birds from one group to another.[12] As noted in chapter 4, under the neutral drift model we would expect diversity, in this case song diversity, to decrease as population size decreases, because rare variants are more likely to be lost due to sampling accidents. Consistent with this prediction, Lynch and Baker observed greater song diversity in the larger populations of chaffinch found on the Azores Islands compared to the smaller mainland populations. Despite the greater attention devoted to studies of chimpanzee culture, studies of birdsong such as Lynch and Baker's remain perhaps the most sophisticated studies of cultural change in any nonhuman species yet conducted.

So several species have been shown to exhibit cultural traditions, that is, stable behavioral differences between different social groups that are the result of social learning. This includes not only big-brained primates and cetaceans, which have cultural traditions of tool use and social customs, but also birds, which have cultural traditions of song dialects, and fish, which exhibit cultural traditions for schooling sites and migratory routes. Sophisticated social learning mechanisms, such as teaching or language, do not appear to be necessary to generate stable cultural traditions.

From Cultural Traditions to Cumulative Cultural Evolution

While chimpanzee nut cracking or dolphin sponging are certainly impressive, they do not seem to be on the same scale as products of human cultural evolution such as computers, spacecraft, constitutional democracy, or quantum physics. One important way in which human culture appears to differ from the culture of any other species is that human culture is *cumulative*. The products of human culture are in many cases the result of the gradual accumulation of many successive modifications, with each incremental modification increasing the effectiveness of the cultural trait in question. Think of elements of technology that we take for granted, such as computers or automobiles. The car is the end product of thousands of years of successive innovations, from the wheel and fire in prehistoric times, to the internal combustion engine, the first workable models of which were developed in the mid-to-late-1800s, right up to recent modifications such as airbags and hybrid electric vehicles. Knowledge also accumulates gradually: the mathematical knowledge taught to schoolchildren today is the accumulated product of over four thousand years of successive modifications, from the invention of written numerical symbols by the Sumerians in 2400 BC, to the addition of the decimal system by the Babylonians, the invention of zero by the Hindus and Mayans, geometry by the Greeks, algebra by the Arabs, calculus by Europeans, and right up to modern-day advances in mathematics.[13]

In such cases, the products of human cultural evolution far exceed anything that a single person could ever invent on their own and in a single lifetime. Imagine a Robinson Crusoe–like character stranded on a desert island. Even if all of the raw materials were present, surely the chances that he or she could ever invent anything like a car or a computer from scratch are practically zero. The cumulative character of human culture has been highlighted by comparative psychologist Michael Tomasello.[14] Tomasello uses the metaphor of a ratchet to describe human culture. A ratchet is a rotating disc that has asymmetrical teeth around the edges that allow movement in one direction, but prevent movement in the other direction. Once the disc rotates a certain distance, the teeth lock the wheel in place to prevent it slipping backward. In the same way, Tomasello argues that the defining characteristic of human culture is that modifications gradually accumulate over time without being lost.[15]

In contrast, none of the examples of nonhuman cultural traditions given above appear to be the product of cumulative culture. The examples in fish of culturally acquired schooling site preferences and migratory routes are in no real sense accumulated in that they cannot be separated out into constituent subcomponents that could potentially have been built up over time. Moreover, a single fish could easily discover a particular schooling site on their own. Birdsong, while showing clear change over time, does not accumulate changes of increasing functional effectiveness. Indeed, the fact that birdsong fits the expectations of neutral drift models shows that different song syllables are functionally neutral. And while the culturally transmitted tool-using behaviors of chimpanzees, orangutans, and dolphins are impressive, they too do not appear to be composed of a series of smaller components that could have accumulated over time in the way that a car or computer does. It also does not seem unreasonable that a single chimpanzee, given nuts, stones, and enough time, could invent nut cracking on his or her own. It might take a lot longer than if they had another chimpanzee to copy, but it seems possible nonetheless, whereas our Robinson Crusoe character surely has no chance whatsoever of inventing an iPod or discovering the double-helical structure of DNA from scratch.

This distinction between cumulative and noncumulative culture is hugely important, because only the former constitutes the gradual evolutionary change that Darwin termed "descent with modification." In other words, only humans exhibit a fully Darwinian process of cultural evolution. In recent years much attention has been devoted to figuring out why this is the case: what crucial cognitive capacity do humans possess, and every other species lack, that makes cumulative cultural evolution possible?

Imitation versus Emulation. An early suggestion put forward by Tomasello concerned the fidelity of cultural transmission.[16] In order to accumulate modifications over time, it is necessary to successfully preserve every previous modification that has gone before. If previously discovered knowledge is easily lost or distorted, then it cannot be added to and built upon by others. Specifically, Tomasello argued that only humans have cumulative culture because only humans are capable of *imitation*, which comparative psychologists define as the copying of another individual's bodily actions. He contrasted this with *emulation*, which is defined as the copying of the end product of another individual's actions, rather than the actions themselves. For example, learning how to serve in tennis by *imitation* would involve observing and copying the bodily movements of an already-proficient tennis player while they execute a serve. Learning how to serve in tennis by *emulation* would involve copying just the end result of serving, that is, that the ball has to land within the serving area. Because emulation does not involve the copying of exact behavior, only the end products of behavior, according to Tomasello it does not provide sufficiently high fidelity to support cumulative culture. In the tennis example, only imitation can preserve the precise technique with which successful players serve; each emulator would have to reinvent the serving technique from scratch, severely limiting the accumulation of effective actions.

Experiments conducted in the 1980s and 1990s appeared to support this idea that nonhuman species are capable of emulation but not imitation, finding that whereas chimpanzees tend to copy the end products of a demonstrator's actions, they do not copy the actions themselves.[17] However, more recent experiments that are more directly designed to simulate the cultural traditions observed in the wild have challenged these initial findings. In a study conducted by Andrew Whiten, Victoria Horner, and Frans de Waal, two separate groups of captive chimpanzees were tasked with using a sticklike tool to get food out of a tubelike apparatus.[18] This apparatus was designed to simulate the kind of tool-based foraging tasks that chimpanzees face in the wild, and for which solutions are thought to be acquired via social learning. In the experimental task, food could be obtained in one of two equally effective ways: either by poking the stick into a hole in the apparatus, which pushed a blockage and allowed the food to roll out, or by using the stick to lift a hook on the top of the apparatus, which lifted the flap and released the food. In the training phase, one chimpanzee was removed from the first group and taught to use the "poke" method, while another chimpanzee was removed from the second group and taught the "lift" method. These two individuals were then put back into their respective original groups and every chimpanzee was given access to the apparatus. Over the next ten days, the researchers tracked the spread of each method through the two groups.

The results re-created the cultural traditions observed in the wild: the majority of chimpanzees in the first group used the poke method, while the majority of chimpanzees in the second group used the lift method. And these differences remained when the groups were retested two months later. This could only have occurred if the chimpanzees were copying, probably by imitation, the exact method exhibited by the taught, demonstrator chimpanzee, rather than just emulating the end result, which after all was the same in both groups (using a stick to get food). Subsequent studies by Whiten and colleagues have shown that tool-use methods can be transmitted faithfully along linear chains of chimpanzees using the same transmission chain method that we saw in chapter 6 has been used to study human cultural transmission, and that tool-use methods can pass from group to group as well as between individuals within groups.[19] While these experiments do not simulate *cumulative* culture, they do show that chimpanzee social learning is of sufficiently high fidelity to preserve specific actions at a group level, suggesting that a lack of imitation is unlikely to be the answer to the question of why chimpanzees, at least, do not have cumulative culture.

Overimitation. Other studies have shown that while chimpanzees *can* imitate, they do not show the seemingly spontaneous compulsion to comprehensively imitate that humans, and especially human children, do. In one experiment demonstrating this, Victoria Horner and Andrew Whiten presented both adult chimpanzees and human children with a box on which a demonstrator performed a mix of relevant and irrelevant actions.[20] The relevant action involved opening a door on the box and using a rod to hook out some food. The irrelevant action involved inserting the rod into a hole in the top of the box and tapping on a solid surface. The box was either opaque, which hid from the participants the fact that the irrelevant action was irrelevant to getting food, or transparent, in which case the irrelevance of the irrelevant action was clear to see.

When allowed to interact with the box following the demonstration, the chimpanzees faithfully copied the irrelevant action in the opaque condition but not in the transparent condition. We might think that this is quite sensible behavior: why waste time performing the irrelevant action when you can see that it clearly has no effect on whether you get food or not? The really interesting finding, however, concerned the human children. For the children, it made no difference whether the box was opaque or transparent. They faithfully imitated every action demonstrated to them, even the irrelevant action, and even on the transparent box where it was clear that the action had no effect on whether the food got released. Subsequent studies have shown that children copy obviously irrelevant actions even when they are alone and unobserved, showing that they are not simply trying to please the experimenter, and even when the demonstrator clearly identifies the irrelevant action as being "silly and unnecessary."[21]

In the words of the authors of these studies, the children were "overimitating"—imitating even when it was unnecessary to do so. This suggests that cumulative culture may depend not only on the *ability* to imitate others but also on the *compulsion* to imitate others. If children compulsively imitate adults' behavior, then cultural modifications are more likely to be preserved and accumulate over successive generations compared to the flexible imitation-emulation switching shown by chimpanzees. The price might be the occasional copying of irrelevant or even maladaptive behaviors, but this might be compensated for by the adaptive benefits provided by the products of cumulative culture. Of course, this compulsion could not be so strong as to prevent new, beneficial traits to ever be invented or acquired, otherwise there would be nothing new to accumulate.

The Stickiness of Nonhuman Culture. Other recent studies with chimpanzees and children have presented an alternative explanation for the former's lack of cumulative culture. Rather than a lack of transmission fidelity, it may be that other species do not possess the ability to easily switch to a newly encountered, better way of doing something. Instead, they show a preponderance to stick with their existing solution to a problem. This "stickiness" prevents nonhuman species from cumulatively building up successively more effective cultural elements.

This idea is supported by a recent experiment conducted by Sarah Marshall-Pescini and Andrew Whiten.[22] A group of chimpanzees was presented with an apparatus consisting of pots with honey inside. These pots could be opened in one of two ways. The first, not very efficient, method involved opening a small trap door, inserting a stick into the trap door, and licking honey off the stick. A second and more efficient method represented a cumulative step up from the previous one: the same stick could be used to poke a small bolt on the side of each pot, after which the entire lid could be opened, giving full access to the honey inside. This second method was a cumulative step up because it contained within it the action involved in the first method—inserting a stick into a hole—but as part of a larger sequence of actions. A group of eleven chimpanzees were first shown the simple dipping technique by a human demonstrator, after which five of the older members learned this skill. In the second phase of the experiment, the five chimpanzees who had mastered the simple dipping technique were shown the more complicated probing technique. Despite the greater effectiveness of the probing method, only one of the five chimpanzees switched to it from the dipping method, and there was evidence that this chimpanzee had discovered the probing method on his own prior to demonstration of the dipping technique. In contrast, eight out of twelve human children given the same task successfully switched from the simpler dipping method to the more efficient probing method. Another study by Christine Hrubesch, Signe Preuschoft, and Carel van Schaik similarly found that chimpanzees who had learned to use sticks to get food from an out-of-reach tray were unwilling to switch to a more effective method of shaking the tray, even when they could see other chimpanzees doing better with this method.[23] Although both of these studies are limited by small sample sizes, the similar findings that chimpanzees are poor at switching to better solutions to problems and prefer to stick with existing solutions, however inefficient, points to a possible explanation for their lack of cumulative culture. If chimpanzees always stick with adequate solutions, then even if a better solution did appear, perhaps by copying error or from a particularly innovative individual, then it would not spread, and beneficial skills would not accumulate over time.

Teaching (and Wanting to Be Taught). Another suggestion for the key to cumulative cultural evolution is teaching. Developmental psychologists Gergely Csibra and Gyorgy Gergely of the Central European University in Hungary argue that humans, uniquely compared to other species, have communication systems that are designed by natural selection to effectively transmit information between individuals.[24] Specifically, they argue that adults are predisposed to tailor their speech and their actions to make it as easy as possible for infants to learn something useful from them. Human infants, in turn, have evolved to assume (not necessarily consciously) that adults' speech and actions are tailored to be maximally relevant. Csibra and Gergely call this system, in which both adults and infants tailor their communication to maximize the likelihood that the infant will acquire useful knowledge from the adult, "natural pedagogy" (I will here use the more reader-friendly term "teaching").

Csibra and Gergely argue that teaching is particularly useful when what has to be learned is "cognitively opaque," that is, when it is not immediately obvious what function other people's actions serve. Much of cumulative culture is likely to involve the transmission of cognitively opaque actions. Think of making even the simplest of tools, such as the Acheulean handaxes encountered in chapter 4. Handaxe construction involves a series of sequential steps: locating raw materials, transporting raw materials to a construction site, slowly chipping off flakes from the rock, and so on, all without any immediate payoff. In such situations, it would pay for infants to simply assume that what adults are doing is in some way useful, and imitate what they do. This is similar to the idea of overimitation encountered above.

Csibra and Gergely have carried out several studies with human infants that indicate that infants automatically assume that adults communicate to them relevant or useful information. For example, six-month-olds only follow an adult's eye gaze toward an object if the adult first makes eye contact with the infant, and/or the adult speaks directly to the infant, suggesting that even at this young age infants understand that certain gestures indicate an adult's intention to communicate useful information.[25] In another study, fourteen-month-olds saw an adult demonstrate the unusual action of switching on a light with their foreheads rather than their hands, before being asked to switch on the light themselves.[26] In a condition where the adults' hands were wrapped under a blanket, the infants tended to ignore the adults' forehead method and instead used their hands to switch on the light. When the adults' hands were free, however, the infants copied the adults exactly and used their heads to switch on the light. Csibra and Gergely interpreted this result as consistent with the assumption that adults' communication is generally designed to transmit useful information. In the latter hands-free condition, the infants assumed that there must be a good reason for the adults' unusual forehead method, and so they copied it. In the other condition, the head method was incidental because the adults' hands were wrapped up, so the infants assumed that the head method was not what the adults intended them to copy.

Do nonhuman species teach their young in this way? For a long time, teaching was believed to be unique to humans, although in recent years a few examples have been documented of teaching in nonhuman species. Adult meerkats, for example, are known to present juvenile meerkats with dead, disabled, or intact scorpions so that the juveniles can practice killing them.[27] Importantly, the state of the scorpion depends on the age of the juveniles: the youngest meerkats are presented with dead scorpions, older juveniles are presented with disabled scorpions, and the oldest juveniles are presented with intact scorpions. The adult meerkats therefore appear to be tailoring their behavior to make it as easy as possible for the juveniles to learn, which certainly resembles teaching in humans. There are two ways in which it differs, however. First, meerkat teaching is restricted to a single behavior, catching and disabling scorpions, whereas human teaching involves the transmission of a much wider range of generalizable knowledge. Second, the juvenile meerkats' learning may be facilitated by the adults, but they still have to learn how to kill the scorpions themselves using individual learning. They do not directly copy the actions of adults via social learning, as human children do. So given these differences, perhaps there is good reason to believe that teaching plays some role in supporting cumulative cultural evolution in humans.

Conclusions: Other Species Have Culture, But Not Cultural Evolution

Although numerous species exhibit one-to-one social learning and regional cultural traditions, no species other than humans appears to exhibit cumulative culture, where increasingly effective modifications are gradually accumulated over successive generations. This might therefore be described as the defining characteristic of human culture, and indeed it is this aspect that makes human culture fully Darwinian, given Darwin's description of evolution as "descent with modification." Without studies of nonhuman culture, it is doubtful that these distinctions between one-to-one social learning, cultural traditions, and cumulative culture would have been recognized, because humans have all three.

Why only humans have cumulative cultural evolution remains unclear. Several suggestions have been proposed, including imitation (rather than emulation), overimitation (imitating even when functionally unnecessary), switching (from existing solutions to novel, better solutions), and teaching. While the first of these—imitation rather than emulation—does not appear to be supported, the others all remain viable candidates for processes that permit cumulative culture. But this is not an exhaustive list by any means. Other suggestions not considered here include theory of mind, symbolic communication, language (spoken or written), and cooperation. Some of these suggestions are already being tested by psychologists in experiments designed to simulate cumulative cultural evolution in the lab. For example, psychologists Christine Caldwell and Ailsa Millen had chains of adult human participants build and fly paper airplane models, with the aim of flying them as far as possible.[28] Different chains varied in how they could learn from previous generations: some could only see the end product of the previous generation (simulating emulation), others could observe the previous generation building their planes (simulating imitation), while others were taught by a participant from a previous generation (simulating teaching). Over successive generations, plane-building skills appeared to accumulate, given that the planes of later generations flew further than planes of early generations. Yet the means of transmission (emulation, imitation, and/or teaching) had absolutely no effect on the extent or rate of accumulation. Although just a single study, this finding seems to count against both the imitation and the teaching explanations for cumulative cultural evolution cited above. No doubt future research with both human and nonhuman participants will build on this initial finding and identify the key to cumulative cultural evolution.

10   Toward an Evolutionary Synthesis for the Social Sciences

I argued in chapter 1 that, despite voluminous evidence that culture affects several important aspects of human behavior, there are three main problems with how the social sciences currently study culture. First, many social science disciplines (e.g., cultural anthropology) have eschewed quantitative scientific methods, thus limiting their ability to generate clear, testable predictions and converge on increasingly more accurate explanations of cultural phenomena. Second, while many other disciplines (e.g., psychology, economics) are fully scientific, rigorous, and quantitative, they either ignore culture and instead focus on the behavior of single individuals, or they treat culture as a static background variable rather than as something that changes over time in response to individual people's behavior. Third, the social sciences are currently so fractionated that different disciplines speak different languages, hold mutually incompatible theoretical assumptions, and seldom communicate findings across disciplinary boundaries. In the chapters that followed, I attempted to show that all these problems can be solved if culture is treated as a Darwinian evolutionary process. Because this involved the discussion of research across several different disciplines, using several different methods, and dealing with several different kinds of phenomena, I will now summarize how each problem has been addressed.

Advantages of Evolutionary Methods

The Benefits of Formal Models. Cultural evolution researchers have borrowed scientific, quantitative tools developed in evolutionary biology for studying genetic change and applied them to aspects of cultural change. In many cases these evolutionary methods have yielded demonstrably better explanations of cultural phenomena than traditional, nonevolutionary social science methods, which often tend to rely on verbal argument and informal comparisons. While informal, qualitative methods are useful as a way of initially generating hypotheses, without translating those hypotheses into quantitative terms it is often impossible to test them against real-world data and, ultimately, determine their validity. And without this formal hypothesis testing, explanations for cultural phenomena often descend into verbal arguments back and forth between scholars, each of whom believes their pet theory to be better than the other's, with no real way to determine who is correct.

For example, the population-genetic-style mathematical models described in chapter 3 formalize several cultural microevolutionary processes that have been informally proposed by social scientists to explain various cultural phenomena, such as conformity (preferentially copying the most common group behavior), prestige bias (preferentially learning from prestigious individuals), and vertical cultural transmission (learning from one's parents). The advantage of formal models is that the macroevolutionary consequences of these microevolutionary processes can be precisely specified and then tested for in real-world data. Joseph Henrich, for example, showed that cultural selection is more likely to be responsible for the diffusion of technological innovations through societies than guided variation because real-life innovations tend to exhibit S-shaped diffusion curves, which models show is consistent with cultural selection, rather than an r-shaped diffusion curve, which models showed to be indicative of guided variation. Similarly, Alex Bentley and colleagues showed that various real-world phenomena, such as first names, patent citations, pottery motifs, and dog breeds, are distributed in a way that is consistent with a purely random copying model, where traits (names, motifs, breeds, etc.) are intrinsically equal in fitness and are copied at random. These nonintuitive findings would not have been possible without the use of quantitative evolutionary models similar to those employed in evolutionary biology.

The phylogenetic methods discussed in chapters 4 and 5 also provide several examples of the advantages of formal evolutionary methods. Phylogenetic methods provide a formal way of reconstructing the historical relationships between culturally transmitted artifacts, behavioral practices, manuscripts, or languages in a way that is more accurate than informal, subjective means of classifying these phenomena. Phylogenetic methods have often been used to resolve outstanding issues in the social sciences, such as Russell Gray and colleagues' findings that Austronesian languages originated in Taiwan rather than Indonesia, and Indo-European languages spread via Anatolian farmers rather than Kurgan horsemen, or Ruth Mace and colleagues' findings that patriliny emerged as a result of the adoption of cattle, and that bridewealth is ancestral to dowry. As Mace has argued, phylogenetic methods provide a solution to Galton's problem—that societies are not always independent data points due to shared descent—that has hindered previous cross-cultural comparisons in anthropology.

Cultural Evolutionary Methods Are Intrinsically Social and Dynamic. Unlike traditional theoretical approaches within economics and cognitive science, which assume that people are independent, asocial creatures, cultural evolutionary theory explicitly acknowledges cultural influences on human behavior. As discussed in chapter 1, these influences are many and significant. In chapter 6, we saw how experimental methods such as the transmission chain method are extending traditional psychology experiments by allowing people to solve problems not only on their own but also by copying others. Often this leads to surprising and illuminating findings, such as Simon Kirby and colleagues' finding that several aspects of real-life languages such as compositionality emerge in an artificial language simply through the act of transmitting that language through successive people, or Andrew Schotter and Barry Sopher's experimental finding that culturally transmitted advice allows participants to coordinate their behavior in an economic transaction. Chapter 8 contained several real-world examples of how culturally transmitted routines shape economic decision making.

Evolutionary methods also, by their very nature, explicitly incorporate change over time. We saw in chapter 8 how Richard Nelson and Sidney Winter used evolutionary concepts and models to update standard nonevolutionary economic models, which tend to focus on static equilibria at a single point in time. This can explain hitherto puzzling aspects of economic markets, such as the failure of companies like Polaroid to change their business model in response to technological change and the rather wasteful proliferation of companies following a novel technological innovation, as observed in the tire industry. Similarly, Peter Turchin's dynamical models of historical change discussed in chapter 5 allow quantitative tests of traditional explanations for the rise and fall of empires during history, pointing to deficiencies of those theories (that they are "first order," i.e., contain only a single state variable) and to what a better explanation might look like (one that contains a second state variable, such as social cohesiveness).

Interdisciplinarity. The traditional social sciences are hindered by the separation of different methods and different subjects into different disciplines: psychologists conduct laboratory experiments, cultural anthropologists conduct ethnographic fieldwork, archaeologists document prehistory, and economists construct models of market systems. Because these different disciplines seldom communicate and do not share a common theoretical framework, findings obtained using one method are seldom used to guide research in other disciplines that use other methods. This is a huge missed opportunity, given that different methods often complement one another's strengths and weaknesses. For example, lab experiments have the advantage of high internal validity, such as control over potentially confounding variables, the ability to "re-run" history multiple times, the ability to manipulate variables, and the access to uninterrupted, complete data sets. Yet these advantages are offset by their lack of external validity, given that an hourlong experiment with (typically) Western undergraduates in the artificial setting of the psychology lab may not accurately capture real-life historical change in bow-and-arrow technology or entire languages over many thousands of years under very different conditions. Yet these strengths and weaknesses are perfectly complemented by the exact opposite strengths and weaknesses of archaeological and historical methods, which have high external validity in their direct measurement of real-life cultural change yet low internal validity in their lack of control over variables, inability to replicate results, and so on. When combined, experimental and historical methods (and mathematical models, and ethnographic methods, and phylogenetic analyses, and so on) provide a more complete understanding of cultural change than any one method alone.

Because cultural evolution theory provides a common language and common set of assumptions, we have come across several cases where multiple methods have been used in this way. For example, in chapter 6 I discussed how Matthew Spencer and colleagues tested the ability of various phylogenetic methods to accurately reconstruct actual manuscript evolution, for which the true historical relationships are not known for certain, by applying them to experimentally generated manuscripts, for which the actual historical relationships were known with absolute certainty. Similarly, links were made in chapter 6 between archaeology and psychology by myself and Michael O'Brien, when we simulated in the psychology lab the cultural evolution of arrowhead designs. The ability to manipulate variables allowed us to test a particular hypothesis—that designs in prehistoric Nevada were influenced by prestige bias whereas designs in prehistoric California were influenced by guided variation—that archaeologists can only infer from incomplete historical records. We also saw a fusion of ethnographic and phylogenetic (i.e., historical) methods in chapter 4, when Jamie Tehrani and Mark Collard used ethnographic findings to explain the strong treelike phylogenetic pattern in Turkmen textile evolution, specifically by showing that social norms prohibiting women from interacting with members of other groups prevent the blending of textile lineages.

Another advantage of interdisciplinary synthesis is the explanation of what appear to be diverse cultural phenomena in terms of a handful of common underlying processes. This is a commonplace in biology, where what appear to be incredibly diverse biological phenomena (e.g., peacock tails, bower bird nests, the antlers of both deer and beetles) are explained in terms of the same basic underlying process (e.g., sexual selection). Yet generalization across societies and languages is much less common in the social sciences, where each case is typically considered in terms of its own unique characteristics. While there are undoubtedly many differences between the way in which different kinds of cultural phenomena (e.g., technology, language, religions, firms) evolve, there may nevertheless be important common underlying microevolutionary processes that are shared by each. Conformity, for example, may explain both the diffusion of technological innovations (chapter 3), the slow mutation rate of commonly used words (chapter 5) and bubbles and crashes in the stock market (chapter 2). Some kind of culturally group-selected cooperative tendency might explain both the historical rise and fall of empires (chapter 5) and the contemporary expansion and contraction of business firms (chapter 8). Identifying common causes across these superficially diverse phenomena might lead to their discovery in yet other cases, once researchers know what to look for.

Toward a Synthesis

Just as evolutionary theory served in the 1930s to synthesize the previously fractured biological sciences within a common and unifying theoretical framework, the interdisciplinary connections highlighted in the previous section suggest that a similar synthesis is possible and may be nearing for the social sciences. In chapter 2, we saw how the synthesis in biology was made possible by the mathematical models of Fisher, Haldane, and Wright, who showed formally how the newly discovered neo-Darwinian microevolutionary principles of particulate and non-Lamarckian genetic inheritance were consistent with observed macroevolutionary patterns such as gradual change and species diversity. The mathematical models of Cavalli-Sforza, Feldman, Boyd, and Richerson outlined in chapter 3 provide a similar bridge between processes of cultural microevolution as studied by psychologists and microeconomists, such as conformity, prestige bias, Lamarckian-like guided variation or blending inheritance (many of which differ from neo-Darwinian microevolutionary processes in biology), and patterns of cultural macroevolution, as studied by anthropologists, archaeologists, historians, historical linguists, and macroeconomists.

But perhaps we can go further than this basic micro-macro link and try to map out exactly what a synthetic evolutionary science of culture might look like.[1] Given the Darwinian parallels between biological and cultural evolution, it is not unreasonable to assume that the structure of any science of cultural evolution might broadly resemble the structure of the science of biological evolution, that is, evolutionary biology. Figure 10.1 attempts to make this mapping explicit. On the left, I have sketched out the structure of evolutionary biology as it has emerged as a science over the last 150 years.[2] On the right is a corresponding structure of a possible science of cultural evolution. For each branch of biology, I have specified an existing or potential branch of the social sciences that shares the same aims and goals, and in many cases the same methods, as its biological counterpart. I have also given the chapter of this book in which that particular strand of cultural evolution research is discussed.

Disciplines near the top of figure 10.1 concern macroevolution, either biological or cultural. On the biological side this includes paleobiology and biogeography, which use the methods of systematics, typically phylogenetic methods such as maximum parsimony, to reconstruct broad temporal (paleobiology) and spatial (biogeography)

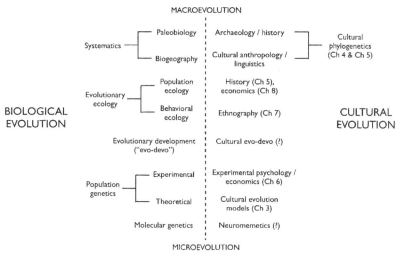

FIGURE 10.1 The structure of a potential science of cultural evolution (*righthand side*), as mapped on to the existing structure of evolutionary biology (*lefthand side*).

patterns in biological macroevolution. In chapters 4 and 5 we saw how archaeologists, historians, cultural anthropologists, and linguists are applying the same methods, predominantly phylogenetic methods, to cultural macroevolution. Evolutionary ecology also concerns macro-evolutionary change to a certain degree, particularly population ecology, the study of how populations interact with the environment including other species. This has a clear parallel on the cultural side in Peter Turchin's models of historical dynamics, as discussed in chapter 5. We might also include here the evolutionary models of cultural change developed by economists and discussed in chapter 8, such as models of how firms interact with other firms within markets, equivalent to how species interact within ecosystems. Further toward the microevolutionary end of the scale comes behavioral ecology, the branch of biology that deals with organisms' behavioral interactions with their environments and each other. This has a parallel in the ethnographic studies discussed in chapter 7, which examine how people interact with other people to generate patterns in culture (e.g., how patterns of food taboos arise from certain cultural transmission pathways or how scientific change arises from scientists' interactions with other scientists).

Evolutionary developmental biology, or "evo-devo" as it has come to be known, is an increasing focus of interest for many biologists. To date, development has received little attention within cultural evolution research, and there is currently no obvious parallel on the cultural side. I'll take up the role of development in cultural evolution in the next section.

The next discipline on the biological side is population genetics, which can be divided into two branches, experimental and theoretical. In experimental population genetics, evolutionary processes are simulated in the lab using, say, fruit flies or bacteria. This has a clear cultural parallel in the experimental studies outlined in chapter 6, incorporating experimental psychology, experimental economics, and other experimental branches of traditional social science disciplines. Theoretical population genetics, as already mentioned, involves the construction and analysis of mathematical models of microevolutionary processes such as natural selection, drift, mutation, migration, and so on. The cultural equivalent of theoretical population genetics is the mathematical modeling work discussed in chapter 3, in which various cultural microevolutionary processes have been modeled using similar mathematical techniques to those used by biologists.

The final biological discipline in figure 10.1 is molecular genetics, the study of how genetic information is encoded in the genome, how this information is translated into proteins to make phenotypes, and how it replicates during genetic inheritance. Like evo-devo, the cultural equivalent of molecular genetics has yet to be discussed here. The next sections discuss these two hitherto unexplored levels of analysis in more detail. Indeed, this highlighting of potential gaps in cultural evolution research is another key benefit of viewing the social sciences within a synthetic evolutionary framework.

Gaps in the Synthesis: Cultural Evo-Devo. Although Darwin discussed topics such as embryology in *The Origin*, development—the processes whereby an organism's genotype becomes, through interactions with the environment, a phenotype—was absent from the evolutionary synthesis of the 1930s and 1940s. In recent years, however, growing numbers of researchers are attempting to incorporate development into evolutionary biology in the form of evolutionary developmental biology, or "evo-devo" for short.[3] Evo-devo concerns how developmental processes are generated by, and constrain, longer-term evolutionary change. For example, much attention has been devoted to Hox genes, a set of genes found across animal species, from fruit flies to mice to humans, that appear to control the development of body parts in the embryo.[4] One Hox gene triggers the formation of limbs, another the head, others trigger different abdominal sections. Most interestingly,

Hox genes can be artificially switched to alter development in dramatic ways. Replacing the fruit fly Hox gene that normally triggers antennae growth with the Hox gene that normally triggers leg growth causes legs to grow out of the fly's head where the antennae usually are. Although this particular mutation would be rather detrimental to a fly's fitness, it is becoming clear that genes such as Hox that are involved in development can play a major role in generating, constraining, and patterning phenotypic diversity, and consequently play a major role in biological evolution.

So what is the equivalent of evo-devo in the science of cultural evolution sketched in figure 10.1? Following the ideational definition of culture given in chapter 1, cultural development would be the process by which information stored in the brain (the equivalent of the genotype) becomes expressed as behavior, speech, artifacts, and institutions (the equivalents of the phenotype). Cultural evo-devo would then concern how this developmental process constrains or facilitates broader, long-term cultural evolution.[5]

One example of how development might affect cultural evolution concerns modularity. In biological evo-devo, it has been suggested that genes such as Hox that trigger the development of entire structures such as limbs or antennae facilitate evolution by making development *modular*. Think of a centipede or millipede, for example, with their many identical body segments. Without high-level genes such as Hox, each segment would have to be coded by separate genes. With Hox genes, you only need one set of genes that specify how to build one segment, and you can simply use Hox genes to repeat that segment (or "module") over and over again. In other words, a modular developmental system eliminates redundancy from the genome. Such a modular structure would also facilitate the evolution of new adaptive forms. A simple change in the expression of a single Hox gene would increase (or decrease) the number of body segments or limbs, rather than having to evolve an entirely new segment or limb from scratch.

Modularity may play a similar role in cultural evolution. Many technological artifacts are composed of partially independent subcomponents that have been imported from other artifacts or technological domains. Consider the Swiss Army Knife, with its numerous functionally specialized blades and devices. Each of these blades can be seen as a module akin to a body segment or a limb of an organism. The inventors of the Swiss Army Knife did not have to reinvent each component (cutting knife, serrated saw, corkscrew, magnifying glass) from scratch; they imported each one from preexisting standalone blades and devices.[6] So just as modularity facilitates biological evolution by reducing the need to independently evolve repeating body parts, so too modularity facilitates cultural evolution by reducing the need to independently evolve repeating technological components, a prediction that is supported by computer simulations of artifact learning.[7] Future research in cultural evo-devo might reveal other general principles that constrain, guide, or facilitate cultural evolution.

Gaps in the Synthesis: Neuromemetics. The second discipline of evolutionary biology that has no clear parallel in the cultural evolution research that we have discussed so far is molecular genetics. Ever since James Watson, Francis Crick, and others worked out the structure of DNA in 1953, molecular geneticists have made huge advances in determining how DNA provides a molecular mechanism for the inheritance of genetic information and how the information represented in DNA is translated into the phenotypic adaptations that natural selection acts upon. The equivalent to molecular genetics in the study of cultural evolution would concern how, at a molecular level, cultural information is stored, transmitted, and expressed. Cultural information is stored primarily in the brain, so this would be the preserve of neuroscience. Indeed, Robert Aunger, in his book *The Electric Meme*, suggests that the field of memetics should really be called "neuromemetics," with memes treated as electrochemical states of multiple neurons.[8] I will follow Aunger's lead and use the term "neuromemetics" to describe the cultural equivalent of molecular genetics.

Compared to molecular geneticists' sophisticated understanding of genetic inheritance, however, neuroscientists have only a very limited understanding of how information is stored in the brain, let alone how that information changes over time, is transmitted from one brain to another, and is translated into behavior and material artifacts. This severely limits our ability to answer the kinds of questions raised earlier in the book, such as whether cultural evolution involves the all-or-nothing transmission of discrete units of inheritance akin to genes and particulate genetic inheritance, or whether there are no discrete units at the neural level and continuous cultural variation instead blends together during transmission. Brain imaging methods such as MRI and PET are not yet sophisticated enough to be able to detect neuronal activity at a level of detail that might reveal whether information is represented in a discrete or continuous fashion. Such methods can tell neuroscientists which general area of the brain is activated during different cognitive tasks, but not yet at the level of single neurons or networks of neurons.

Very rarely, an alternative and more direct method of studying the brain is possible. Some kinds of epilepsy are caused by small lesions within the brain, such as the result of a tumor. When seizures are severe and fail to respond to anticonvulsive drugs, surgeons will sometimes perform brain surgery to remove the lesion and hopefully stop or reduce the seizures. Before this happens, the surgeons need to know exactly where in the brain the lesion is located. Because noninvasive brain imaging methods such as MRI are often not fine-grained enough to locate very small lesions, some patients instead have electrodes implanted directly into their brains for several days. When a seizure occurs, these electrodes record exactly which neurons were firing, and therefore the likely location of the lesion responsible.

A team of neuropsychologists led by Rodrigo Quian Quiroga took advantage of this procedure to examine how knowledge is represented in the brain.[9] Eight epileptic patients with electrode implants had their neuron activity directly recorded as they were shown various pictures of people, animals, objects, landmarks, and words. The rather unexpected finding was that some neurons showed remarkable specificity, only firing in response to a single concept, object, or person. One neuron fired only in response to photographs of Jennifer Aniston. It did not respond to any other female celebrity, nor any of the other people or objects used in the test. And it seemed to respond to the *identity* of Jennifer Aniston, not just to specific photographs. She could be in different poses, wearing different clothes, or viewed from different angles, the neuron would respond to all of them. Another neuron fired only in response to pictures of Halle Berry, as well as line drawings of Halle Berry and the printed words "Halle Berry." Another responded only to the Sydney Opera House. These remarkable findings seem to suggest that the brain represents information in terms of discrete, high-level units, somewhat like discrete genes. We should perhaps not get carried away, however. Studies such as Quian Quiroga et al.'s are rare. Only a very small number of neurons were recorded from, and only a very small number of pictures presented to the patients. And just because information is represented in a discrete fashion, it might not be transmitted in a discrete fashion. Much more research is needed before the full implications of these preliminary findings are known.

Another area of neuropsychological research that may turn out to have important implications for cultural evolution involves *mirror neu-*

rons. These neurons, first discovered through invasive single-neuron recordings in monkeys, fire both when the monkey performs an action and when the monkey observes another monkey perform that same action.[10] Different mirror neurons respond to different actions, and only to those actions. For example, some neurons respond only when the monkey grasps a piece of food or sees another monkey grasp a piece of food in the same way; other neurons fire only when the hand of the monkey (own or observed) rotates clockwise; others fire only to anti-clockwise rotation. This link between the observation of an action and the performance of the same action has suggested to some researchers that mirror neurons might form the neural basis of imitation, the process whereby one individual copies an action observed being performed by another.[11] And, of course, imitation constitutes one very important mechanism of cultural transmission.

Again, however, we should not get carried away with these initial findings. The fact that mirror neurons have only been directly observed in a species that cannot imitate—macaque monkeys—should make us hesitant to accept any simple link between mirror neurons and imitation. Evidence for mirror neurons in humans is limited to neuroimaging studies which show that the same region of the brain (Broca's area, which is homologous to the area in the macaque brain where mirror neurons are found) is active when people observe an action and perform that same action.[12] While this is suggestive of a mirror neuron system in the human brain, the rather indirect level of analysis afforded by neuroimaging methods does not help to answer detailed questions about the neural basis of imitation and other forms of cultural transmission in human cultural evolution.

These rather sketchy speculations concerning the neural basis of cultural evolution illustrate the limitations of current neuroimaging methods. As these methods become more sophisticated and fine-grained, we can anticipate future cultural equivalents of Watson and Crick making key discoveries concerning how information is stored in the brain, expressed as behavior, and transmitted to other brains. If this has anything like the impact in the study of cultural evolution that the work of the actual Watson and Crick had in biology, then we can expect major repercussions in all of the other disciplines shown in figure 10.1.

Other Future Directions. As well as these big gaps in any future science of cultural evolution, several outstanding questions have also been encountered in previous chapters that warrant further study. A key question raised in chapter 9 concerned why only humans appear to possess the capacity for cumulative culture. Whereas many species can acquire information from other individuals via social learning, and in many cases this results in distinct behavioral differences between different groups, only humans appear to be able to accumulate modifications over successive generations in a way that results in complex cultural adaptations such as cars or computers that a single individual could not invent on their own. And it is this cumulative property of human culture, in which beneficial modifications are accumulated to form complex adaptations, that makes it an evolutionary process. Early suggestions that cumulative culture depends on imitation are unlikely to be correct given findings that other species, in particular chimpanzees, can imitate yet do not have cumulative culture. More recent suggestions include an ability to switch from adequate to better solutions to a task (rather than stick with the adequate solution, which is what other species appear to do), and a sophisticated form of teaching in which adults tailor what they say and do to maximize the likelihood that other people, particularly children, will learn useful information from them. No doubt future comparative studies of cultural learning in a variety of species will provide more definitive answers to this key question.

A second area that deserves further attention concerns large-scale cooperative social institutions, from prehistoric tribes to historical empires to modern business firms. The tendency for our species to live in such highly cooperative groups, as well as the frequency with which different groups (e.g., tribes, empires, firms) come into conflict with one another, has led several researchers to propose that cultural evolution can usefully be analyzed at the level of the group rather than the individual. We saw this in chapter 5 with Peter Turchin's theory of empire growth and decline, where more internally cohesive social groups outcompete less internally cohesive groups to become dominant empires. This idea of cultural group selection was elaborated upon in chapter 8. According to Robert Boyd, Peter Richerson, Joseph Henrich, Herbert Gintis, and others, a lengthy process of cultural group selection during human evolution has led to the genetic evolution of behavioral predispositions to cooperate with ingroup members. This makes possible large-scale cooperative institutions such as nation-states and business firms. These institutions then undergo their own process of cultural group selection, such as when firms compete within the marketplace. Yet the mechanisms by which cultural group selection operates remain poorly understood. Various mechanisms thought to play a crucial role in cultural group selection have been modeled mathematically, such as conformity (which maintains between-group variation), third-party punishment (to prevent free riders exploiting groups), payoff-biased imitation (where prosocial norms are preferentially copied from neighboring groups), and payoff-biased migration (where people choose to join groups that have relatively high prosocial norms).[13] Which of these processes are actually operating in particular instances of cultural group selection has yet to be empirically tested. Ethnographic studies might test for the presence and effects of such processes in small-scale societies and business organizations, cultural group selection might be simulated experimentally in the lab, and historians might quantitatively measure the strength of cultural group selection during history. While sociologists since Émile Durkheim have explained cultural change in terms of group level selection, such explanations have remained entirely informal and qualitative. Quantitative models of economic behavior, on the other hand, have focused at the level of the individual. Cultural group selection provides a middle way between these two extremes, allowing quantitative tests of group-level explanations.

Finally, there is a need to greatly expand the ethnographic studies of cultural evolution under real-world conditions, as outlined in chapter 7. While the studies mentioned in that chapter constitute initial attempts to quantify the cultural transmission pathway (e.g., vertical, horizontal, oblique) involved in particular instances of cultural change, there is a need to quantitatively measure under natural conditions the other cultural processes described in chapter 3. These might include the strength of content-biased cultural selection, predicting how quickly a novel, beneficial innovation would spread through a society, or the strength of conformist and prestige-biased cultural selection. Evolutionary biologists have developed several methods for detecting the strength of natural selection in the wild that could be adapted to detect and measure cultural selection in societies.[14] For example, if natural selection is acting, then biologists would expect to observe two closely related species living in the same environment to diverge in their morphological or behavioral characters, a phenomenon known as character displacement. Convergent evolution also constitutes evidence for natural selection, as unrelated species living in similar environments evolve similar adaptations to that environment (e.g., the independently evolved streamlined body shape of fish, penguins, and dolphins, which increases swimming efficiency). A third example involves perturbations of wild populations, either natural perturbations such as earthquakes, droughts, or disease epidemics, or artificial perturbations such as the introduction of an invasive species into an area. Perturbations frequently change a naturally occurring population in some way, such as a reduction in average body size following a severe drought as larger individuals are more likely to die. If the trait returns back to its original value following the perturbation, then this constitutes evidence for natural selection operating on that trait.

All of these methods, and others, could be adapted to detect cultural selection in actual human societies.[15] Cultural character displacement might occur when people of different religious beliefs occupy the same geographical region, resulting in stronger and more divergent beliefs (e.g., Protestantism and Roman Catholicism in Northern Ireland, or Judaism and Islam in the West Bank). We have already encountered possible examples of convergent cultural evolution in chapter 2, such as the independent invention of writing or Darwin and Wallace's independent discoveries of natural selection, although such examples remain quite informal compared to the way in which biologists identify the specific selection pressures that are purported to be responsible for convergence. And finally, researchers might test how cultural traits respond to perturbations, both natural perturbations such as disease epidemics or earthquakes, and artificial perturbations such as political revolutions or civil wars.

Practical Benefits

A better understanding of cultural change, facilitated by the evolutionary methods outlined in this book, may also lead to improved practical, real-world benefits. Many behaviors that are detrimental to our health, such as smoking, drinking, and poor dietary habits have been shown to be culturally transmitted.[16] Yet while some kind of social influence has been implicated in the spread of such behaviors, the precise form that this influence takes in each specific case remains sketchy. Our understanding of such phenomena, and any efforts to prevent their spread, may benefit from a consideration of the detailed cultural microevolutionary processes outlined in chapter 3. Take the phenomenon of copycat suicide, for example. Sociologists have documented small but significant increases in national suicide rates in response to celebrity suicides, as well as local clusters of suicides within networks of close school friends.[17] In terms of the microevolutionary processes listed in chapter 3, the former appear to be cases of prestige bias magnified by the one-to-many transmission pathway of the mass media, while the latter appear to be similarity bias via one-to-one transmission. Formal evolutionary models can be used to explicitly simulate these microevolutionary processes to see whether they really are consistent with the macroevolutionary clustering documented by sociologists, and consequently where to best target individual-level interventions.[18]

A better understanding of economic systems will hopefully come from the assumptions that economic actors have culturally group-selected prosocial motivations and behavior that is shaped by culturally transmitted norms and routines, rather than actors who are purely self-interested and asocial.[19] For example, the knowledge that stock market bubbles and crashes are caused at least in part by myopic, herdlike conformist behavior, and an understanding of the initial macroevolutionary (i.e., marketwide) trends that are indicative of such a process, might allow the construction of an early warning system that would either motivate traders to stop an oncoming crash or allow the government to intervene to stop it.

Conclusions

The vast majority of the research reviewed in this book is extremely recent, only having appeared in the last decade or so. In a sense (or perhaps in hindsight) this is to be expected. Just as evolutionary biology only became the successful and synthetic enterprise that it is today after Fisher, Haldane, and Wright laid out the quantitative foundations of biological evolution in the early twentieth century, the recent explosion of cultural evolution research is, I think, a consequence of Cavalli-Sforza, Feldman, Boyd, and Richerson's equally pioneering work in the 1970s and 1980s laying the quantitative foundations of cultural evolution. A new generation of evolutionarily minded scholars has emerged who are well versed in both quantitative evolutionary theory and traditional ethnographic, experimental, or historical methods, and who are eschewing the traditional disciplinary divisions that have for so long impeded a fully scientific understanding of culture. Yet while evolutionary analyses of culture represent a significant advance over nonevolutionary and nonscientific approaches to the study of culture, which have for so long been prevalent within the social sciences, there is much that is still to be worked out given the sheer complexity and diversity of cultural phenomena past and present.

Notes

PREFACE
1. Darwin 1871, 90–91.
2. James 1880, 441.

CHAPTER ONE
1. The hundreds of definitions are listed by Kroeber and Kluckohn 1952 and Baldwin et al. 2006. The definition given in the text follows the most influential anthropological definition of culture given by Edward Burnett Tylor in 1871: "[T]hat complex whole which includes knowledge, belief, art, law, morals, custom, and any other capabilities and habits acquired by man as a member of society" (Tylor 1871, 1). Ignoring the Victorian sexism in restricting culture to the male half of the species, and the anthropocentrism in restricting culture to humans, the key phrase here is "acquired as a member of society," that is, socially transmitted. Definitions of culture given by modern-day cultural evolution researchers similarly stress social transmission, such as the following: "Culture is information capable of affecting individuals' behaviour that they acquire from other members of their species through teaching, imitation, and other forms of social transmission" (Richerson and Boyd 2005, 5). Note that this definition does not restrict culture to humans. Indeed, much recent research has demonstrated that many nonhuman species make use of socially transmitted information and so can be said to possess culture (see chapter 9). Finally, by "social sciences" I mean those academic disciplines concerned with the study of culture. I would argue that this includes virtually all of the social and

behavioral sciences in one way or another (e.g., psychology, social/cultural anthropology, archaeology, linguistics, history, economics, sociology), given my definition of culture.

2. Cronk 1999, 10–14.

3. On genetic basis of alcohol dependence, see Soyka et al. 2008; on alcohol intolerance in East Asia, Peng et al. 2010.

4. Rice and Feldman 1997. Note that I have changed their term "civic culture" to "civic duty" in order to avoid confusion over the use of the word "culture."

5. Rice and Arnett 2001. See also Putnam 1993, who carried out similar analyses for different regions in Italy.

6. See Roth 1995 and Camerer and Thaler 1995 for details of the ultimatum game as conducted on US college students.

7. These findings have received a great deal of attention from economists because they fly in the face of classical "rational actor" theories of human economic behavior. Such theories predict that people should behave as if they are maximizing the amount of money (or whatever it is they value) that they can receive. In the ultimatum game this would result in extreme selfishness. Responders should accept any offer that isn't zero, because any amount of money is better than no money. Knowing this, the proposer should offer the smallest amount of money possible, say $1, keeping $99 for themselves. The responder accepts this $1, because it is better than the $0 that they would receive if they rejected the offer. The issue of how to explain this seemingly irrational human fairness is discussed in chapter 8. I will here focus on cross-cultural variation in ultimatum game responses.

8. Henrich et al. 2005, 2010.

9. For reviews, see Heine and Norenzayan 2006; Henrich, Heine, and Norenzayan 2010.

10. Jones and Harris 1967.

11. Morris and Peng 1994.

12. For cognitive dissonance, see Heine and Lehman 1997. For attention and memory of objects see Masuda and Nisbett 2001. For analytic vs. holistic thinking, see Nisbett et al. 2001. For an overview of cultural psychology research, see Heine and Norenzayan 2006 and Heine 2008.

13. The classic criticism of cognitive psychologists' failure to distinguish properly between individual and social influences is Bandura 1977; for a more recent critique, see Goldstone, Roberts, and Gureckis 2008. For a critique of economists' individualistic focus, see Gintis 2007. For examples of cultural ecology, see Steward 1955 and M. Harris 1989.

14. See, for example, Tooby and Cosmides 1992; Gangestad, Haselton, and Buss 2006.

15. Hewlett, De Silvestri, and Guglielmino 2002. See also a similar earlier study by Guglielmino et al. 1995, which found no cultural traits associated with ecology. Cultural phylogenies also provide evidence for the role of cultural descent, as discussed in chapter 4.

16. Plomin et al. 2003.

17. On genetic variation between versus within population, Rosenberg

et al. 2002; on genetic versus cultural between-population variation, Bell, Richerson, and McElreath 2009. See also Nisbett 1998 for evidence against between-group genetic differences in IQ.

18. See, for example, Norenzayan et al. 2002; for further references, see Heine and Norenzayan 2006, 261.

19. See Basalla 1988, Petroski 1994, and Vincenti 1993 on technological change, and Wilder 1968 and Hull 1988 on scientific change.

20. Bentley, Hahn, and Shennan 2004.

21. McMurray 2007.

22. Lyons, Young, and Keil 2007.

23. Herrmann et al. 2007.

24. See reviews by Tomasello et al. 2005 and Csibra and Gergely 2009, as well as chapter 9.

25. Aoki, Wakano, and Feldman 2005; Boyd and Richerson 1995.

26. A. Rogers 1988 pointed out a problem with the idea that culture is adaptive because it is less costly than individual learning: if too many individuals in the population are cultural learners, then there may be too few individual learners to detect any further environmental change and the cultural learners will be left copying incorrect, out-of-date information. Boyd and Richerson 1995 showed that cultural learning is in fact favored over individual learning when individuals can switch between the two, only employing cultural learning when individual learning is particularly costly, and when culture is cumulative, as noted in the text.

27. Guiso, Sapienza, and Zingales 2006, 23.

28. Tooby and Cosmides 1992, 41.

29. See, for example, the *Ethnographic Atlas* of Murdock 1967.

30. Slingerland 2008, especially chapters 2 and 3, is an excellent source of further information on, as well as a potent attack on, these hermeneutic and social constructionist approaches. Aunger 1995, 2004 discusses the problem of reflexivity and potential solutions to it.

31. See Aunger 2004 for equivalent methods using multiple observers and statistical correction in ethnography.

32. Nisbett et al. 2001; Markus and Kitayama 1991.

33. Nisbett et al. 2001.

34. Nelson and Winter 1982.

35. See Lenski and Travisano 1994 for experimental simulations of punctuated equilibria; Endler 1986 for a review of studies measuring natural selection in the wild.

CHAPTER TWO

1. Darwin 1859; Ghiselin 2003.

2. See Mesoudi, Whiten, and Laland 2004 for a fuller exposition of this comparison

3. Lewontin 1970.

4. Grant 1986.

5. Darwin 1859, 83.

6. Darwin 1859, 102.

7. On species number, see Wilson 2006, although this is only species known to science, so the actual number of species will be higher. On gene numbers, Carninci and Hayashizaki 2007.

8. Darwin 1859, 202.

9. Petroski 1994, 135.

10. US Patent and Trademark Office (http://www.uspto.gov/)

11. Barrett, Kurian, and Johnson 2001.

12. Grimes 2002.

13. Mehl et al. 2007.

14. http://en.wikipedia.org/wiki/Wikipedia:Size_comparisons.

15. It is interesting to compare the extent of human cultural variation with that of other species. Our closest living relative, the chimpanzee, has been shown to exhibit just 39 geographically variable behaviors, such as differences in the use of tools, that are thought to be culturally acquired (Whiten et al. 1999), with a comparable figure of 24 for orangutans (van Schaik et al. 2003). This may be due to the noncumulative basis of nonhuman culture, such that cultural traits are not accumulated over time, as discussed in chapter 9.

16. Darwin 1859, 130.

17. Darwin 1859, 116.

18. Lewontin 1970; Endler 1986.

19. On Oceania, Rivers 1926; on Tasmania, Diamond 1978. Of course, these technologies and practices survived in other regions and later diffused back in, but to these isolated populations they were to all intents and purposes extinct.

20. Krauss 1992.

21. Lieberman et al. 2007.

22. Darwin 1871, 91.

23. On pottery, Kroeber 1916; on the bow and arrow, Nassaney and Pyle 1999.

24. McGeoch and McDonald 1931.

25. Darwin 1859, 154.

26. Darwin 1859, 75.

27. Darwin 1859, 76.

28. Bandura, Ross, and Ross 1961.

29. Asch 1951.

30. Cavalli Sforza et al. 1982.

31. Basalla 1988. See Petroski 1994 and Vincenti 1993 for other examples of cumulative technological change.

32. Wilder 1968.

33. Darwin 1859, 114–115.

34. Henrich 2008.

35. E. Rogers 1995.

36. Basalla 1988, 107.

37. Darwin 1859, 223.

38. Diamond 1998.

39. Petroski 1994.

40. Tylor 1871; Morgan 1877.

41. Spencer 1857; see also Freeman 1974.

42. Morgan 1877, 18.

43. Morgan 1877, 18.

44. Gould 1990.

45. Boas 1920.

46. While the explanations for progressive cultural evolution proposed by early scholars such as Tylor and Morgan are inadequate, and the inevitability and discrete stagelikeness of that progression are empirically unsupported, a case can be made that cultural change does exhibit some general increase in social or technological complexity that warrants an explanation. Johnson and Earle 2000, for example, argue that societies have, in several regions and in parallel, passed through a series of broadly similar stages of increasing social complexity, from small-scale, kin-based, egalitarian hunter-gatherer societies to large-scale, socially stratified, market-based societies with extensive division of labor. Richerson and Boyd 2001 provide a potential explanation of this increasing social complexity in terms of many of the Darwinian cultural evolutionary processes described in subsequent chapters of this book, such as conformist cultural transmission (see chapter 3) and cultural group selection (see chapter 8). These theories are different from the early progressive theories in providing actual mechanisms by which societies increase in complexity. And importantly, the same mechanisms can also result in the loss of complexity under certain conditions, as shown by Henrich 2004b (see chapter 4).

47. See, for example, White 1959a.

48. Mayr 1982.

49. Cadieu et al. 2009.

50. Dawkins 1976.

51. Dennett 1995; Blackmore 1999.

52. Bloch 2000, 194.

53. Lehmann 1992.

54. Sherif 1936.

55. Another complication is that genes are not in fact as discrete as is commonly thought (Portin 2002; Stotz and Griffiths 2004). In the early days of genetics, genes were indeed seen as discrete units of information that are transmitted whole, that mutate independently from other genes, and that code for a single protein. Over the last century, however, the concept of the gene has changed considerably, and become much less clear-cut. Biologists have found *overlapping genes*, where the same stretch of DNA codes for more than one protein;, *movable genes*, which move around the genome;, and *nested genes*, which reside inside other genes. In *alternative splicing*, the same gene codes for different proteins depending on the action of other genes. This new concept of a gene, one with fuzzy boundaries that changes its function depending on its context, resembles the fuzzy-boundary, context-dependent concept of a cultural trait that is commonly held by social scientists (Laland and Brown 2002, 225–228).

56. Unfortunately much confusion surrounds the term "Lamarckian." As well as describing the inheritance of acquired characteristics, it is also occasionally used to describe the role that an organism's intentionality plays in evolution (biological or cultural). See Hull 1988 and Hodgson and Knudsen 2006 for more details.

57. While this is the standard textbook account, there have been increasing calls to revise this neo-Darwinian prohibition on the inheritance of acquired characteristics. Jablonka and Lamb 2005, for example, argue that phenomena such as epigenetic inheritance and, indeed, cultural transmission, where information is transmitted from individual to individual nongenetically, mean that the Lamarckian inheritance of acquired characteristics plays an important role in biological evolution.

58. Gould 1991, 65.

59. Hodgson and Knudsen 2006, 2010; Hull 1988.

60. Basalla 1988, 35–37.

61. Luria and Delbrück 1943.

62. Campbell 1965.

63. Simonton 1999.

64. Benton 2000, 216.

65. Simonton 1999.

66. Mesoudi 2008a.

67. Gould 1991, 65.

68. Maynard Smith 1986.

69. See Nelson 2007 and Mesoudi 2007 for similar arguments.

70. Mayr 1982, 566.

71. Mayr and Provine 1980, 15–17.

72. Mayr 1982, 542–550.

73. Haldane 1927; Fisher 1930; Wright 1932.

74. Although Fisher, Haldane, and Wright used mathematical techniques such as differential calculus to determine long-term equilibria, biologists today also use computers to simulate long-term changes in gene frequencies or interactions between organisms.

75. Haldane 1927; Fisher 1930.

76. Huxley 1942; Mayr and Provine 1980; Mayr 1982.

77. Mayr 1963, 586–587.

78. Kroeber 1917, 192–193.

79. Durkheim 1938 [1966].

80. See Slingerland 2008 for a critique of the mind-body dualism that pervades the social sciences and humanities.

81. Note that this does not necessarily conflict with the previous problem: macrolevel phenomena may be both caused by, and in turn influence, microlevel individual behavior. Indeed, the complexity of this circularity may be one of the reasons why the micro-macro divide has persisted for so long in the social sciences. The formal models used in evolutionary biology offer one way of dealing with this complexity.

82. Lux 1995.

83. Gintis 2007, 7.

CHAPTER THREE

1. Cavalli-Sforza and Feldman 1981; Boyd and Richerson 1985.

2. Often this transmission is not directly modeled at the individual-to-individual level. In population-genetic-style models (both biological and cultural), big simplifying assumptions are made such as infinite population sizes, and processes are modeled as averaged across the entire hypothetical population. Other models *do* explicitly simulate separate individuals and the transmission of cultural information between them. These are known as agent-based models: see Epstein and Axtell 1996; Epstein 2007.

3. This list is assembled from several sources, primarily Cavalli-Sforza and Feldman 1981; Boyd and Richerson 1985; Henrich and McElreath 2003; Richerson and Boyd 2005. Unfortunately, not all of these sources, even those by the same authors, consistently use the same terms. There are, therefore, terminological differences between this list and some of the original work. Some confusion surrounds the use of the term "cultural selection." I have followed the definition of "cultural selection" given by Cavalli-Sforza and Feldman 1981, 15: "the rate or probability that a given [cultural trait] will be accepted in a given time unit by an individual representative of the population." Richerson and Boyd 2005: 79 eschew the term "cultural selection," preferring instead "biased transmission" to avoid confusion with the terms "guided variation" and "natural selection." However, I think that the advantage of using a recognizable term such as "selection" outweighs any potential confusion, particularly if "guided variation" and "natural selection" are explicitly listed as different processes, as I have done in table 3.1. Also note that in Boyd and Richerson 1985, "content bias" was originally called "direct bias" and "model-based biases" were originally called "indirect bias"; I have used the new terms from Richerson and Boyd 2005.

4. McElreath and Boyd 2007, 4–8.

5. For horizontal gene transfer, see Rivera and Lake 2004; Doolittle 2009. For genomic imprinting, see Reik and Walter 2001.

6. Cavalli-Sforza and Feldman 1981, see summary on 351–357. The vertical transmission line in Figure 3.1a is constructed using Cavalli-Sforza and Feldman 1981, 79, equation 2.26, with $b_3 = 1$, $b_0 = 0$, $b_1 = b_2 = 0.6$. The horizontal transmission line uses equation 3.41 on p.151, with the same b_i parameters plus $f = 0.5$.

7. Cavalli Sforza et al. 1982.

8. Cavalli-Sforza and Feldman 1981, 267–286; Boyd and Richerson 1985, 71–76. See also Henrich and Boyd 2002 for a detailed discussion of why cultural evolution does not require discrete replicators.

9. The reduction of variation caused by blending inheritance was an early criticism of Darwin's theory of biological evolution, pointed out most forcefully by Fleeming Jenkin. If biological inheritance is blending, then variation would disappear, and there would be nothing for selection to act upon. Darwin considered this to be a serious problem for his theory, one that was not resolved until the rediscovery of Mendel's particulate rules of inheritance.

10. Cavalli-Sforza and Feldman 1981, 267–286; Boyd and Richerson 1985, 71–76.

11. The classic demonstration of this is Bartlett 1932; see chapter 6 for further discussion.

12. Christakis and Fowler 2009, 206. See also McPherson, Smith-Lovin, and Cook 2001 for evidence that people preferentially associate with others who are similar to them ("homophily").

13. Guided variation resembles what cognitive anthropologists have called "cultural attraction" (Sperber 1996; Atran 2001), where people transform the beliefs and ideas that they acquire from others according to their own biologically evolved cognitive processes. Guided variation also resembles what some cognitive psychologists (e.g., Griffiths, Kalish, and Lewandowsky 2008) have called "inductive bias," where culturally transmitted information converges on a preexisting prior that is present in each individual. Both cultural attraction and inductive bias are predicted to have the same macroevolutionary consequences as guided variation, that is, convergence on the individually favored representation/prior.

14. Campbell 1960.

15. Boyd and Richerson 2005, 69.

16. Heath, Bell, and Sternberg 2001. See also Heath and Heath 2007 for a range of other potential content biases (albeit not framed in cultural evolution terminology).

17. Boyer 1994; Atran 2002.

18. Norenzayan et al. 2006.

19. E. Rogers 1995.

20. E. Rogers 1995, 244–246.

21. E. Rogers 1995, 1–5.

22. This is equivalent to Fisher's Fundamental Theorem in population genetics, which states that the strength of selection is proportional to the amount of variation in a population.

23. E. Rogers 1995; Sultan, Farley, and Lehmann 1990.

24. Henrich 2001. Strictly, Henrich showed that any form of cultural selection could be responsible for S-shaped diffusion curves. Alternative forms of cultural selection might be prestige bias or conformist bias, as discussed in the following two sections. However, although Rogers does note prestige effects in the diffusion of innovations, most of the drivers of diffusion appear to be content biases such as the ones discussed previously (trialability, observability, etc.). Henrich also notes that conformity generates the long tails that prevent innovations from taking off, as discussed later in the chapter. However, conformity alone (in the absence of content bias) cannot account for the S-shaped curves because a rare innovation would never take off at all unless there were some content bias favoring it.

25. The guided variation curve in figure 3.1b is derived from Boyd and Richerson 1985, 97, equation 4.11, with $a = 0.8$ and $H = 1$.

26. The content bias curve in figure 3.1b is derived from Boyd and Richerson 1985, 138, equation 5.2, with $B = 0.2$ and initial frequency of favored trait 0.01.

27. Sherif 1936; Asch 1951.

28. The unbiased transmission line in figure 3.1c is derived from Boyd and Richerson 1985, 66, equation 3.12; the conformity curve is from equation 7.1 on page 208 of same publication with $D = 0.2$. Initial frequency of the trait plotted on the vertical axis is 0.55.

29. McElreath et al. 2005; Efferson et al. 2008. See Mesoudi 2009a for further criticisms of social psychology conformity experiments.

30. Content bias plus conformity line in Figure 3.1b derived from equation 10 in Henrich 2001, with $b = 0.2$ and $\alpha = 0.1$. Initial frequency of the trait favored by content bias is 0.01.

31. For more on how conformity maintains between-group differences see Henrich and Boyd 1998. Boyd and Richerson, and others, have also noted that these conditions—low within-group variation plus high between-group variation—are ideal conditions for selection to operate at the level of cultural groups. So far we have considered cultural selection acting on individual traits (beliefs, practices etc.), where one trait is more likely to survive and reproduce than another trait. Cultural *group* selection occurs when some groups are more likely to survive and reproduce than other groups. Chapter 8 explores further the consequences of cultural group selection in potentially explaining the unusually strong cooperation with non-kin that is characteristic of our species.

32. Boyd and Richerson 1985, chapter 8 (note that they called prestige bias "indirect bias"). See Henrich and Gil White 2001 for further discussion of prestige bias.

33. For the art director study, see Mausner 1953; for the student activism study, Ryckman, Rodda, and Sherman 1972; for the horse betting study, Rosenbaum and Tucker 1962. See also McElreath et al. 2008.

34. E. Rogers 1995, chapter 8.

35. Labov 1972.

36. See Boyd and Richerson 1985, 259–271, for the runaway selection model of prestige bias.

37. To check these frequencies for yourself, go to www.national-lottery. co.uk.

38. Kimura 1983.

39. Bentley, Hahn, and Shennan 2004 present an overview of the cultural drift model as applied to first names, patents and pottery.

40. See Mesoudi and Lycett 2009 for details of the agent-based simulations used to generate figure 5.1d.

41. Mesoudi and Lycett 2009.

42. Data taken from http://www.ssa.gov/OACT/babynames/decades/names2000s.html. Interestingly, boys' names appear to be more conservative than girls' names. This may be because boys are more often named after their fathers or grandfathers.

43. Durham 1991, chapter 7.

44. Cavalli-Sforza and Feldman 1981, 101–107; Boyd and Richerson 1985, chapter 6.

45. Bramanti et al. 2009.

CHAPTER FOUR

1. Harvey and Pagel 1991.

2. From Samonte and Eichler 2002.

3. Technically, similarities that arise independently may be classified into those that result from convergent evolution, where the two species have ancestors that were dissimilar to each other; parallel evolution, where the two species have ancestors that were similar to each other; and reversals, where a recently evolved character reverts back to its ancestral state. For ease of exposition I will only describe "convergent evolution" in the text.

4. This example is adapted from O'Brien, Darwent, and Lyman 2001; a more detailed discussion of the phylogenetic method can be found in that paper as well as in O'Brien and Lyman 2003.

5. Nei and Kumar 2000.

6. O'Brien, Darwent, and Lyman 2001; O'Brien and Lyman 2003.

7. O'Brien, Darwent, and Lyman 2001.

8. Galton 1889.

9. Goodwin, Balshine-Earn, and Reynolds 1998.

10. Goodwin, Balshine-Earn, and Reynolds 1998.

11. Mace and Pagel 1994.

12. Holden and Mace 2003.

13. Aberle 1961.

14. Fortunato, Holden, and Mace 2006.

15. Jackson and Romney 1973.

16. Gould 1991; Moore 1994. For a critique of cultural phylogenetics that is nevertheless supportive of cultural evolution theory, see Borgerhoff Mulder, Nunn, and Towner 2006.

17. Note that this is a slightly different use of the term "blend" than in "blending inheritance," encountered in chapter 3. *Blending inheritance* describes the microevolutionary process whereby a single individual adopts the average of two or more demonstrators' continuous cultural traits, as opposed to particulate inheritance, where only one of the demonstrators' discrete traits would be copied. *Blending across lineages* describes the macroevolutionary process whereby traits cross from one ethnic group to another ethnic group (equivalent to cultural diffusion). The two are logically distinct. For example, cultural macroevolution can be entirely treelike, with no blending across lineages/groups, despite lots of blending inheritance going on within those lineages/groups. Or conversely, cultural macroevolution might be not at all treelike, with lots of cross-lineage blending, yet that cross-lineage transmission is entirely particulate rather than blending at the microevolutionary level.

18. Kroeber 1948, 260.

19. Gould 1991, 63–65.

20. Doolittle 2009.

21. Rivera and Lake 2004.

22. Tehrani and Collard 2002.

23. Collard, Shennan, and Tehrani 2006.

24. Durham 1991.

25. On ethnocentrism in anthropology, see LeVine and Campbell 1973; in social psychology, Tajfel 1982.

26. Tehrani and Collard 2009.

27. Jordan and Shennan 2003.

28. Kimura 1983.

29. Neiman 1995.

30. Shennan and Wilkinson 2001.

31. Shennan and Wilkinson 2001, 592.

32. Ambrose 2001.

33. Lycett and von Cramon-Taubadel 2008.

34. Prugnolle, Manica, and Balloux 2005.

35. Henrich 2004b.

36. Powell, Shennan, and Thomas 2009.

CHAPTER FIVE

1. Fitch 2008; Whitfield 2008; Pagel 2009.

2. The following history is taken from van Wyhe 2005.

3. Darwin 1871, 90–91.

4. Not to be confused with the phylogenetic comparative method in biology, which is used to test for correlated changes on a phylogenetic tree as was used in Holden and Mace's 2003 study discussed in the previous chapter.

5. McMahon and McMahon 2003.

6. See Gray, Greenhill, and Ross 2007 and Pagel 2009 for overviews.

7. See Diamond and Bellwood 2003 for the express-train model as applied to several regions, including Southeast Asia, and Diamond 2000 on Austronesian languages.

8. The Indonesian origin was suggested by Oppenheimer and Richards 2001; Terrell et al. 2001 argue that intergroup transmission prevents accurate historical reconstruction.

9. Gray and Jordan 2000.

10. Dixon 1997, 48.

11. See Renfrew 1990 for details of these hypotheses.

12. Gray and Atkinson 2003.

13. Atkinson et al. 2008.

14. Cited in Atkinson et al. 2008.

15. Pagel, Atkinson, and Meade 2007.

16. See Rubin 1995 for how memory biases can distort orally transmitted folktales.

17. Barbrook et al. 1998; Howe et al. 2001.

18. The classic narrative account of the fall of the Roman Empire is Bury 1923, while modern accounts include Heather 2005.

19. Turchin 2003, 2008. Note that the dynamical models discussed in this section have also been used in physics (e.g., mechanics) and chemistry (e.g., kinetics) as well as biology (e.g., population ecology). I focus here on the latter examples from population ecology because these are more applicable to human cultural change, given that both biological and cultural systems can be described as Darwinian (unlike physical and chemical systems).

20. In the interests of readability I will not include actual mathematical expressions for these functions. See Turchin 2003 for details.

21. The following discussion is based on Turchin 2003.

22. Collins 1995; see Turchin 2003, chapter 2. Note that for ease of exposition I have excluded "marchland position" from my discussion and illustration in the figure. However, Turchin shows that the conclusions remain the same if marchland position is considered.

23. Turchin 2003, chapter 2. Figure 5.2c is derived using Turchin's equation 2.11, with $c = 2$, $b = 1$, and $a = 1$. Starting points for empires 1, 2, and 3 are $A = 2.2, 2.3$, and 9.5 units, respectively.

24. Following Ibn Khaldun, Turchin calls collective solidarity "asabiya." I will use the more familiar term "cohesiveness."

25. Boyd and Richerson 1985, 2009. See also chapter 8.

26. Tajfel 1982.

27. Turchin 2003, figure 4.4.

28. Turchin 2003, table 5.1.

29. Fracchia and Lewontin 1999, 77–78; see also Ingold 2007.

30. Fracchia and Lewontin 1999, 77.

CHAPTER SIX

1. See Elena and Lenski 2003 for an overview of this research.

2. Wright 1932.

3. See Mesoudi 2009a and Mesoudi and Whiten 2008 for an expanded discussion of the benefits of experiments for studying cultural evolution. For a related argument in favor of the use of experiments in the social sciences, but from a nonevolutionary perspective, see Falk and Heckman 2009.

4. See Levitt and List 2007 for a typical critique of experiments in economics.

5. Bartlett 1932.

6. Bartlett 1932, 123.

7. Source: http://www.google.com/trends. There was at least one positive side effect of the scandal, however, in that many people appeared to have learned a new word. Google searches for the single word "transgressions" increased 28-fold at exactly the same time as Woods made his public apology, presumably because people who didn't know what "transgressions" meant were desperately trying to find out exactly what sordid activity he was admitting to having done.

8. Humphrey 1976; Byrne and Whiten 1988; Dunbar 2003.

9. Dunbar 2003.

10. Mesoudi, Whiten, and Dunbar 2006.

11. Boyer 1994; Atran 2002.

12. Barrett and Nyhof 2001, experiment 2.

13. Kirby, Cornish, and Smith 2008.

14. See also Kirby, Dowman, and Griffiths 2007 and Chater, Reali, and Christiansen 2009 for challenges to nativist theories of language structure from a cultural evolution perspective.

15. Gintis 2007; Thaler and Sunstein 2008.

16. Schotter and Sopher 2003.

17. Spencer et al. 2004.

18. Bettinger and Eerkens 1999.

19. Betinger and Eerkens called it "indirect bias" following Boyd and Richerson's original terminology, but I will call it "prestige bias" to maintain consistency with previous chapters.

20. Bettinger and Eerkens 1999, 237.

21. Mesoudi and O'Brien 2008a; see also Mesoudi and O'Brien 2008b; Mesoudi 2008b.

22. In the original paper we describe three phases; for simplicity I have here combined the first two phases into a single phase.

23. This is similar to the argument proposed by Fisher 1930 for the evolution of sexual reproduction in biological organisms. Fisher argued that sexual reproduction allows different beneficial mutations that have arisen in separate individuals to be brought together through recombination. In asexual organisms, in contrast, different beneficial mutations will not co-occur unless they independently evolve in the same individual lineage. Hence, both asexual reproduction (biology) and guided variation (culture) will drive individuals to locally optimal peaks in an adaptive landscape, whereas both sexual reproduction/recombination (biology) and prestige bias (culture) allow individuals to jump to higher peaks in the adaptive landscape.

24. Mesoudi 2008b.

25. Cheshier and Kelly 2006.

26. On conformity, Jacobs and Campbell 1961; Efferson et al. 2008; on intergroup processes, Insko et al. 1983; on migration, Gurerk, Irlenbusch, and Rockenbach 2006; on cultural drift, Salganik, Dodds, and Watts 2006; on social learning mechanisms, Caldwell and Millen 2009.

CHAPTER SEVEN

1. Grant and Grant 1989.

2. See Endler 1986 for a review of studies of natural selection in wild populations.

3. See Aunger 1995, 2004 for a comprehensive discussion of the limitations of ethnographic methods and statistical methods for overcoming such limitations.

4. Hewlett and Cavalli-Sforza 1986.

5. It should be stressed that there is no suggestion that the Aka, or any of the hunter-gatherer societies discussed in this chapter, represent a "primitive" stage of cultural evolution. As made clear in chapter 2, this assumption was made by early cultural evolution scholars such as Tylor and Morgan, but is emphatically not implied by contemporary theories of cultural evolution, which do not classify societies into stages and focus on variation within societies as much as variation between societies. So the Aka are to be studied as a human society in their own right, not as a more primitive version of Western society.

6. J. R. Harris 1995.

7. E.g., Ohmagari and Berkes 1997.

8. Nisbett and Wilson 1977.

9. Aunger 2000.

10. In order to quantitatively measure similarity between individuals, Aunger 2000 used optimal scaling to reduce multiple categorical (i.e., taboo present/taboo absent) response variables into a single position within a three-dimensional space, and then calculated the Euclidean distance between individuals within this response space. Tukey-Kramer t-tests were then used to determine whether the similarity between a pair of individuals was statistically significant.

11. This and the following quotes are from Aunger 2000, 452–453. Italics and square brackets are in the original.

12. Tehrani and Collard 2009.

13. Reyes García et al. 2009.

14. McDade et al. 2007.

15. See also models of vertical, oblique, and horizontal transmission by McElreath and Strimling 2008.

16. Hull 1988.

17. Popper 1979, 261.

18. Hull 1988, 353.

19. Planck 1950, 33.

20. Hull 1988, 357.

21. Watts 1999.

22. Bentley and Shennan 2005.

CHAPTER EIGHT

1. Hodgson 2005.

2. Nelson and Winter 1982; see Nelson and Winter 2002 for an updated but briefer account.

3. Simon 1955.

4. Lux 1995.

5. Nelson and Winter 1982, 14.

6. Tripsas and Gavetti 2000.

7. Quoted in Tripsas and Gavetti 2000, 1157.

8. Klepper 1997.

9. See Klepper and Simons 2000 for the following tire industry example.

10. See also Basalla 1988; Petroski 1994.

11. Brockhurst et al. 2007.

12. Henrich et al. 2005.

13. Gintis et al. 2003; Fehr, Goette, and Zehnder 2009.

14. Krueger and Mas 2004.

15. Lee and Rupp 2007.

16. Fehr, Goette, and Zehnder 2009.

17. Gintis et al. 2003; Henrich 2004a; Richerson and Boyd 2005.

18. Cultural group selection should not be confused with genetic group selection. The latter requires there to be genetic variation between genetically homogenous groups, with groups comprising genes for ingroup altruism out-reproducing groups that are genetically less altruistic toward ingroup members. While this kind of explanation was common in biology prior to the

1960s, biologists such as W. D. Hamilton 1964 showed that genetically altruistic groups are vulnerable to invasion by selfish free riders. These free riders reap the benefits of being in an altruistic group but do not pay the cost of ever helping others. Since Hamilton's work, altruism in nonhuman species has been explained in terms of either kin selection, where individuals help other individuals who are genetically related to themselves (e.g., offspring, siblings) because those relatives share genes for kin selection, or reciprocal altruism, where one individual helps another (unrelated) individual in return for an equal amount of help in the future. All nonhuman cooperation can seemingly be explained in terms of these two principles. Even chimpanzees, our closest relative species, do not cooperate with unfamiliar nonkin. In the ultimatum game, for example, chimpanzees behave in an entirely selfish way by failing to reject any nonzero offer (Jensen, Call, and Tomasello 2007). Human altruism, in contrast, is frequently directed toward nonkin and in situations in which there is no possibility of future reciprocation, as is the case in most experimental economic games. As such it cannot be explained solely in terms of kin selection and reciprocal altruism. Cultural group selection does not suffer the problem of free riders that genetic group selection does because cultural evolutionary processes such as conformity act to make groups internally homogenous. This would make it more difficult for free riders to emerge, given that conformity inhibits the spread of rare free-riding behavior. For further details see Gintis et al. 2003; Henrich 2004a; Richerson and Boyd 2005.

19. Richerson, Collins, and Genet 2006.

20. Cordes et al. 2008.

21. Orlitzky, Schmidt, and Rynes 2003.

CHAPTER NINE

1. Tylor 1871, 1.

2. Kroeber 1948, 253.

3. Baldwin et al. 2006.

4. For overviews of the research discussed in this chapter, see the contributions in Laland and Galef 2009.

5. For the following examples, see Galef and Laland 2005; Leadbeater and Chittka 2007.

6. Boyd and Richerson 1985.

7. Whiten et al. 1999.

8. On orangutans, see van Schaik et al. 2003; on capuchins, Perry et al. 2003; on whales and dolphins, Rendell and Whitehead 2001; Krutzen et al. 2005.

9. See Whiten and Mesoudi 2008 for a review of experimental studies, and Lycett, Collard, and McGrew 2007 for an application of phylogenetic methods to chimpanzee culture.

10. Laland and Hoppitt 2003.

11. Helfman and Schultz 1984.

12. Lynch and Baker 1993.

13. See Basalla 1988 and Wilder 1968 for details of the cumulative cultural evolution of technology and knowledge, respectively.

14. Tennie, Call, and Tomasello 2009; Tomasello, Kruger, and Ratner 1993.

15. Note that Tomasello does not imply that culture is progressive in the sense described in chapter 2 and as used by early cultural evolutionists such as Tylor and Morgan. There is no implication that the ratcheting up of culture is inevitable or follows fixed stages, simply that human culture *can* accumulate modifications, whereas nonhuman culture cannot.

16. Tomasello 1996.

17. Nagell, Olguin, and Tomasello 1993.

18. Whiten, Horner, and de Waal 2005.

19. Horner et al. 2006; Whiten et al. 2007.

20. Horner and Whiten 2005.

21. Lyons, Young, and Keil 2007.

22. Marshall-Pescini and Whiten 2008.

23. Hrubesch, Preuschoft, and van Schaik 2009.

24. Csibra and Gergely 2009; see also the earlier relevance theory of Sperber and Wilson 1986 related to adult communication.

25. Senju and Csibra 2008.

26. Gergely, Bekkering, and Kiraly 2002.

27. Thornton and McAuliffe 2006.

28. Caldwell and Millen 2009.

CHAPTER TEN

1. For a full discussion of the structure of a possible science of cultural evolution, see Mesoudi, Whiten, and Laland 2006; Mesoudi 2007.

2. I have constructed this primarily from the popular undergraduate textbook *Evolutionary Biology* by Douglas Futuyma 1998, especially 12–14. Note that I have categorized paleobiology as a branch of systematics, which is not commonly done but suits my purposes here.

3. Carroll 2005.

4. Pearson, Lemons, and McGinnis 2005.

5. For further discussion of cultural evo-devo, see Reader 2006; Wimsatt 2006.

6. This example points to a potential difference between cultural and biological evolution: whereas modules in biological evolution are typically repeated or borrowed from within the same organism (e.g., a repeated body segment), the greater possibility for horizontal transmission in cultural evolution means that modules can be imported from one invention to another (e.g., a corkscrew imported into a Swiss Army Knife).

7. Mesoudi and O'Brien 2008c.

8. Aunger 2002.

9. Quian Quiroga et al. 2005.

10. Rizzolatti et al. 1996.

11. Rizzolatti et al. 2002.

12. Keysers 2009.

13. Boyd and Richerson 2009.

14. See Endler 1986, especially chapter 3, for methods for detecting natural selection in the wild.

15. For more on how these methods might be applied to cultural evolution, see Laland and Brown 2002; Mesoudi, Whiten, and Laland 2006.

16. Christakis and Fowler 2009.

17. Joiner 1999.

18. Mesoudi 2009b.

19. Lux 1995; Gintis 2007; Thaler and Sunstein 2008.

Works Cited

Aberle, D. F. 1961. Matrilineal descent in cross-cultural perspective. In *Matrilineal kinship*, edited by D. M. Schneider and K. Gough 655–730. Berkeley: University of California Press.

Ambrose, S. H. 2001. Paleolithic technology and human evolution. *Science* 291:1748–1753.

Aoki, K., J. Y. Wakano, and M. W. Feldman. 2005. The emergence of social learning in a temporally changing environment: A theoretical model. *Current Anthropology* 46:334–340.

Asch, S. E. 1951. Effects of group pressure on the modification and distortion of judgments. In *Groups, leadership and men*, edited by H. Guetzkow, 177–190. Pittsburgh, PA: Carnegie Press.

Atkinson, Q. D., A. Meade, C. Venditti, S. J. Greenhill, and M. Pagel. 2008. Languages evolve in punctuational bursts. *Science* 319:588.

Atran, S. 2001. The trouble with memes: Inference versus imitation in cultural creation. *Human Nature* 12:351–381.

———. 2002. *In gods we trust: The evolutionary landscape of religion.* New York: Oxford University Press.

Aunger, R. 1995. On ethnography: Storytelling or science. *Current Anthropology* 36:97–130.

———. 2000. The life history of culture learning in a face-to-face society. *Ethos* 28:1–38.

———. 2002. *The electric meme.* New York: Free Press.

———. 2004. *Reflexive ethnographic science.* Walnut Creek, CA: Altamira.

Baldwin, J. R., S. L. Faulkner, M. L. Hecht, and S. L. Lindsley.

2006. *Redefining culture: Perspectives across disciplines.* Mahwah, NJ: Lawrence Erlbaum.

Bandura, A. 1977. *Social learning theory.* Oxford: Prentice-Hall.

Bandura, A., D. Ross, and S. A. Ross. 1961. Transmission of aggression through imitation of aggressive models. *Journal of Abnormal and Social Psychology* 63:575–582.

Barbrook, A. C., C. J. Howe, N. Blake, and P. Robinson. 1998. The phylogeny of the *Canterbury Tales. Nature* 394:839.

Barrett, D. B., G. T. Kurian, and T. M. Johnson. 2001. *World Christian encyclopedia: A comparative survey of churches and religions in the modern world:* Oxford: Oxford University Press.

Barrett, J. L., and M. A. Nyhof. 2001. Spreading non-natural concepts: The role of intuitive conceptual structures in memory and transmission of cultural materials. *Journal of Cognition and Culture* 1:69–100.

Bartlett, F. C. 1932. *Remembering.* Oxford: Macmillan.

Basalla, G. 1988. *The evolution of technology.* Cambridge: Cambridge University Press.

Bell, A. V., P. J. Richerson, and R. McElreath. 2009. Culture rather than genes provides greater scope for the evolution of large-scale human prosociality. *Proceedings of the National Academy of Sciences* 106:17671–17674.

Bentley, R. A., M. W. Hahn, and S. J. Shennan. 2004. Random drift and culture change. *Proceedings of the Royal Society B* 271:1443–1450.

Bentley, R. A., and S. J. Shennan. 2005. Random copying and cultural evolution. *Science* 309:877–879.

Benton, T. 2000. Social causes and natural relations. In *Alas, poor Darwin,* edited by H. Rose and S. Rose, 206–224. New York: Harmony.

Bettinger, R. L., and J. Eerkens. 1999. Point typologies, cultural transmission, and the spread of bow-and-arrow technology in the prehistoric Great Basin. *American Antiquity* 64:231–242.

Blackmore, S. 1999. *The meme machine.* Oxford: Oxford University Press.

Bloch, M. 2000. A well-disposed social anthropologist's problems with memes. In *Darwinizing culture,* edited by R. Aunger, 189–204. Oxford: Oxford University Press.

Boas, F. 1920. The methods of ethnology. *American Anthropologist* 22: 311–321.

Borgerhoff Mulder, M., C. L. Nunn, and M. C. Towner. 2006. Cultural macroevolution and the transmission of traits. *Evolutionary Anthropology* 15:52–64.

Boyd, R., and P. J. Richerson. 1985. *Culture and the evolutionary process.* Chicago: University of Chicago Press.

———. 1995. Why does culture increase human adaptability? *Ethology and Sociobiology* 16:125–143.

———. 2009. Culture and the evolution of human cooperation. *Philosophical Transactions of the Royal Society B* 364:3281.

Boyer, P. 1994. *The naturalness of religious ideas: A cognitive theory of religion.* Berkeley: University of California Press.

Bramanti, B., M. G. Thomas, W. Haak, M. Unterlaender, P. Jores, K. Tambets, I. Antanaitis-Jacobs, M. N. Haidle, R. Jankauskas, and C. J. Kind. 2009. Genetic discontinuity between local hunter-gatherers and central Europe's first farmers. *Science* 326:137.

Brockhurst, M. A., N. Colegrave, D. J. Hodgson, and A. Buckling. 2007. Niche occupation limits adaptive radiation in experimental microcosms. *PLOS One* 2:e193.

Bury, J. B. 1923. *History of the later Roman empire*. London: Macmillan.

Byrne, R. W., and A. Whiten, eds. 1988. *Machiavellian intelligence: Social expertise and the evolution of intellect in monkeys, apes, and humans.* Oxford: Clarendon Press.

Cadieu, E., M. W. Neff, P. Quignon, K. Walsh, K. Chase, H. G. Parker, B. M. VonHoldt, A. Rhue, A. Boyko, and A. Byers. 2009. Coat variation in the domestic dog is governed by variants in three genes. *Science* 326:150–153.

Caldwell, C., and A. E. Millen. 2009. Social learning mechanisms and cumulative cultural evolution: Is imitation necessary? *Psychological Science* 20:1478–1483.

Camerer, C., and R. H. Thaler. 1995. Anomalies: Ultimatums, dictators and manners. *Journal of Economic Perspectives* 9:209–219.

Campbell, D. T. 1960. Blind variation and selective retentions in creative thought as in other knowledge processes. *Psychological Review* 67:380–400.

———. 1965. Variation and selective retention in socio-cultural evolution. In *Social change in developing areas*, edited by H. R. Barringer, G. I. Blanksten, and R. W. Mack, 19–49. Cambridge, MA: Schenkman.

Carninci, P., and Y. Hayashizaki. 2007. Noncoding RNA transcription beyond annotated genes. *Current Opinion in Genetics and Development* 17:139–144.

Carroll, R. L. 2005. *Endless forms most beautiful*. New York: W. W. Norton.

Cavalli-Sforza, L. L., and M. W. Feldman. 1981. *Cultural transmission and evolution*. Princeton: Princeton University Press.

Cavalli Sforza, L. L., M. W. Feldman, K. H. Chen, and S. M. Dornbusch. 1982. Theory and observation in cultural transmission. *Science* 218:19–27.

Chater, N., F. Reali, and M. H. Christiansen. 2009. Restrictions on biological adaptation in language evolution. *Proceedings of the National Academy of Sciences* 106:1015–1020.

Cheshier, J., and R. L. Kelly. 2006. Projectile point shape and durability: The effect of thickness:length. *American Antiquity* 71:353–363.

Christakis, N. A., and J. H. Fowler. 2009. *Connected: The surprising power of our social networks and how they shape our lives.* New York: Little, Brown and Co.

Collard, M., S. J. Shennan, and J. J. Tehrani. 2006. Branching versus blending in macroscale cultural evolution: A comparative study. In *Mapping our ancestors: Phylogenetic methods in anthropology and prehistory*, edited by C. P. Lipo, M. J. O'Brien, S. Shennan, and M. Collard, 53–63. Hawthorne, NY: Aldine de Gruyter.

Collins, R. 1995. Prediction in macrosociology: The case of the Soviet collapse. *American Journal of Sociology* 100:1552–1593.

Cordes, C., P. J. Richerson, R. McElreath, and P. Strimling. 2008. A naturalistic approach to the theory of the firm: The role of cooperation and cultural evolution. *Journal of Economic Behavior and Organization* 68:125–139.

Cronk, L. 1999. *That complex whole: Culture and the evolution of human behavior.* Boulder, CO: Westview Press.

Csibra, G., and G. Gergely. 2009. Natural pedagogy. *Trends in Cognitive Sciences* 13:148–153.

Darwin, C. 1859. *The origin of species.* London: Penguin, 1968. Original edition, 1859.

———. 1871. *The descent of man.* London: Gibson Square, 2003. Original edition, 1871.

Dawkins, R. 1976. *The selfish gene.* Oxford: Oxford University Press.

Dennett, D. 1995. *Darwin's dangerous idea.* New York: Simon & Schuster.

Diamond, J. 1978. The Tasmanians: The longest isolation, the simplest technology. *Nature* 273:185–186.

———. 1998. *Guns, germs and steel.* London: Vintage.

Diamond, J., and P. Bellwood. 2003. Farmers and their languages: The first expansions. *Science* 300:597–603.

Diamond, J. M. 2000. Taiwan's gift to the world. *Nature* 403:709.

Dixon, R. M. W. 1997. *The rise and fall of language.* Cambridge: Cambridge University Press.

Doolittle, W. F. 2009. The practice of classification and the theory of evolution, and what the demise of Charles Darwin's tree of life hypothesis means for both of them. *Philosophical Transactions of the Royal Society B* 364:2221.

Dunbar, R. I. M. 2003. The social brain. *Annual Review of Anthropology* 32:163–181.

Durham, W. H. 1991. *Coevolution: Genes, culture, and human diversity.* Stanford: Stanford University Press.

Durkheim, É. 1938 [1966]. *The rules of sociological method.* Translated by S. A. Solovay and J. H. Mueller. Edited by G. E. G. Catlin. 8th ed. New York: Free Press.

Efferson, C., R. Lalive, P. J. Richerson, R. McElreath, and M. Lubell. 2008. Conformists and mavericks: The empirics of frequency-dependent cultural transmission. *Evolution and Human Behavior* 29:56–64.

Elena, S. F., and R. E. Lenski. 2003. Evolution experiments with microorganisms: The dynamics and genetic bases of adaptation. *Nature Reviews Genetics* 4:457–469.

Endler, J. A. 1986. *Natural selection in the wild.* Princeton: Princeton University Press.

Epstein, J. M. 2007. *Generative social science: Studies in agent-based computational modeling.* Princeton, NJ: Princeton University Press.

Epstein, J. M., and R. Axtell. 1996. *Growing artificial societies.* Cambridge: MIT Press.

Falk, A., and J. J. Heckman. 2009. Lab experiments are a major source of knowledge in the social sciences. *Science* 326:535.

Fehr, E., L. Goette, and C. Zehnder. 2009. A behavioral account of the labor market: The role of fairness concerns. *Annual Review of Economics* 1:355–384.

Fisher, R. A. 1930. *The genetical theory of natural selection.* Oxford: Clarendon Press.

Fitch, W. 2008. Glossogeny and phylogeny: Cultural evolution meets genetic evolution. *Trends in Genetics* 24:373–374.

Fortunato, L., C. Holden, and R. Mace. 2006. From bridewealth to dowry? *Human Nature* 17:355–376.

Fracchia, J., and R. C. Lewontin. 1999. Does culture evolve? *History and Theory* 38:52–78.

Freeman, D. 1974. The evolutionary theories of Charles Darwin and Herbert Spencer. *Current Anthropology* 15:211–237.

Futuyma, D. J. 1998. *Evolutionary biology.* Sunderland, MA: Sinauer.

Galef, B. G., and K. N. Laland. 2005. Social learning in animals: Empirical studies and theoretical models. *BioScience* 55:489–499.

Galton, F. 1889. Comment on Tylor, E. B., On a method of investigating the development of institutions, applied to laws of marriage and descent. *Journal of the Royal Anthropological Institute* 18:270.

Gangestad, S. W., M. G. Haselton, and D. M. Buss. 2006. Evolutionary foundations of cultural variation: Evoked culture and mate preferences. *Psychological Inquiry* 17:75–95.

Gergely, G., H. Bekkering, and I. Kiraly. 2002. Rational imitation in preverbal infants. *Nature* 415:755.

Ghiselin, M. T. 2003. *The triumph of the Darwinian method.* Mineola, NY: Dover.

Gintis, H. 2007. A framework for the unification of the behavioral sciences. *Behavioral and Brain Sciences* 30:1–61.

Gintis, H., S. Bowles, R. Boyd, and E. Fehr. 2003. Explaining altruistic behavior in humans. *Evolution and Human Behavior* 24:153–172.

Goldstone, R. L., M. E. Roberts, and T. M. Gureckis. 2008. Emergent processes in group behavior. *Current Directions in Psychological Science* 17:10–15.

Goodwin, N. B., S. Balshine-Earn, and J. D. Reynolds. 1998. Evolutionary transitions in parental care in cichlid fish. *Proceedings of the Royal Society B* 265:2265–2272.

Gould, S. J. 1990. *Wonderful life: The burgess shale and the nature of history.* New York: W. W. Norton.

———. 1991. *Bully for brontosaurus.* New York: W. W. Norton.

Grant, B. R., and P. R. Grant. 1989. *Evolutionary dynamics of a natural population: The large cactus finch of the Galapagos.* Chicago: University of Chicago Press.

Grant, P. R. 1986. *Ecology and evolution of Darwin's finches.* Princeton, NJ: Princeton University Press.

Gray, R. D., and Q. D. Atkinson. 2003. Language-tree divergence times support the Anatolian theory of Indo-European origin. *Nature* 426:435–439.

Gray, R. D., S. J. Greenhill, and R. M. Ross. 2007. The pleasures and perils of Darwinizing culture (with phylogenies). *Biological Theory* 2:360–375.

Gray, R. D., and F. M. Jordan. 2000. Language trees support the express-train sequence of Austronesian expansion. *Nature* 405:1052–1055.

Griffiths, T. L., M. L. Kalish, and S. Lewandowsky. 2008. Theoretical and empirical evidence for the impact of inductive biases on cultural evolution. *Philosophical Transactions of the Royal Society of London B* 363:3503–3514.

Grimes, B. F. 2002. *Ethnologue: Languages of the world.* 14th edition. Summer Institute of Linguistics.

Guglielmino, C. R., C. Viganotti, B. Hewlett, and L. L. Cavalli-Sforza. 1995. Cultural variation in Africa. *Proceedings of the National Academy of Sciences* 92:585–589.

Guiso, L., P. Sapienza, and L. Zingales. 2006. Does culture affect economic outcomes? *Journal of Economic Perspectives* 20:23–48.

Gurerk, O., B. Irlenbusch, and B. Rockenbach. 2006. The competitive advantage of sanctioning institutions. *Science* 312:108–111.

Haldane, J. B. S. 1927. A mathematical theory of natural and artificial selection, part v: Selection and mutation. *Proceedings of the Cambridge Philosophical Society* 23:838.

Hamilton, W. D. 1964. The genetical evolution of social behaviour I and II. *Journal of Theoretical Biology* 7:1–52.

Harris, J. R. 1995. Where is the child's environment? A group socialization theory of development. *Psychological Review* 102:458–489.

Harris, M. 1989. *Cows, pigs, wars and witches: The riddles of culture.* New York: Vintage.

Harvey, P. H., and M. D. Pagel. 1991. *The comparative method in evolutionary biology.* Oxford: Oxford University Press.

Heath, C., C. Bell, and E. Sternberg. 2001. Emotional selection in memes: The case of urban legends. *Journal of Personality and Social Psychology* 81:1028–1041.

Heath, C., and D. Heath. 2007. *Made to stick.* London: Random House.

Heather, P. 2005. *The fall of the Roman empire*: London: Macmillan.

Heine, S. J. 2008. *Cultural psychology.* New York: Norton.

Heine, S. J., and D. R. Lehman. 1997. Culture, dissonance, and self-affirmation. *Personality and Social Psychology Bulletin* 23:389.

Heine, S. J., and A. Norenzayan. 2006. Toward a psychological science for a cultural species. *Perspectives on Psychological Science* 1:251–269.

Helfman, G. S., and E. T. Schultz. 1984. Social transmission of behavioral traditions in a coral-reef fish. *Animal Behaviour* 32:379–384.

Henrich, J. 2001. Cultural transmission and the diffusion of innovations. *American Anthropologist* 103:992–1013.

———. 2004a. Cultural group selection, coevolutionary processes and large-scale cooperation. *Journal of Economic Behavior and Organization* 53:3–35.

———. 2004b. Demography and cultural evolution: How adaptive cultural processes can produce maladaptive losses—the Tasmanian case. *American Antiquity* 69:197–214.

———. 2008. A cultural species. In *Explaining culture scientifically*, edited by M. Brown, 184–210. Seattle: University of Washington Press.

Henrich, J., and R. Boyd. 1998. The evolution of conformist transmission and the emergence of between-group differences. *Evolution and Human Behavior* 19:215–241.

———. 2002. On modeling cognition and culture: Why cultural evolution does not require replication of representations. *Journal of Cognition and Culture* 2:87–112.

Henrich, J., R. Boyd, S. Bowles, C. Camerer, E. Fehr, H. Gintis, R. McElreath, M. Alvard, A. Barr, J. Ensminger, N. S. Henrich, K. Hill, F. Gil-White, M. Gurven, F. W. Marlowe, J. Q. Patton, and D. Tracer. 2005. "Economic man" in cross-cultural perspective: Behavioral experiments in 15 small-scale societies. *Behavioral and Brain Sciences* 28:795–855.

Henrich, J., J. Ensminger, R. McElreath, A. Barr, C. Barrett, A. Bolyanatz, J. C. Cardenas, M. Gurven, E. Gwako, N. Henrich, C. Lesorogol, F. W. Marlowe, D. Tracer, and J. Ziker. 2010. Markets, religion, community size, and the evolution of fairness and punishment. *Science* 327:1480–1484.

Henrich, J., and F. J. Gil White. 2001. The evolution of prestige. *Evolution and Human Behavior* 22:165–196.

Henrich, J., S. J. Heine, and A. Norenzayan. 2010. The weirdest people in the world? *Behavioral and Brain Sciences* 33:61–135.

Henrich, J., and R. McElreath. 2003. The evolution of cultural evolution. *Evolutionary Anthropology* 12:123–135.

Herrmann, E., J. Call, M. V. Hernandez-Lloreda, B. Hare, and M. Tomasello. 2007. Humans have evolved specialized skills of social cognition: The cultural intelligence hypothesis. *Science* 317:1360–1366.

Hewlett, B., and L. L. Cavalli-Sforza. 1986. Cultural transmission among Aka pygmies. *American Anthropologist* 88:922–934.

Hewlett, B., A. De Silvestri, and C. R. Guglielmino. 2002. Semes and genes in Africa. *Current Anthropology* 43:313–321.

Hodgson, G. M. 2005. Generalizing Darwinism to social evolution: Some early attempts. *Journal of Economic Issues* 39:899–914.

Hodgson, G. M., and T. Knudsen. 2006. Dismantling Lamarckism: Why descriptions of socio-economic evolution as Lamarckian are misleading. *Journal of Evolutionary Economics* 16:343–366.

———. 2010. *Darwin's conjecture: The search for general principles of social and economic evolution.* Chicago: University of Chicago Press.

Holden, C. J., and R. Mace. 2003. Spread of cattle led to the loss of matrilineal descent in Africa: A coevolutionary analysis. *Proceedings of the Royal Society B* 270:2425–2433.

Horner, V., and A. Whiten. 2005. Causal knowledge and imitation/emulation switching in chimpanzees (*Pan troglodytes*) and children (*Homo sapiens*). *Animal Cognition* 8:164–181.

Horner, V., A. Whiten, E. Flynn, and F. B. M. de Waal. 2006. Faithful replication of foraging techniques along cultural transmission chains by chimpanzees and children. *Proceedings of the National Academy of Sciences* 103:13878.

Howe, C. J., A. C. Barbrook, M. Spencer, P. Robinson, B. Bordalejo, and L. R. Mooney. 2001. Manuscript evolution. *Trends in Genetics* 17:147–152.

Hrubesch, C., S. Preuschoft, and C. van Schaik. 2009. Skill mastery inhibits adoption of observed alternative solutions among chimpanzees (*Pan troglodytes*). *Animal Cognition* 12:209–216.

Hull, D. L. 1988. *Science as a process*. Chicago: University of Chicago Press.

Humphrey, N. K. 1976. The social function of intellect. In *Growing points in ethology*, edited by P. P. G. Bateson and R. A. Hinde, 303–317. Cambridge: Cambridge University Press.

Huxley, J. S. 1942. *Evolution, the modern synthesis*. London: Allen & Unwin.

Ingold, T. 2007. The trouble with 'evolutionary biology.' *Anthropology Today* 23:3–7.

Insko, C. A., R. Gilmore, S. Drenan, A. Lipsitz, D. Moehle, and J. W. Thibaut. 1983. Trade versus expropriation in open groups: A comparison of two types of social power. *Journal of Personality and Social Psychology* 44:977–999.

Jablonka, E., and M. J. Lamb. 2005. *Evolution in four dimensions*. Cambridge: MIT Press.

Jackson, G. B., and A. K. Romney. 1973. Historical inference from cross-cultural data: The case of dowry. *Ethos* 1:517–520.

Jacobs, R. C., and D. T. Campbell. 1961. The perpetuation of an arbitrary tradition through several generations of a laboratory microculture. *Journal of Abnormal and Social Psychology* 62:649–658.

James, W. 1880. Great men, great thoughts, and the environment. *Atlantic Monthly* 46:441–459.

Jensen, K., J. Call, and M. Tomasello. 2007. Chimpanzees are rational maximizers in an ultimatum game. *Science* 318:107–109.

Johnson, A. W., and T. K. Earle. 2000. *The evolution of human societies: From foraging group to agrarian state*. Stanford: Stanford University Press.

Joiner, J. T. E. 1999. The clustering and contagion of suicide. *Current Directions in Psychological Science* 8:89–92.

Jones, E. E., and V. A. Harris. 1967. The attribution of attitudes. *Journal of Experimental Social Psychology* 3:1–24.

Jordan, P., and S. Shennan. 2003. Cultural transmission, language, and basketry traditions amongst the California Indians. *Journal of Anthropological Archaeology* 22:42–74.

Keysers, C. 2009. Mirror neurons. *Current Biology* 19:R971–R973.

Kimura, M. 1983. *The neutral theory of molecular evolution*. Cambridge: Cambridge University Press.

Kirby, S., H. Cornish, and K. Smith. 2008. Cumulative cultural evolution in the laboratory: An experimental approach to the origins of structure in human language. *Proceedings of the National Academy of Sciences* 105:10681–10686.

Kirby, S., M. Dowman, and T. L. Griffiths. 2007. Innateness and culture in the evolution of language. *Proceedings of the National Academy of Sciences* 104:5241–5245.

Klepper, S. 1997. Industry life cycles. *Industrial and Corporate Change* 6:145–182.

Klepper, S., and K. L. Simons. 2000. The making of an oligopoly: Firm survival and technological change in the evolution of the U.S. tire industry. *Journal of Political Economy* 108:728–760.

Krauss, M. 1992. The world's languages in crisis. *Language* 68:1–42.

Kroeber, A. L. 1916. Zuni potsherds. *American Museum of Natural History, Anthropological Papers* 18:1–37.

———. 1917. The superorganic. *American Anthropologist* 19:163–213.

———. 1948. *Anthropology.* New York: Harcourt, Brace and Co.

Kroeber, A. L., and C. Kluckohn. 1952. *Culture.* New York: Vantage.

Krueger, A. B., and A. Mas. 2004. Strikes, scabs, and tread separations: Labor strife and the production of defective Bridgestone/Firestone tires. *Journal of Political Economy* 112:253–289.

Krutzen, M., J. Mann, M. R. Heithaus, R. C. Connor, L. Bejder, and W. B. Sherwin. 2005. Cultural transmission of tool use in bottlenose dolphins. *Proceedings of the National Academy of Sciences* 102:8939–8943.

Labov, W. 1972. *Sociolinguistic patterns.* Philadephia: University of Pennsylvania Press.

Laland, K. N., and G. R. Brown. 2002. *Sense and nonsense.* Oxford: Oxford University Press.

Laland, K. N., and B. G. Galef. 2009. *The question of animal culture.* Cambridge: Harvard University Press.

Laland, K. N., and W. Hoppitt. 2003. Do animals have culture? *Evolutionary Anthropology* 12:150–159.

Leadbeater, E., and L. Chittka. 2007. Social learning in insects—from miniature brains to consensus building. *Current Biology* 17:703–713.

Lee, D., and N. G. Rupp. 2007. Retracting a gift: How does employee effort respond to wage reductions? *Journal of Labor Economics* 25:725–761.

Lehmann, W. P. 1992. *Historical linguistics: An introduction.* London: Routledge.

Lenski, R. E., and M. Travisano. 1994. Dynamics of adaptation and diversification—a 10,000-generation experiment with bacterial-populations. *Proceedings of the National Academy of Sciences* 91:6808–6814.

LeVine, R. A., and D. T. Campbell. 1973. *Ethnocentrism: Theories of conflict, ethnic attitudes, and group behavior.* New York: Wiley.

Levitt, S. D., and J. A. List. 2007. What do laboratory experiments measuring social preferences reveal about the real world? *Journal of Economic Perspectives* 21:153–174.

Lewontin, R. C. 1970. The units of selection. *Annual Review of Ecology and Systematics* 1:1–18.

Lieberman, E., J. B. Michel, J. Jackson, T. Tang, and M. A. Nowak. 2007. Quantifying the evolutionary dynamics of language. *Nature* 449:713–716.

Luria, S. E., and M. Delbrück. 1943. Mutations of bacteria from virus sensitivity to virus resistance. *Genetics* 28:491–511.

Lux, T. 1995. Herd behaviour, bubbles and crashes. *Economic Journal* 105:881–896.

Lycett, S. J., M. Collard, and W. C. McGrew. 2007. Phylogenetic analyses of behavior support existence of culture among wild chimpanzees. *Proceedings of the National Academy of Sciences* 104:17588.

Lycett, S. J., and N. von Cramon-Taubadel. 2008. Acheulean variability and hominin dispersals: A model-bound approach. *Journal of Archaeological Science* 35:553–562.

Lynch, A., and A. J. Baker. 1993. A population memetics approach to cultural-evolution in chaffinch song—meme diversity within populations. *American Naturalist* 141:597–620.

Lyons, D. E., A. G. Young, and F. C. Keil. 2007. The hidden structure of overimitation. *Proceedings of the National Academy of Sciences* 104:19751–19756.

Mace, R., and M. D. Pagel. 1994. The comparative method in anthropology. *Current Anthropology* 35:549–564.

Markus, H. R., and S. Kitayama. 1991. Culture and the self: Implications for cognition, emotion, and motivation. *Psychological Review* 98:224–253.

Marshall-Pescini, S., and A. Whiten. 2008. Chimpanzees (*Pan troglodytes*) and the question of cumulative culture: An experimental approach. *Animal Cognition* 11:449–456.

Masuda, T., and R. E. Nisbett. 2001. Attending holistically versus analytically. *Journal of Personality and Social Psychology* 81:922–934.

Mausner, B. 1953. Studies in social interaction: Effect of variation in one partner's prestige on the interaction of observer pairs. *Journal for Applied Psychology* 37:391–393.

Maynard Smith, J. 1986. Natural selection of culture? *New York Review of Books*, Nov. 6, 33.

Mayr, E. 1963. *Animal species and evolution*. Cambridge: Harvard University Press.

———. 1982. *The growth of biological thought*. Cambridge: Harvard University Press.

Mayr, E., and W. Provine, eds. 1980. *The evolutionary synthesis*. Cambridge: Harvard University Press.

McDade, T. W., V. Reyes-García, P. Blackinton, S. Tanner, T. Huanca, and W. R. Leonard. 2007. Ethnobotanical knowledge is associated with indices of child health in the Bolivian Amazon. *Proceedings of the National Academy of Sciences* 104:6134–6139.

McElreath, R., A. V. Bell, C. Efferson, M. Lubell, P. J. Richerson, and T. M. Waring. 2008. Beyond existence and aiming outside the laboratory: Estimating frequency-dependent and pay-off-biased social learning strategies. *Philosophical Transactions of the Royal Society B* 363:3515–3528.

McElreath, R., and R. Boyd. 2007. *Mathematical models of social evolution*. Chicago: University of Chicago Press.

McElreath, R., M. Lubell, P. J. Richerson, T. M. Waring, W. Baum, E. Edsten, C. Efferson, and B. Paciotti. 2005. Applying evolutionary models to the laboratory study of social learning. *Evolution and Human Behavior* 26:483–508.

McElreath, R., and P. Strimling. 2008. When natural selection favors imitation of parents. *Current Anthropology* 49:307–316.

McGeoch, J. A., and W. T. McDonald. 1931. Meaningful relation and retroactive inhibition. *American Journal of Psychology* 43:579–588.

McMahon, A., and R. McMahon. 2003. Finding families: Quantitative methods in language classification. *Transactions of the Philological Society* 101:7–55.

McMurray, B. 2007. Defusing the childhood vocabulary explosion. *Science* 317:631.

McPherson, M., L. Smith-Lovin, and J. M. Cook. 2001. Birds of a feather: Homophily in social networks. *Annual Review of Sociology* 27:415–444.

Mehl, M. R., S. Vazire, N. Ramirez-Esparza, R. B. Slatcher, and J. W. Pennebaker. 2007. Are women really more talkative than men? *Science* 317:82.

Mesoudi, A. 2007. A Darwinian theory of cultural evolution can promote an evolutionary synthesis for the social sciences. *Biological Theory* 2:263–275.

———. 2008a. Foresight in cultural evolution. *Biology and Philosophy* 23: 243–255.

———. 2008b. An experimental simulation of the 'copy-successful-individuals' cultural learning strategy: Adaptive landscapes, producer-scrounger dynamics and informational access costs. *Evolution and Human Behavior* 29:350–363.

———. 2009a. How cultural evolutionary theory can inform social psychology and vice versa. *Psychological Review* 116:929–952.

———. 2009b. The cultural dynamics of copycat suicide. *PLoS ONE* 4:e7252.

Mesoudi, A., and S. J. Lycett. 2009. Random copying, frequency-dependent copying and culture change. *Evolution and Human Behavior* 30:41–48.

Mesoudi, A., and M. J. O'Brien. 2008a. The cultural transmission of Great Basin projectile point technology I: An experimental simulation. *American Antiquity* 73:3–28.

———. 2008b. The cultural transmission of Great Basin projectile point technology II: An agent-based computer simulation. *American Antiquity* 73:627–644.

———. 2008c. The learning and transmission of hierarchical cultural recipes. *Biological Theory* 3:63–72.

Mesoudi, A., and A. Whiten. 2008. The multiple roles of cultural transmission experiments in understanding human cultural evolution. *Philosophical Transactions of the Royal Society B* 363:3489–3501.

Mesoudi, A., A. Whiten, and R. I. M. Dunbar. 2006. A bias for social information in human cultural transmission. *British Journal of Psychology* 97:405–423.

Mesoudi, A., A. Whiten, and K. N. Laland. 2004. Is human cultural evolution Darwinian? Evidence reviewed from the perspective of *The Origin of Species*. *Evolution* 58:1–11.

———. 2006. Towards a unified science of cultural evolution. *Behavioral and Brain Sciences* 29:329–383.

Moore, J. H. 1994. Putting anthropology back together again: The ethnogenetic critique of cladistic theory. *American Anthropologist* 96:925–948.

Morgan, L. H. 1877. *Ancient society*. New York: Henry Holt.

Morris, M. W., and K. Peng. 1994. Culture and cause: American and Chinese attributions for social and physical events. *Journal of Personality and Social Psychology* 67:949–949.

Murdock, G. P. 1967. *Ethnographic atlas*. Pittsburgh, PA: University of Pittsburgh Press.

Nagell, K., R. S. Olguin, and M. Tomasello. 1993. Processes of social learning in the tool use of chimpanzees (*Pan troglodytes*) and human children (*Homo sapiens*). *Journal of Comparative Psychology* 107:174–186.

Nassaney, M. S., and K. Pyle. 1999. The adoption of the bow and arrow in eastern North America: A view from central Arkansas. *American Antiquity* 64:243–263.

Nei, M., and S. Kumar. 2000. *Molecular evolution and phylogenetics*. Oxford: Oxford University Press.

Neiman, F. D. 1995. Stylistic variation in evolutionary perspective. *American Antiquity* 60:7–36.

Nelson, R. R. 2007. Universal Darwinism and evolutionary social science. *Biology and Philosophy* 22:73–94.

Nelson, R. R., and S. G. Winter. 1982. *An evolutionary theory of economic change*. Cambridge: Harvard University Press.

———. 2002. Evolutionary theorizing in economics. *Journal of Economic Perspectives* 16:23–46.

Nisbett, R. E. 1998. Race, genetics, and IQ. In *The black-white test score gap*, edited by C. Jencks and M. Phillips, 86–102. Washington, DC: Brookings Institution.

Nisbett, R. E., K. Peng, I. Choi, and A. Norenzayan. 2001. Culture and systems of thought: Holistic versus analytic cognition. *Psychological Review* 108:291–310.

Nisbett, R. E., and T. D. Wilson. 1977. Telling more than we can know: Verbal reports on mental processes. *Psychological Review* 84:231–259.

Norenzayan, A., E. E. Smith, B. J. Kim, and R. E. Nisbett. 2002. Cultural preferences for formal versus intuitive reasoning. *Cognitive Science* 26: 653–684.

Norenzayan, A., S. Atran, J. Faulkner, and M. Schaller. 2006. Memory and mystery: The cultural selection of minimally counterintuitive narratives. *Cognitive Science* 30:531–553.

O'Brien, M. J., J. Darwent, and R. L. Lyman. 2001. Cladistics is useful for reconstructing archaeological phylogenies: Palaeoindian points from the southeastern United States. *Journal of Archaeological Science* 28:1115–1136.

O'Brien, M. J., and R. L. Lyman. 2003. *Cladistics and archaeology*. Salt Lake City: University of Utah Press.

Ohmagari, K., and F. Berkes. 1997. Transmission of indigenous knowledge and bush skills among the Western James Bay Cree women of subarctic Canada. *Human Ecology* 25:197–222.

Oppenheimer, S. J., and M. Richards. 2001. Polynesian origins: Slow boat to Melanesia? *Nature* 410:166–167.

Orlitzky, M., F. L. Schmidt, and S. L. Rynes. 2003. Corporate social and financial performance: A meta-analysis. *Organization Studies* 24:403–441.

Pagel, M. 2009. Human language as a culturally transmitted replicator. *Nature Reviews Genetics* 10:405–415.

Pagel, M., Q. D. Atkinson, and A. Meade. 2007. Frequency of word-use predicts rates of lexical evolution throughout Indo-European history. *Nature* 449:717–721.

Pearson, J. C., D. Lemons, and W. McGinnis. 2005. Modulating hox gene functions during animal body patterning. *Nature Reviews Genetics* 6:893–904.

Peng, Y., H. Shi, X. Qi, C. Xiao, H. Zhong, R. Z. Ma, and B. Su. 2010. The ADH1B Arg47His polymorphism in East Asian populations and expansion of rice domestication in history. *BMC Evolutionary Biology* 10:15.

Perry, S., M. Baker, L. Fedigan, J. Gros-Louis, K. Jack, K. C. MacKinnon, J. H. Manson, M. Panger, K. Pyle, and L. Rose. 2003. Social conventions in wild white-faced capuchin monkeys—evidence for traditions in a neotropical primate. *Current Anthropology* 44:241–268.

Petroski, H. 1994. *The evolution of useful things.* New York: Vintage.

Planck, M. 1950. *Scientific autobiography and other papers.* Translated by F. Gaynor. London: Williams & Norgate.

Plomin, R., J. C. DeFries, I. W. Craig, and P. McGuffin. 2003. *Behavioral genetics in the postgenomic era.* Washington, DC: American Psychological Association.

Popper, K. R. 1979. *Objective knowledge: An evolutionary approach.* Oxford: Clarendon Press.

Portin, P. 2002. Historical development of the concept of the gene. *Journal of Medicine and Philosophy* 27:257–286.

Powell, A., S. Shennan, and M. G. Thomas. 2009. Late pleistocene demography and the appearance of modern human behavior. *Science* 324: 1298–1301.

Prugnolle, F., A. Manica, and F. Balloux. 2005. Geography predicts neutral genetic diversity of human populations. *Current Biology* 15:159–160.

Putnam, R. 1993. *Making democracy work. Civic traditions in modern Italy.* Princeton, NJ: Princeton University Press.

Quian Quiroga, R., L. Reddy, G. Kreiman, C. Koch, and I. Fried. 2005. Invariant visual representation by single neurons in the human brain. *Nature* 435:1102–1107.

Reader, S. M. 2006. Evo-devo, modularity, and evolvability: Insights for cultural evolution. *Behavioral and Brain Sciences* 29:361.

Reik, W., and J. Walter. 2001. Genomic imprinting: Parental influence on the genome. *Nature Reviews Genetics* 2:21–32.

Rendell, L., and H. Whitehead. 2001. Culture in whales and dolphins. *Behavioral and Brain Sciences* 24:309–324.

Renfrew, C. 1990. *Archaeology and language: The puzzle of Indo-European origins*. Cambridge: Cambridge University Press.

Reyes García, V., J. Broesch, L. Calvet-Mir, N. Fuentes-Peláez, T. W. McDade, S. Parsa, S. Tanner, T. Huanca, W. R. Leonard, and M. R. Martínez-Rodríguez. 2009. Cultural transmission of ethnobotanical knowledge and skills: An empirical analysis from an Amerindian society. *Evolution and Human Behavior* 30:274–285.

Rice, T. W., and M. Arnett. 2001. Civic culture and socioeconomic development in the United States: A view from the states, 1880s–1990s. *Social Science Journal* 38:39–51.

Rice, T. W., and J. L. Feldman. 1997. Civic culture and democracy from Europe to America. *Journal of Politics* 59:1143–1172.

Richerson, P. J., and R. Boyd. 2001. Institutional evolution in the holocene: The rise of complex societies. *Proceedings of the British Academy* 110:197–204.

———. 2005. *Not by genes alone*. Chicago: University of Chicago Press.

Richerson, P. J., D. Collins, and R. M. Genet. 2006. Why managers need an evolutionary theory of organizations. *Strategic Organization* 4:201–211.

Rivera, M. C., and J. A. Lake. 2004. The ring of life provides evidence for a genome fusion origin of eukaryotes. *Nature* 431:152–155.

Rivers, W. H. R. 1926. *Psychology and ethnology*. London: Kegan Paul, Trench, Trubner.

Rizzolatti, G., L. Fadiga, L. Fogassi, and V. Gallese. 1996. Premotor cortex and the recognition of motor actions. *Brain Research* 3:131–141.

———. 2002. From mirror neurons to imitation: Facts and speculations. In *The imitative mind: Development, evolution and brain bases*, edited by A. N. Melzhoff and W. Prinz, 247–266. Cambridge: Cambridge University Press.

Rogers, A. R. 1988. Does biology constrain culture? *American Anthropologist* 90:819–831.

Rogers, E. 1995. *The diffusion of innovations*. New York: Free Press.

Rosenbaum, M. E., and I. F. Tucker. 1962. The competence of the model and the learning of imitation and nonimitation. *Journal of Experimental Psychology* 63:183–90.

Rosenberg, N. A., J. K. Pritchard, J. L. Weber, H. M. Cann, K. K. Kidd, L. A. Zhivotovsky, and M. W. Feldman. 2002. Genetic structure of human populations. *Science* 298:2381–2385.

Roth, A. E. 1995. Bargaining experiments. In *Handbook of experimental economics*, edited by J. H. Kagell and A. E. Roth, 253–348. Princeton, NJ: Princeton University Press.

Rubin, D. C. 1995. *Memory in oral traditions*. Oxford: Oxford University Press.

Ryckman, R. M., W. C. Rodda, and M. F. Sherman. 1972. Locus of control and expertise relevance as determinants of changes in opinion about student activism. *Journal of Social Psychology* 88:107–114.

Salganik, M., P. Dodds, and D. Watts. 2006. Experimental study of inequality and unpredictability in an artificial cultural market. *Science* 311:854–856.

Samonte, R. V., and E. E. Eichler. 2002. Segmental duplications and the evolution of the primate genome. *Nature Reviews Genetics* 3:65–72.

Schotter, A., and B. Sopher. 2003. Social learning and coordination conventions in intergenerational games: An experimental study. *Journal of Political Economy* 111:498–529.

Senju, A., and G. Csibra. 2008. Gaze following in human infants depends on communicative signals. *Current Biology* 18:668–671.

Shennan, S. J., and J. R. Wilkinson. 2001. Ceramic style change and neutral evolution: A case study from neolithic Europe. *American Antiquity* 66:577–593.

Sherif, M. 1936. *The psychology of social norms.* Oxford: Harper.

Simon, H. A. 1955. A behavioral model of rational choice. *Quarterly Journal of Economics* 69:99–118.

Simonton, D. K. 1999. Creativity as blind variation and selective retention: Is the creative process Darwinian? *Psychological Inquiry* 10:309–328.

Slingerland, E. 2008. *What science offers the humanities.* Cambridge: Cambridge University Press.

Soyka, M., U. W. Preuss, V. Hesselbrock, P. Zill, G. Koller, and B. Bondy. 2008. GABA–A2 receptor subunit gene (GABRA2) polymorphisms and risk for alcohol dependence. *Journal of Psychiatric Research* 42:184–191.

Spencer, H. 1857. Progress: Its law and cause. *Westminster Review* 67:244–67.

Spencer, M., E. A. Davidson, A. C. Barbrook, and C. J. Howe. 2004. Phylogenetics of artificial manuscripts. *Journal of Theoretical Biology* 227:503–511.

Sperber, D. 1996. *Explaining culture: A naturalistic approach.* Oxford: Oxford University Press.

Sperber, D., and D. Wilson. 1986. *Relevance: Communication and cognition.* Oxford: Blackwell.

Steward, J. 1955. *Theory of culture change.* Illinois: University of Illinois Press.

Stotz, K., and P. Griffiths. 2004. Genes: Philosophical analyses put to the test. *History and Philosophy of the Life Sciences* 26:5–28.

Sultan, F., J. U. Farley, and D. R. Lehmann. 1990. A meta-analysis of applications of diffusion models. *Journal of Marketing Research* 27:70–77.

Tajfel, H. 1982. Social psychology of intergroup relations. *Annual Review of Psychology* 33:1–39.

Tehrani, J. J., and M. Collard. 2002. Investigating cultural evolution through biological phylogenetic analyses of Turkmen textiles. *Journal of Anthropological Archaeology* 21:443–463.

———. 2009. On the relationship between interindividual cultural transmission and population-level cultural diversity: A case study of weaving in Iranian tribal populations. *Evolution and Human Behavior* 30:286–300.

Tennie, C., J. Call, and M. Tomasello. 2009. Ratcheting up the ratchet: On the evolution of cumulative culture. *Philosophical Transactions of the Royal Society B* 364:2405–2415.

Terrell, J. E., K. M. Kelly, P. Rainbird, P. Bellwood, J. Bradshaw, D. V. Burley, R. Clark, B. Douglas, R. C. Green, and M. Intoh. 2001. Foregone conclusions? In search of "Papuans" and "Austronesians." *Current Anthropology* 42:97–124.

Thaler, R. H., and C. R. Sunstein. 2008. *Nudge: Improving decisions about health, wealth, and happiness*. New Haven: Yale University Press.

Thornton, A., and K. McAuliffe. 2006. Teaching in wild meerkats. *Science* 313:227–229.

Tomasello, M. 1996. Do apes ape? In *Social learning in animals: The roots of culture*, edited by C. Heyes and B. G. Galef, 319–346. San Diego, CA: Academic Press.

Tomasello, M., M. Carpenter, J. Call, T. Behne, and H. Moll. 2005. Understanding and sharing intentions: The origins of cultural cognition. *Behavioral and Brain Sciences* 28:675–691.

Tomasello, M., A. C. Kruger, and H. H. Ratner. 1993. Cultural learning. *Behavioral and Brain Sciences* 16:495–552.

Tooby, J., and L. Cosmides. 1992. The psychological foundations of culture. In *The adapted mind*, edited by J. H. Barkow, L. Cosmides, and J. Tooby, 19–136. New York: Oxford University Press.

Tripsas, M., and G. Gavetti. 2000. Capabilities, cognition, and inertia: Evidence from digital imaging. *Strategic Management Journal* 21:1147–1161.

Turchin, P. 2003. *Historical dynamics: Why states rise and fall*. Princeton, NJ: Princeton University Press.

———. 2008. Arise 'cliodynamics.' *Nature* 454:34–35.

Tylor, E. B. 1871. *Primitive culture*. London: John Murray.

van Schaik, C. P., M. Ancrenaz, G. Borgen, B. Galdikas, C. D. Knott, I. Singleton, A. Suzuki, S. S. Utami, and M. Merrill. 2003. Orangutan cultures and the evolution of material culture. *Science* 299:102–105.

van Wyhe, J. 2005. The descent of words: Evolutionary thinking, 1780–1880. *Endeavour* 29:94–100.

Vincenti, W. G. 1993. *What engineers know and how they know it*. Baltimore: Johns Hopkins University Press.

Watts, D. J. 1999. Networks, dynamics, and the small-world phenomenon. *American Journal of Sociology* 105:493–527.

White, L. A. 1959a. *The evolution of culture*. New York: McGraw-Hill.

———. 1959b. The concept of culture. *American Anthropologist* 61:227–251.

Whiten, A., J. Goodall, W. C. McGrew, T. Nishida, V. Reynolds, Y. Sugiyama, C. E. G. Tutin, R. W. Wrangham, and C. Boesch. 1999. Cultures in chimpanzees. *Nature* 399:682–685.

Whiten, A., V. Horner, and F. B. M. de Waal. 2005. Conformity to cultural norms of tool use in chimpanzees. *Nature* 437:737–740.

Whiten, A., and A. Mesoudi. 2008. An experimental science of culture: Animal social diffusion experiments. *Philosophical Transactions of the Royal Society of London B* 363:3477–3488.

Whiten, A., A. Spiteri, V. Horner, K. E. Bonnie, S. P. Lambeth, S. J. Schapiro, and F. B. M. de Waal. 2007. Transmission of multiple traditions within and between chimpanzee groups. *Current Biology* 17:1038–1043.

Whitfield, J. 2008. Across the curious parallel of language and species evolution. *PLOS Biology* 6:e186.

Wilder, R. L. 1968. *Evolution of mathematical concepts.* Milton Keynes: Open University Press.

Wilson, E. O. 2006. *Naturalist.* Washington, DC: Island Press.

Wimsatt, W. C. 2006. Generative entrenchment and an evolutionary developmental biology for culture. *Behavioral and Brain Sciences* 29:364.

Wright, S. 1932. The roles of mutation, inbreeding, crossbreeding and selection in evolution. *Proceedings of the Sixth International Congress of Genetics* 1:356–366.

Index

Made in the USA
Las Vegas, NV
09 January 2025

16151357R00163